The Obligations of the Harp

The Obligations of the Harp

Essays

Arthur Saltzman

Parlor Press
West Lafayette, Indiana
www.parlorpress.com

Parlor Press LLC, West Lafayette, Indiana 47906

Some essays in *Obligations of the Harp* originally appeared in the following journals and magazines: "Castaways" (*Drunken Boat*); "Clique Song"(*Under the Sun*); "Falling with Style" (*Lake Effect*); "From the Notebook of the Human Cannonball" (*Asphodel*); "Get Up and Get Away" (*nidus*); "On Reading with a Pen" (*Gihon River Review*); "Reason Not the Need" (*Columbia: A Journal of Literature and Art*); "The Table on the Planet" (*Delmar*); "Taking Pains" (*Prague Literary Review*); "Time Out" (*Slow Trains*); "Watch This Space" (*Mid-American Review*); "What All the Fuss Is For" (*Center: A Journal of Literary Arts*).

Printed in the United States of America

S A N: 2 5 4 - 8 8 7 9

Library of Congress Cataloging-in-Publication Data

Saltzman, Arthur M. (Arthur Michael), 1953-
The obligations of the harp : essays / Arthur Saltzman.
   p. cm.
ISBN 978-1-60235-115-8 (pbk. : alk. paper) -- ISBN 978-1-60235-116-5
   (adobe ebook)
I. Title.
AC8.S227 2009
081--dc22
                              2009021504

Cover image: "MASS Ensemble with Earth Harps in the Utah Salt Flats."
   Used by permission of MASS Ensemble.
Cover design by David Blakesley.
Thanks to Susan Bales for providing editorial assistance on this project.
Printed on acid-free paper.

Parlor Press, LLC is an independent publisher of scholarly and trade titles in print and multimedia formats. This book is available in paper, cloth and Adobe eBook formats from Parlor Press on the World Wide Web at http://www.parlorpress.com or through online and brick-and-mortar bookstores. For submission information or to find out about Parlor Press publications, write to Parlor Press, 816 Robinson St., West Lafayette, Indiana, 47906, or e-mail editor@parlorpress.com.

Contents

The Obligations of the Harp

The way things work
is that eventually
something catches.

—Jorie Graham, "The Way Things Work"

The heart's full cargo is so immense it's not
hard to feel the weight of the word
shift, and we might as well admit it's easy
to think of the spites and treacheries
and worse the poised word had to bear
lest some poor heart break unexplained, inept.

—William Matthews, "Wrong"

1 The Table on the Planet

The arrangement contains the desire of
The artist. But one confides in what has no
Concealed creator.

—Wallace Stevens, "So-and-So Reclining on Her Couch"

It may never have happened, or it may not have happened precisely as the theory would have us believe, but if evolution happened, it apparently happened according to one of three models, for they are the models that have endured.

One is the racetrack, along whose color-coded lanes the earliest vertebrates, given a running Precambrian start, sprint through 500-plus million years toward the here and now. The planet has been fraught with offspring for a few *billion* years, in fact, and the majority fail to complete the marathon, their collapses occurring invisibly and ages before they'd have come into view of the grandstands. Indeed, most of the dinosaurs whose fragments we're familiar with cannot leap the steeple from the Mesozoic Era to the Cenozoic, and the next contestants tread upon their fossils. Some who do survive the marathon do not survive as they began it. Eohippus, for instance, drops out, leaving the modern horse to deliver the mail. A given lizard may streamline every thousand centuries or so, sloughing a dozen or more precedent semblances on its way, dumping ballast for the long haul. Certain amphibians carry the baton legless ancestors brought the first half-million generations. Meanwhile, a few mischievous species prominent in the Holocene stretch slipped in recently, perhaps ducking in from behind a dying herd during that catastrophe's distraction; some would say their success is tempered by the deceit. The fittest are left standing, slithering, soaring, or treading water at the ever-receding finish line, leaving immeasurable time and carnal tonnage in their wake.

Tolstoy wrote that happy families are all alike. From the long view of biology, unhappy families are all alike, too. Been there. Been them.

A second viable diagram shows Creation coursing in several unpredictable directions from a hypothetical seminal event. Call it biology's own version of the Big Bang. Here the way species spread from the center recalls how cracks in the windshield can continue for years after it's been struck by a BB or a pebble a truck kicked up. Whatever existed during the first eons—that rudimentary zodiac—was presumably packed close to the core, after which the traces of random gambits, impasses, and mysteriously juried amendments to the constitution of life on Earth become visible. Everything about this depiction is unsettling: not only the unlucky animals born too close to the epicenter but all successive creatures as well are perched precariously over faults, which, based on what we know of faults, are liable to grow. Logic dictates that because those fractures have persisted for so long, we, too, will eventually tumble in after the majority.

Then there is the so-called Tree of Life, a metaphor bequeathed to us by Darwin himself. Many find this the most appealing of the three models: whereas the racetrack model emphasizes lethal competition and the shattered glass model accident, the Tree of Life is a community roost, consolingly organic, with a different beast blooming from every bud. Single-celled animals hug the trunk, while increasingly complex organisms roost and ramify further out. Trilobites and other unimaginably ancient entities verified only by the barest carbon outlines make the oldest claims nearest the bole, with millions of insects and other biological minutiae infesting ground level with them. The lower branches are hung with cuttlefish and tube coral, decked with plankton, caterpillars, and blood stars as if to celebrate a Christmas held millennia before the arrival of the putative guest of honor. A jungle of more advanced vertebrates nest in the canopy—as in New York City, priority manifests as altitude—until finally, Man, having alighted last, rides highest of the higher mammals; he commands the branch closest to heaven, his eminence depending on the slightest twig.

These models are models of necessity: they ordain a trackable past and a reasonably foreseeable future for every constituent, from plants to prime ministers, from mollusks to Machiavelli, from algae to Elvis. It's safe to say that they are not the only options. Once the standing committee rescinded the biblical image of the ark, with every current animal and animal to come coupled in its impossible cargo, once the suspicion arose that our souls are not outsourced by the Lord Himself, there must have been other proposals that received a hearing. Consider a layout on the order of the London Underground, with each species stationed on its isolated platform; some will catch expresses, some will get stuck on local lines, and some bygone animals will remain stranded altogether. Picture the whirling Earth as a centrifuge whose populations separate and resolve. What about an Escher-inspired digestive system, whose contents are constantly being circulated, absorbed, or expelled? Or a bank of elevators. A miraculously engendering rainfall that precipitates everyone in its spill. The interstate highway system. A charm bracelet. The ultimate gumbo. An immense Pachinko game, whose random paths and probabilities our advents take. The interstices of the U.S. Tax Code—how many have perished trying to navigate its narrows?—or the financial agent's ledger, in which each of us is listed as a credit and a debit together, as once and future dust. Try the declension of government powers, with its Hobbesian population vying for perks and office space, and with its cubicles checked and balanced against one another. A theater, whose structured seating chart ranges from the simplest groundlings to the lucky personages occupying the royal box. Then again, maybe Creation comes down to a construction as common as boxes stacked in a closet. (Going by such a diagram, with all species wrapped in boxed sets, it is obvious that caskets are the main thing living things share.) These and a hundred other wayward arrangements might serve the idiosyncrasies science encounters.

All this proves is that the details of evolution (whether God, the devil, or any engineer is in the details or not) are maddeningly obscure, like an argument in a distant room. Life has been conceived in the conditional tense. We might think of these depictions as "whether patterns," if we may be pardoned the pun. Because in a sense every animal update puns on the shape and function of its parent, by punning ourselves we are merely borrowing from evolution's own figurative history, anyway. Out of the ocean's endless approaches and approximations life began, and ever since, approaches and approximations describe its perpetuation and perpetuate its description.

Given a choice of metaphors, I prefer a flip book: even though agile handling provides the illusion of a smooth evolution, closer inspection reveals gaps in the manuscript, which current findings in the fossil record confirm. The gaps, though, are what gall us most. The unseen shoving that upsets the queue. Some species prevail, some are plowed over, and if nothing else is known for certain, it is clear that it isn't virtue that got us and any other chosen taxonomy through the gate.

One might say, in an attempt to appease the creationists, that the Tree of Life doesn't fall far from the apple. Breaks in the terrestrial manuscript, however, do not mean that creationists win the day, much less the definition of time. If the evolutionists' version of the world is based on generation after generation of subtle paraphrase, the creationists' is a stupor of continuity plagiarized verbatim from God. No said-and-done scheme they might devise accommodates any organic scrap we've encountered so well as the incremental Genesis evolution subscribes to.

The ascension of cells, whether envisioned as a race, a ripple effect, or a totemic orchard, may conclude with humanity, but recent studies make mankind look less and less mandatory. Lest we get too smug about our fifteen seconds of geologic dominance, Stephen Jay Gould reminds us that "progress does not rely (and is not even a primary thrust of) the evolutionary process." The same disclaimers go for Homo sapiens. Organisms earn no extra credit for complexity. There is no special award for gorgeousness, either. Human supremacy, for what it's worth and so long as it lasts, smacks of some vague exchange of favors behind the scenes. The history of habitation is narrated as a *bildungsroman,* and human beings are the author, hero, and happy ending. But once we "see the Earth again, / Cleared of its stiff and stubborn, man-locked set," as Wallace Stevens's angel of reality advises we do, existence becomes a shell game. Furthermore, fossil evidence is hearsay that doesn't automatically hold up in court, and whatever chart we employ is an elaborate confession of extenuating circumstances. And when we add to that the fact that man's recent reign has lasted, oh, about two percent as long as the frog's did, it's pretty hard to muster much arrogance.

Scientists bandy the beaks of finches and debate the opalescence of the inshore squid, but surely there is no more relevant concern for the layman than by what sort of ape the scientists themselves were fathered. In *Herzog,* Saul Bellow's hero devotes one of his notorious mental letters to the issue of our issue: "Latest intelligence from the Olduvai Gorge in East Africa gives grounds to suppose that man did not descend from a peaceful arboreal ape, but from a carnivorous, ter-restrial ape, a beast that hunted in packs and crushed the skulls of prey with a club or femoral bone." Even if genetics is not the whole of our destiny, the news still packs a wallop. "It sounds bad," Herzog concludes, but "bad" is not the half of it. If the apes we're made from conquered through combat rather than diplomacy, it is not simply military strategy but their own essences that would-be peacemakers dispute. Not beneficence but blood is in our blood, in which human beings may have been marinating ever since the first hominids rose up with whatever weaponry they could get their opposable thumbs around some two million years or so ago.

Nevertheless, a propensity for violence is not the exception that rules us, much less guarantees our rule. Classification is primarily con-cerned with uniqueness, so man's task is to determine what special quality determines us as us. What, in other words, is the most singular behavior in our biology? Glancing at some of the Latin we've usu-ally assigned our ancestors, who derived from one or another set of comparatively ambitious apes, we discover men who walked upright, arrived from the south, developed fire, or were handy enough with tools to leave incisions for Homo sapiens to brood about. Those pos-sessing several of these credentials, of course, got past the early rounds of natural selection. As humans grew used to their status, their devi-ance from other creatures took on other forms, including an interest in tradition, communication through symbols, cost accounting, and cooking their kill before consuming it.

As for building monuments, bringing gifts, establishing neighbor-hood watch programs, whispering endearments during intercourse, or sandbagging ourselves with babies we educate and adore, these are noble attributes, but they are not unique to people and hence, cannot properly designate us. Although they are less flattering, subtler charac-teristics may home in our identity better . . . once we realize the right Latin-activated phrase for them. We humans root for the Raiders, hail taxis, shop for shoes, use the latrine, and alter our wills, any one of which sets us apart from all who, if we buy the Tree of Life concept, are forever mired in the flora they adorn. Maybe we've been especially hard-wired for wonder or for worry—both proposals compel and could sustain lobbies. We feel remorseful and ashamed; we pine and we pray. In these ways and countless others, we will not be subsumed.

One zoologist I heard being interviewed on NPR—yes, subscribing to public radio is another candidate for distinguishing people—contended that monogamy is the signature perversity of our species. By comparison, flight is less startling, mutation from a larval stage less sensational, urinating to certify one's property and committing suicide less peculiar. A sea urchin's busy cilia, a western banded gecko's detachable tail, a glass fish's transparency, an oyster's variable foot, a mother pelican's washing down its fledglings' dinner with her own blood—none of these raises an eyebrow anywhere in the animal kingdom the way our wedding vows do. Even the other members of our genus find the exclusivity of bride and groom peculiar. Research proves that even cannibalism is more typical than allowing the same presence to make the same depression forever in the same bed and, under extreme circumstances, more practical as well.

Or perchance by our neuroses you may know us. Doctor Seuss tells the story of a bear, a rabbit, and a worm competing for bragging rights. The bear could smell the subtlest odor at a remarkable distance; the rabbit could hear a sound just as faint and far away; but the worm defeated the other animals with his amazing vision. In a memorable illustration, he launched his eyesight beyond the horizon, over the curve of the Earth, and all the way around the globe until he was able to see himself from behind. One of the good doctor's reliable delights was designing beings that embodied obsessions just this side of what even children recognize as our own. The worm's ambushing himself with self-regard may not be one of Doctor Seuss's most fantastic inventions, but it is definitely one that profoundly implicates his readers.

As if by reflex, we believe that Nature is as abuzz with us as we are consumed with ourselves. If not Seuss's conceited annelid, the hero of Vladimir Nabokov's "Signs and Symbols," who is convinced that he is shadowed and colluded over by everything else in nature, may serve as the mascot of our species. "Clouds in the staring sky transmit to one another, by means of slow signs, incredibly detailed information regarding him. His inmost thoughts are discussed at nightfall, in manual alphabet, by darkly gesticulating trees." But if this "referential maniac" is paranoid, his disease has reach. To be sure, ever since the self invented "the self" (arguably around the time Renaissance painters made faces to crowd out the landscape and intercept the sky, possibly as early as early man first clutched his own chest in his death throes), we have been installing more mirrors than windows, until today there are more personal websites than persons to warrant them.

And no websites see our penchants better than those continuous visual diaries whose subjects so effectively surround themselves with surveillance equipment that they are under inspection twenty-four hours a day. Evidently, rather than feel orphaned for a single unattended moment, they encourage Big Brother to adopt them. To be is to be perceived, they reason, and it does not appear to matter whether the agent of that perception is an angel touching the shoulder or a stranger casing the shower. "See me," they say, which is, after all, the aim of every input, as well as every petrified vestige and artifact, every claw print and songline. It would take a model coterminous with the world to guarantee it. If the perpetually Web-cast are correct, an inadvertently tripped switch could snuff out a species; a computer virus could trigger a catastrophe on the order of the Cretaceous-Tertiary extinction. While it is not the exclusive fate of human beings to suffer that or any other fatality, it is their exclusive fate to realize it.

In order to inspire its patrons to increase their endowments, the board of directors for the San Diego Zoo came up with a novel idea: an art sale. Specifically, they decided to sell the works of the zoo creatures themselves, thereby enabling them to help earn their keep. Paws and pelts, muzzles and tails were loaded with paint, and in an orgy of aleatory technique, the animals scored, strafed, swatted, stamped, mauled, or bellied about their canvases. It was all in good fun and for a good cause, and there was no question of alerting the ASPCA. Those creatures that could not be induced to use this medium still contributed: a shark-bitten steel rod, a hornbill's shed feathers, and the castings of a python, for example, were combined in a glass tray to constitute a collage that went for a thousand dollars. The canvases were cajoled from the cages of the artists, framed, and auctioned off at prices that, while they wouldn't have impressed Sotheby's, nevertheless earned a considerable sum for the zoo.

One of the canvases in particular bears noting because it was the only one from the exhibit that was not abstract. A Silver Back gorilla produced a piece of admittedly minimalist but nonetheless representational art. He had taken a brush and painted a series of parallel vertical lines. Critics debated its significance, as critics are wont to do. (It is characteristic of the species.) Some suggested that he had depicted an insistent rain. Others thought that the lines of descent indicated a race history. A few said that he had merely painted the bars of his cell.

"See me," they said.

Do not despair: all the data and excavations agree that life is a project. Do not presume, either. As Gould explains, "For all practical purposes, we're not evolving. There's no reason to think we're going to get bigger brains or smaller toes or whatever—we are what we are." As well as all we'll ever be. We as a species may feel like a rough copy—we still have cancer, a cramped birth canal, and a number of atavisms to work out—but we're what Nature has submitted as a final draft.

We are stuck in our cells. We paint the bars. See us?

So where did we leave off? Once upon a time, two ape-like contingencies, while trudging toward eternity, parted ways. One made its way into oblivion quickly, as "quickly" is understood against epochs. The other began a fifty-million-year game of evolutionary telephone, with each generation speaking its genetic message to the next, who did not exactly understand it but passed it on, until it ended up in a botch of modern consciousness. And if it happened anything like that, the phenomenon left us wanting, and what's worse, knowing that we are wanting and what's worse. And that is that the race will have run its course, to trace that figure as far as it, and we, can go. Then may we be inscribed for a blessing in the Book of Life, as we say in my religion. It is one more abiding model, in whose infinite index all may be ordered, familiar, and found.

2 Get Up and Get Away

It may not be the most often quoted or sighed-over scene in *Casablanca,* but I propose that the one that has proved the most prescient features an elderly couple who have come to Rick's *Café Americain* to celebrate their impending departure for America. They ask Karl, the maitre d' (played so indelibly by the cream-centered S. Z. "Cuddles" Sakall), to join them in a toast to their future. (Anticipating their invitation, Karl has brought out the good brandy.) Having agreed to speak nothing but English so that they will feel at home when they arrive, they proceed to demonstrate their command of American idioms:

"*Liebchin,* er, sweetness heart, what watch?"

"Ten watch."

"Such watch!"

Karl buttons the scene with the following verdict: "You will get along beautifully in America."

Let me suggest that what makes this interchange important, beyond the comic relief, which in the context of the film had become as precious and rare as exit visas under the German occupation, is the unintentional recognition of the American emphasis on time. Karl is right: American prosperity was and continues to be characterized, guaranteed, and rewarded by time management. If they plan to live in this country, they will need to master that priority. American bustle is conducted in the shadow of the clock, whose hands threaten to swipe fatally down upon us like Poe's pendulum. Or, as Pablo Neruda observed as those hands scythed away at the night, time grinds silently, incessantly away as if his watch were a mill relentlessly working, abrading the hours into minutes and the minutes into seconds, with the seconds crushed still further down until they (and we) are dust. Time is the essential American commodity, at once the impetus and the cost of our getting and spending. Thus we not only want it all, we want it all at once. This is the philosophy that has sanctified the remote control, the cell phone, the laptop computer, the combination laundromat / tanning salon and pedicure / kidney dialysis center, and, perhaps most notoriously, the fast-food restaurant.

Every social critic worth his strictly limited salt intake argues that the proliferation of fast-food restaurants throughout America is a national tragedy. Well, "tragedy" is wrong, but it is certainly a truth universally disparaged, at least by anyone old enough that a Happy Meal does not immediately lift his spirits but sets off something tectonic in his gut. Dieticians deplore the fat calories and the relegation of the food pyramid to another neglected wonder of the ancient world. City planners denounce the numbing sameness of franchise-infested landscapes, whereby locales lose their unique architectural flavors along with their culinary ones, and any city of any size at all comes to look like Anywhere, U.S.A. Editorialists of every stripe bemoan the casualties of convenience. The complaints are as predictable as the standardized patties they target.

And there is no denying the unfortunate fact that children salivate over the prospect of a trip to McDonald's while routinely leaving the time-consuming dinners their mothers dutifully prepare unconsumed. What inestimable damage they do to their digestive tracts! Nietzsche's horror at the prospect of a "detestable, grimacing death, which advances on its belly like a thief" may aptly be compared to the sludgy lunches that advance on the belly of each unwitting child who eats there. Yet the shape of McDonald's has shaped his craving. Pre-schoolers who struggle with their ABC's manage to have the commercial jingles down, and grown-ups can only wring their hands. (Meanwhile, truth to tell, grown-ups themselves are likelier to remember the entire theme to *Gilligan's Island* than be able to recite a line of Shakespeare or solve a single binomial equation). You have to hand it to the advertisers. They have imprinted the configuration and colors of McDonald's so successfully that kids can recognize that topographic dominant at twenty times the distance that they can make out their own parents. At the same time, they have instilled in them the belief that going to what is the most obvious, ubiquitous establishment in town is a treat.

Do not be fooled by mottoes. Although they advocate their eagerness to serve us according to our idiosyncratic schedules and to respond precisely to the way we savor, McDonald's, Dairy Queen, Wendy's, Hardee's, and Burger King have us *their* way. That's the conventional wisdom: awful to contemplate, impossible to cure.

I testify as one who was shackled early on by this same addiction and (say it!) endures it still. Well, "endure" and "addiction" are wrong, but my heart leaps up when I behold a McDonald's golden double rainbow in the sky. I leave it to Proust to remember more elegantly while plucking crumbs of overpriced madeleine from his teeth. (There is nothing French about my reverie save the fries.) Disdaining to sup on anything wrapped in paper or to gorge on anything less than gorgeous is snobbery, pure and simple. Along with Cole Porter, I get no kick from champagne, but the Number Eight Combo hits me where I live. And where I live, in a town of only forty thousand, my populist palate may be served by seven strategically spaced locations. Only in America, you say? Well, so far.

My mundane indulgences are indulgences nonetheless. With the sole exception of those slimy disks of salami I remember my father sawing off the gnarled club he hung in the hall closet to stiffen still further for bagel sandwiches—salami the color and consistency I imagined hardened arteries to be—no taste so satisfies my irremediably rude yearning, no aroma wakens my nostalgia better, than a Quarter Pounder can. Vegetarians, they say, find ample bliss by abstaining from all but salads, with meatless meals martyring themselves; others cultivate a cautious passion for health foods or ruminate over the sensory poverty of the sensible portions they have trained themselves to settle for. By contrast, I confess to numbering myself among the cholesterol-unconscious majority, managing to suspend for the space of the odd meal knowing better. Only hours after my annual doctor's visit, only hours after having studied the diagram framed in the waiting room which shows the way plaque can lodge near the heart like a sated grizzly slumped against the wall of its cave, I find myself dreaming of such a form as greasy goldsmiths make of hamburgers gold and gold polyurethane to keep a growly customer slaked.

How could such dependable contentment be wholly unwholesome? There must be more to the menu here than misgiving. McDonald's suffers the tiny, unchurched children; McDonald's harbors the wayward, distempled teens. All who have shirt and shoes may eat FDA-inspected flesh. Here, in this place at once familiar and special, you can feel at once familiar and special, as religious mentors purport every soul to be. Here, among the billions and billions counted, you count.

I contend that McDonald's offers more than blight so bright we cannot see past the scandalous appetites it manufactures and caters to.

("Blight" is wrong, but cynics maintain that for all their popularity McDonald's and other franchises are disfigurements, unmistakably and nonetheless. Let them eat sugar-free cake.) For one thing, because it spreads the same cuisine, décor, and chipper disposition everywhere, McDonald's reifies the feeling that wherever you are, you are never far from home. The Golden Arches rise like idyllic staples out of the surf and swarm of the chaos of the everyday and hold fast, where bleary-eyed truckers and the roaming homeless may find hot coffee, clean restrooms, and central heat. Centuries from now, some hypothetical Schliemann will hook a buried franchise by one of its fallen arches and winch out a representative and undeteriorated McDonald's, salvaging a significant part of our social history along with it. Presuming, that is, that there ever comes a future when McDonald's has gone under—one tends to predict that McDonald's is the cockroach of our contemporary service economy and will survive any geopolitical debacle or revolution of taste.

McDonald's is also an ideal starter restaurant. It is a place where children can learn to function in public without repercussion. Here they may mix, choose, and invent condiment combinations with an impunity denied even government-funded chemists; they may subject their sandwiches to whatever Boolean options suit their fancies. Free of metal silverware and sharp edges, purged of breakable glasses and plates, McDonald's is the culinary equivalent of vinyl books, padded crib rails, and children's car seats. Let the flattened ketchup packets fly and the sodden crusts fall: it takes less than half an hour to wipe down the Formica and hose off the plastic at the end of each day. Until they are ready for better than Neanderthal etiquette and real, discrepant eating, children can practice their rudimentary manners and desires at McDonald's and insult no protocol, disturb no one. After all, anyone who might be offended by the noise or the noxious combinations kids customarily make from their meals knows not to come to McDonald's in the first place. Here there is no aesthetic to transgress against, business meeting or lovers' tryst to contaminate, or delicate sensibility to sully no matter how much mustard is spattered or "special sauce" slopped about. At McDonald's, there is nothing to ruin.

A third benefit of McDonald's is that it provides a setting where divorced parents can facilitate their joint custody and exchange their kids. It is a weigh station for relationships that circumstances have forced to persist beyond the reach of love. McDonald's is easy to locate and (a particular advantage for the father whose displacement has landed him in a different city) typically set close to the cloverleaf, so awkward meetings between estranged parents can be handled expeditiously. On Saturdays, especially, McDonald's teems with drop-offs and getaways. In this sense, McDonald's is a sort of roundhouse for coupling and uncoupling, where quickly and with minimum stress, families can come together and come apart.

"Your father is late again," grumbles Mom. "Isn't that just like him." Fortunately, they can get a Coke or visit the Play Place while they wait.

When Dad does show up, offering explanation instead of apology, there is no need for the parents to prolong the scene or even to interfere with their child's navigation through the massive plastic intestine in the other room. Mom took off Lauren's tennis shoes before she entered the contraption. Dad joins the other occasional dads swarming at the orifice to collect his charge when she's excreted. Henry Ford could have devised no smoother assembly-line logic, which also, by the way, mimics the conduction of the McDonald's meal in its passage through many hands from order to tray. "Where should we go for lunch, Champ?" asks one weekend father, who has found his son swimming in a cage of colored whiffle balls. He speaks to him through the mesh like an attorney colluding with his client over the chances of getting him paroled. "We already ate, Dad," he says. "I see. Well, what would you like to do next? Where would you like to go? Name it." "Can't I just stay here?" Like his parents, if the boy is guilty of anything, it is of loving not wisely but too well.

There is a rumor at large regarding the construction of the first McDonald's on the moon. Needless to say, it would not be a functioning restaurant, only a hollow mock-up mounted for the glory of the imprimatur alone. There would be just the renowned logo and arches adorning a husk, those rooted commas punctuating the vacancy, interrupting the ash. It would make as firm a purchase on eternity as those other human contributions to the lunar surface do: the abandoned NASA equipment, Alan Shepard's golf ball, a brittle, ripple-free flag. Imagine peering through a high-powered telescope at the black of space. Then suddenly, like a lost traveler starved for landmarks, starved for sustenance and company, you detect something, a flash at the farthest reach of your vision to satisfy your hunger and lift your heart—a touch of gold. And you are saved.

Well, "saved" is wrong, but you get the message. I currently live no more than an hour away from what is, in terms of square footage, the largest McDonald's in the world. Its arches are superimposed upon the overpass of Highway 44, clamping it off and heralding the otherwise unexceptional outskirts of Vinita, Oklahoma. For devotees of McDonald's and defenders of the tourist trade in the Sooner State, it represents a truer Gateway to the West and its mythical promise than does its more celebrated counterpart in St. Louis (where, by the way, souvenirs and concessions are both less plentiful). Long glass cases display the evolution of layouts, logos, and all the jolly products of business calculation like phylogenetic charts. Out of the primordial fifteen-cent burgers emerge hearty subspecies and once-unforeseeable strains, establishing from those humble beginnings one of the most abundant, redoubtable corporate organisms on Earth. In an isolated housing lies a concordance of all the variants that have ever issued from the ur-burger, a record of every modification that's ever been spatula'd off the grill and every mutation that's ever risen from the first fry vat on down to whatever it was you just devoured. Plastic heads and torsos of the company clown preside throughout the complex in unmitigatable glee; in fact, the whole garish, hyperactive, make-believe population of Mc-Donaldland have been figured into party favors and plush toys, banks and balloons, collectibles past and yet to come on the market. They've rounded up the usual suspects, as it were. As so, on view through the glass walls facing east and west over I-44, are we.

"Louie, I think this is the beginning of a beautiful friendship," Rick remarks as the two of them stroll off the tarmac, out of *Casablanca*'s closing scene and into our collective unconsciousness. It will occur to contemporary audiences that as good a place as any for them to dedicate their alliance might be McDonald's. Having sacrificed Ingrid Bergman and the sanction of the occupying army between them, who better deserves a break today than these two? Undoubtedly, to stay a step ahead of the Nazi pursuit, they'd get whatever they get to go.

And so I wish our heroes safe passage and fast food. But *Casablanca* always did bring out the romantic in me.

3 Castaways

each scrap has a shadow—each shadow cast
by a different light.

—Sharon Olds, "The Unswept"

It should be moving water. A pond may provide the requisite serenity, and for contemplative depths a lagoon will do, but either will eventually clog with wrongdoing. Moving water, however, keeps recrimination from building by bearing it away. Tradition may respect all bodies of water equally, but because we are more effectively consoled by the sensation of opening up a distance between our selves and our sins, a river is preferable to a stew of group renunciation. Landlocked urban worshippers have to improvise by seeking out streams, creeks, or drainage canals to accommodate the ceremony. For grace is centrifugal, redemption transitive. And if even minor indiscretions need leaching out, just imagine the rinse cycle an entire race requires.

Dry seasons present special challenges. Consider the way children make miniature rafts out of Popsicle sticks to ripple down the gutters toward the sewer at the corner. In case of drought, they will create the course by running the hose. In a pinch, when cramped quarters limit the participation of larger Jewish populations or, conversely, when one finds himself marooned in Kansas and there's not a minyan's worth of Jews within miles, flushing one's failings down the toilet may suffice. While such a practice lacks the dignity and conventional setting we have come to associate with holy offices, the purpose of the service may in spite of everything be preserved.

If separation and departure are the sources of assurance, airports and train stations might eventually replace the pastoral origins of this and many other ancient rituals anyway. Modern American Jews cluster in cities and must adapt. Would not the Old Testament prophets have benefited from today's telecommunications? Would scribes have abjured the printing press for compromising the glory of the Word? There is no blasphemy inherent in taking advantage and making do.

We might remember how Herakles cleaned the Aegean stables by diverting a river's flow to flood the floor. We might pause to think of that resultant rush of dung and muddy straw, with all the massed and baffled animals looking on, were that not the myth of another culture. Still, the principle holds true today.

Many crumble bread to cast upon the waters and lend their efforts symbolic heft. The practice not only resonates liturgically but also satisfies the ecologically minded in attendance since bread readily biodegrades. But well before that process gets under way, birds congregate along the banks to carry off the offerings. A televised contingent from Temple Sholom gathered for *tashlicht* one September morning at a channel of the Chicago River. By the time the slices had been distributed, the place was dense with starlings, jays, and grackles, who kibbitzed and competed more loudly than the Jews who'd come to demonstrate their duty to the viewing audience. Most of the bread was borne off the minute it hit the water. The most impertinent birds ganged up on the smallest kids, spooking them into dropping their provender and high-tailing it back to their parents, while their tasty sins were quickly divvied up and devoured. Birds are fairly indiscriminate about it—so much the better, for our divestiture has such variety, and its contents from year to year can be hard to predict.

Much of what the birds miss, the fish will nip or the nosy squirrels will loot—nature is full of culprits. The rest will melt and mix in with the river's other impurities, as if passing down a digestive tract.

It will go better for us if it is moving water. A common philosophy says that consciousness is a stream, but conscience could be a stream as well. "Nothing outside of the flux secures the issue of it," wrote William James, and that presumably includes our imperfections and that very formulation. You needn't take faith's word for the futility of trying to fix belief on solid ground.

As for the children, who had to be coaxed by the prospect of physical activity to endure the services that preceded the ceremony, they, too, have their budding cruelties and tiny crimes to purge. (It was surely no easy matter to convince them that, full of breakfast and on the brink of Burger King, from another perspective they are famished. Clad in Adidas and Levi's, they are nonetheless in need. What worked was the suggestion that, given the right attitude, their repentance might be fun.) They craved their neighbors' answers on math tests and took the Lord's name in vain when the ground ball ducked through a teammate's legs. They cadged matches and thrilled to the sight of ants shrunk to miniscule black buttons by the fire; they transformed worms into licorice and dropped their bundled skins on a catafalque of twigs. Every one of their recesses contains a little history of affronts and revenges. When they grow up, they will simply expand the perimeter of sin and retribution. Only then will their machinations alert the courts and make the papers. Still, the principle holds true today.

For the time being, they are absorbed, until the whole slices of Wonder Bread that the mischievous try to race take only seconds to capsize and swamp. Although *tashlicht* implies that their juvenile records have been destroyed, the kids kick miserably at the leaves: the adventure was hardly worth the transgression and whatever punishment might come of it.

People unconsciously curse the assailing birds and call for more bread.

Many depend on paper. Those who have not drafted their misgivings in advance simply settle for conventional prayers and shred blank pages to consign to the water. Others have committed their pleas to writing; they arrive at the water's edge like attorneys with briefs to file. The adults, having a greater range of error to encompass, admit their sins more generally. They have signed away "resentment," "envy," and "pride." Essentially, they see their hearts as furnaces and have come to shovel out the accumulated ash. On the other hand, the kids, at least the literate among them, confess with explicitness; they forego the dissembling of simile and Hebrew, and write about the particular vulgarity uttered, the stolen gum.

I have seen older orthodox Jews, men who have not gone swimming in decades or showered with others at a gymnasium for even longer, wade in up to their knees with their papers. They assemble at a depth of about twelve inches, shivering, their trousers hiked over white legs to no avail. The rabbi, their spiritual admiral, ventures farthest out. Davening, they seem to be engaging in the sort of rickety water aerobics the elderly practice on those afternoons they take over the pool at the Y.

Doing this in company emphasizes how common our afflictions are. No one is unforgivable or exempt, so take comfort, take care. It is also a rare something outside of algebra or Monopoly for families to do together. Mothers urge their toddlers to flick their meager share of sin away. Three other members of the temple steady an old woman's wheelchair against the rain-slick slope so she can dribble her documents in. Some pieces cling to her dress, and several hands brush at them like flies.

We send our petitions piecemeal over the water. It is an epidemic unique to our religion. This is our bad dander we shed, like the slips of fortune you find in cookies and decide to pay no mind. This is our insistent litter and supplication. Together we rid ourselves of things forbidden and annually foresworn. To the unsuspecting, it may look as though we are sending confetti after an absent ship.

The children, however, will not be daunted by the demands of ritual; nor are they deterred by the substitution of paper for bread. Being outside is too unusual and precious an event during Sabbath services for them to lose to solemnity. They have secretly twisted their pages into makeshift boats—"There is no Frigate like a Book," Dickinson promises, and perhaps the poetry will prove out. Even though the grown-ups glower, already some of the kids are dashing ahead to see whose sins will prove swiftest or survive the current longest. Most take on water too fast and, too far from shore for bailing, become pulpy, clump, and drown.

Only the smallest scribbles, torn to pieces in a flurry of atonement, stay afloat. A few vile modifiers dangle from some overhanging brush as, here and there, improper nouns slide by. A scrap of misdemeanor snags on something secret beneath. A bit of sin gets snookered behind a stone. Parts of other repudiations find their way back ashore; wayward phrases lodge in the mud. Not all of these free-floating disavowals disperse, however, but vaguely superimpose and fuse into new indictments. Lust and covetousness collide, lending greater intensity to one another. Assorted gluttonies gather downstream. All in all, a manifesto of regret. The jettison spreads, giving God's forgiveness a run for its money.

We can only guess how disjointed words are recollected. A mysterious syntax emerges as sodden verbs clutch at objects that the water has randomly redirected. The ad-lib of our atonement, our extravagant shame and curling, spindrift sin. Estranged clauses find one another to form bizarre acknowledgments. Lied my sister cursing even after without asking them. Took bothering in vain without returning after midnight. Fighting again that didn't belong to despair me. Hate said only shouldn't anyway. Wasn't pretended to be mean to him the last piece. Sundered passions and mixed metaphors. The huddled bunch of us, drawn up like a pucker or a fist, united to scatter our faults, our crimes, and His name. Our wake is just the shape of our trespasses.

When it comes to putting you in an intricate hold, wrestlers have nothing on telemarketers. Yesterday night I succumbed to a conversation—less a conversation than a script at my expense—having to do with a credit card that I was being offered at an "embarrassingly low initial interest," all thanks to my spotless record. (More to the point, I have incurred sufficient debt in my life to be worth the trouble of contacting.) The catch to these deals, of course, is that sooner than you expect the interest rate will skyrocket. They're betting on your attention lapsing and your commitment to sensible spending losing steam; they're betting that you can't sustain virtue for six months. I have several friends who shift their debts from card to card to evade the impending crush. Financially speaking, they live on the lam. It took me a good fifteen minutes and several demurrals to escape this time.

This morning I join Joplin's tidy contingent of Jews at Shoal Creek. According to our respective inclinations, we drop our crusts and crib sheets in. The creek is sluggish today, drowsy and imperturbable, as if to say there's nothing new here, it's all been said before. We're nothing if not expeditious about our business. There is no evidence of fever in our efforts, no paroxysm of rapture in our midst. This year's ceremony is as smoothly dutiful as shaving. For some reason even the younger kids are towing the line. They are transfixed for the moment by the illusion that they are receding from the debris they've left rather than the other way around.

We end up accomplishing *tashlicht* in less time than it took me to get off the phone last night. As we conclude, there is nothing of the sun coming cleanly out of an eclipse; it is more like stretching after a nap. Some of us look up as we climb the bank back to our cars, but I suspect that it is to consider the weather or the scenery rather than the revised condition of our souls.

I come home to poetry—specifically, the fastidious Elizabeth Bishop, whom I'm preparing to teach tomorrow. First, I examine her poem about the sandpiper, that relentless inspector of the shoreline. Like the birds that bore witness this morning, he comes to evaluate and glean what he can from the endlessly "dragging grains." Like the rest of us, "looking for something, something, something," both poet and bird stand for scrutiny. We would be judged kindly. We would be cherished not according to our worth.

As I read, I find a fragment from another poet drifting through my mind. It is about a different twitchy bird, another of nature's migrant workers, who likewise wonders "what to make of a diminished thing." Strange, what comes together in water and what comes apart.

I will also undertake "The Man-Moth" on Monday. About its origins, Bishop gives us this: "I've forgotten what it was that was supposed to be 'mammoth.' But the misprint seemed meant for me." What I can make out so far is a fable of failed transcendence—that much I remember, that much I've got—whose hero "must investigate as high as he can climb," only to fall back. He cannot discover any Beyond beyond this world, either because there is none or because he "always seats himself facing the wrong way" on the pale subways he invariably returns to.

It must be hard for him to determine whether the train is crossing over the ties beneath him or if the ties themselves are being pulled out from under him. Point of view is everything, I guess. The principle holds true regardless.

It's been only hours since the ritual ended, yet already I've forgotten what it was that was supposed to be mammoth. Or it has changed, as is ever the case with moving water, whose solutions are only temporary. It was something about words that get mangled or miscast, sundered or absorbed, but nevertheless seemed meant for me. Something about climbing out and falling back and, guided by instinct, tradition, and the flow of others, climbing out again.

4 The History Channelers

One of the paradoxes of being an English professor at a small local college is that while you are seldom appreciated for the expertise you do have, you are also occasionally credited for expertise you do not. I was therefore not surprised to learn that when the sponsor of the junior high's History Day competitors needed someone to direct her students in the finer points of performance, my name came up. After all, shrewdly trading on my prestige and string of degrees—I think it was George in *Who's Afraid of Virginia Woolf?* who thinks that "ABMAPHID" sounds like a wasting disease, or perhaps a creature whose extinction is guaranteed—I'd judged the district elementary school spelling bee, served as toastmaster for the dedication of the refurbishment of the public library, and arbitrated countless conflicts between bosses and their secretaries via our department's Grammar Hotline. I promoted and produced language for a living, I went by "Doctor" more or less honestly, and, to put it bluntly, I came cheap. If not especially momentous, I was still, clearly, the man of the moment. Hence, I heeded the call of history.

Predictably, most of the problems I encountered came down to issues of authority. Not mine—as I said, I carried sufficient mystery and uncontestable, if elusive, esteem to compel the attention of the players. (I also made a point of wearing a sport coat and tie when I visited, emblems I reserve for the world beyond campus when I need to summon prestige. Similarly, a retired colonel will don his dress blues for a funeral or a judge will allude to his title to secure a table at a crowded restaurant.) No, it was the kids' believability that needed bolstering. In order to impersonate eminent historical figures with any effectiveness at all, they had to transform themselves more fully than any Stanislavsky-bred actor ever did when dissolving into his role. Basically, they all had to deal with being twelve-to-fourteen years old. The judges would excuse the artifice of our having to expedite each life we dis-

23

played, cramming its span into a ten-minute thesis. They would over-look the cardboard scenery moms had helped their kids cut from boxes cadged from the grocery store. Their willing suspension of disbelief could withstand the occasional chirp of a wristwatch in the audience as General Lee conceded at Appomattox Courthouse or excuse the ring of a cell phone outside the cell of soliloquizing Sir Thomas More, whose very walls swayed with the air conditioning. But something had to be done to distract from the fact that these junior high kids, for all their honorable effort and commitment to something other than video games and gateway drugs, were still, undeniably, junior high kids.

Acting is deception, granted, and like all adolescents, those in my charge had undoubtedly had plenty of practice. But acting upped the ante considerably, and considerably beyond their scope. It was one thing to lie convincingly about having brushed one's teeth, done one's homework, or pocketed the dollar that disappeared from the dresser. It was quite another to do so as Caesar. Yeats's claim to the contrary, the ceremony of innocence was not so easily drowned. I might tempo-rarily subdue their teen-aged squirms and instruct their pulses to slow down, but the truth was that by junior high, our actors hadn't lived long enough to credibly inhabit their *own* adult futures, much less anyone else's adult past. They were as yet too unassembled themselves to dissemble successfully—not according to the script, anyway, and not on cue.

Costumes and make-up could disguise their true stature only so far. Actually, the combination of vague, hasty tailoring and clumsy, almost clownish application of cosmetics had the opposite effect, em-phasizing the masquerade they were intended to conceal. Anything we used to accessorize the lie—borrowed briefcases and purses, babushkas and watch fobs, stopgap armor and sartorial ruses as given celebrities required—actually made it harder for the kids to be convincing, not to mention maintain their balance. Our few props—assorted sextants and scepters, plastic swords and quills—merely exposed how small our operating budget was. The students swam in their pseudo-period cloth-ing, struggling as much with the merchandise as with the lines they had to deliver. (Just try finding military gear, waistcoats, and tunics in the Children's Department of any store in the mall.) So our would-be Booker T. Washington had to contend not only with racial stereotyp-ing but also with the oversized suit that kept threatening to subdue him before he completed his speech. Our Abe Lincoln's estimable head kept sliding up his famous stovepipe as if he were a chimney sweep, and the embattled president had to free himself at least once during each rehearsal in order to issue his Emancipation Proclamation. In the midst of deliberations about his death, a toga scissored and sewn from a bed sheet caused our Socrates to revert to a boy who needed to be cajoled back to sleep. "You have to *amplify*," I implored them, referring to more than the projection of their voices to the back wall of the theater. But they could manage only so much dimension. The History Day theme for that year, "Triumph and Tragedy," connoted pinnacles and depths; my junior high players could neither aspire nor plummet very far and still keep their ill-fitting costumes intact.

As for the make-up, the kids depended on rickety miracles of deception, variously comprised of shoe polish, Scotch tape, spirit gum, Vaseline, and lipstick applied like plumber's caulk. It was as if they were engaged in a kind of goofy kabuki. With washable thin-line markers they slashed wrinkles on their foreheads like staves that could be read from the mezzanine; with talcum they excessively pomaded their hair as if elderly characters rose like phoenixes from the ashes of autos-da-fe held eras ago. Smudged with charcoal and rouge, Molly Pitcher's and Kit Carson's respective skins, meant to look weathered, looked necrotic instead. Cotton ball beards did not create sages but ramshackle Santas or, rather, based on the size of the players, Santa's scrabbling elves. The kids wore wigs that shifted on their heads like ice floes. They pancaked on the powder, making their faces seem to slop like boiled chickens loose on their bones. They sported breasts and bellies made of wadded toweling, which would slide off kilter and turn the kids into botched outcomes of plastic surgery, Cubist nightmares.

The conclusion of all of this counterfeiting was to render the pantheon of human history, from Garibaldi to Indira Gandhi, from Galileo to Thomas Edison, from Leonardo da Vinci to John Dillinger . . . well, cute. Watching from the vantage of authentic adulthood, I feared that parents, teachers, and judges might be charmed by the sputtering history staged for their benefit, but they'd never be edified, implicated, or truly moved.

Nonetheless, I did what I could to counteract the actors' unerasable nature. I helped to edit some of the scripts, removing telltale anachronistic diction from their dialogues. "It's unlikely that Anne Boleyn would have uttered the phrase 'Yeah, *right!*' under any circumstances," I argued. "And I'd bet anything that General Patton never referred to his junior officers as 'you guys.'" I also rooted out instances of unnatural exposition. History would have to survive the absence of such admittedly functional but wholly incredible lines as "Well, there's never a dull moment when you're Thomas Jefferson, the third president of the United States. It's almost 1803 already, and I still haven't purchased the Louisiana Territory!"

Mostly, though, I urged the actors to manifest the physical differences their adopted selves required. Eleanor Roosevelt doesn't throw herself into her seat the way a child does, I said; rather, she reaches for it gingerly, befitting a woman of consequence, pomp, and excess poundage. Then, when she rises, she doesn't launch herself out of the chair like one of the White House pups but works her way up in stages, pressing up with both hands. The pre-teens in particular were used to rocking back and forth as they spoke as if needing the bathroom. My would-be soldiers, scientists, and labor leaders were sprawlers who swung their bodies about as recklessly as they used slang. I tried to explain that older workers are not called "working stiffs" for nothing. I reminded them of the arthritis and equity that increase over time and encouraged them to show both in their carriage. Thus I grounded Lindbergh and Earhart. I bent springy senior statesmen into ampersands. I laid gravity upon Joplin Junior High School's brace of notables and bade them stay.

In short, I tried to teach the kids to cultivate a semblance of the heft of decades in only a month. (The alternative, I told them, was to whittle history down and compete solely as distinguished children: say, a bunch of boy King Tuts and a squad of Shirley Temples.) Hamlet took pains to tutor the players he commissioned in plausibility, admonishing them not to bellow, strut, or saw the air in such ways as to strain patience and crack the mirror he'd have them hold up to Nature. But at least the prince was dealing with grown men, and professionals at that. *My* troupe's problem was not tempering their passions but mimicking passions they'd never had.

Unfortunately, even when I convinced them that they must not only speak the speech but act their assumed ages as well, the result was pretty comical. Grown-up moods take years to cook into the countenance. For example, kids get sad, certainly, but their sadnesses are comparatively shallow; richer recriminations and profounder sorrows take time to bed down in the core of the people we become—a great deal more time than we could devote to the process. Asked to do languor, our Queen Elizabeth I merely looked bored, as if she'd been closeted away from court society to finish her algebra homework. Asked to do hauteur, our Napoleon stalked about the stage with what seemed to be a bad nosebleed. Instead of ennui, I got petulance; instead of dignity, daze; instead of studied contempt, the look of someone who'd swallowed sour milk with his cereal. Contemplation came off as constipation, existential crisis as ADHD.

Yet dutifully I drilled them late into the evenings they'd have preferred to fill with television and soccer. A veritable encyclopedia of despots, generals, rebel leaders, artists, martyrs, and other luminaries kept hours after class in rarefied detention that spanned centuries. Those who did not know their history, who did not have every jerry-built gesture and syllable of it down pat, were doomed to repeat it and, every afternoon for nearly a month, repeat it again. Such was the history they inherited: a show that must go on.

And on they went, serving up bite-sized highlights of Western civilization like turns on a bill. Twenty-three elite personalities dredged out of the archives. (Dredged, indeed, going by the baggy, overblown figures they presented.) Twenty-three sundry tragedies strung together to constitute a pageant, our very own ruin with a view, which we offered up gamely to enchant an audience ready and willing to be enchanted.

And going by the applause and the judging sheets, we got away with it. We apparently pulled off Pericles without tarnishing the Golden Age of Greece. We led out Lenin and the putsch went unpunished. We paraded our Columbus, Kennedy, and Sacagawea, and their reputations somehow survived. And afterward, all clutching certificates of merit, our miniature diplomats and makeshift sovereigns were embraced by grateful teachers and parents, who felt, for once, that the dustbin of history had been redeemed, that the past, theirs and ours, was not lost time. Because it clearly featured students from their own school district, because their own children headed the cast, history was assured a level of significance that no textbook, file tape, or document under glass could match. Nothing was as preposterous as the version of posterity we put on that day. As it turned out, though, intimacy, not integrity, was the point of it.

I used to wonder what it would be like to watch the network news as if I knew everyone involved. If the nightclub fire had exclusively claimed my classmates, the eight-car pile-up had restricted itself to the relatives with whom I'd just shared Thanksgiving turkey, and the evening's inventory of burglary, rape, and murder victims had all had my last name, how would I bear up? How would I persevere under all that personal implication? Then I'd realize that, of course, every assault and battery, every killing blizzard and embezzlement, every accident and spectacle *had* sought out *someone's* husband, wife, parent, or child. Everyone who was interviewed on screen or made the papers was someone's significant other, just like everyone who did not.

"What seest thou else / In the dark backward and abysm of time?" asks Shakespeare's Prospero. The answer is always the same: the faces of our children, which remind us of our own, long since ravaged and irretrievable. The children, flushed with their performances, will discover that, too. For parents are fated to let their sons and daughters in on their mutual doom. That was one definite lesson that came out of the day's proceedings. All of us, sooner or later, will be history.

5 Watch This Space

We work in the dark—we do what we can—we give what we have. Our doubt is our passion and our passion is our task. The rest is the madness of art.

—Henry James, "The Middle Years"

Unpack any molecule and you'll find it's mostly empty space—like space itself, chiefly composed of soots. A monotony of black, an ecstasy of it, with barely a break in the mute and unremitting night. "From Blank to Blank—/ A Threadless Way," went Emily Dickinson, whose groping disclosed nothing more definite than the determination that "'Twas lighter—to be Blind." True, one might find a brief gash of star or an arguable flicker of intention somewhere, but in the main it's a formal evening every evening, and nature's wardrobe is basic black.

The overall lack of habitation goes against the psychic grain. We prefer to interpret our Solar System, with its massive planets running unopposed, conducting their ancient oval offices around an eternally tenured sun, as the result of the primary election, when actually it represents only the returns from the nearest precincts, which are not very reliable in the long run. In the main, science finds only a modest ration of atoms allotted to every astronomical acre—the monopoly of darkness is that undeniable, a comprehensive locking out and locking down. The chances of anything occupying a random shovelful of universe, much less of any *being* being there, are so scant that they barely bear mention.

John Updike wrote about the need to edit our ambition: in the absence of supernatural certainty, he suggested the consolation of "the small answer of a texture." But on a macrocosmic scale, even that may be too much to ask. Our constant barrage of radio waves, television

signals, and other electronic sorties notwithstanding, no technological "Marco" is likely to get anything resembling a "Polo" in response.
No, from all reports, it's an agony of emptiness all around, a crush of
nothing, and just looking up is enough to threaten your religion. Talk
about vistalessness. Talk about empyreal disease. We yearn for surfaces
for eyes or instruments to light upon, something to satisfy our starving for contact and contradict the nil, but in the big picture—and in
the last analysis, there is no other picture showing tonight—matter is
a smattering. In sum, the universe is an exaggerated zero, with barely
an erg or iota to wrap your mind around.

And doesn't the brain conceive of itself in much the same way, not
as the wormy clod that surgery exposes, not as any solid per se, but as
all sheen, unblemished atmosphere, infinite sky?

As I say, as for sentient company, apart from the usual terrestrial
subjects, forget it. According to textbook illustrations of the Milky
Way, astronomers have placed us far from the metropolitan center,
in the lower left-hand corner of the spill, which is still hypothetically
dribbling off the page. We're in the equivalent of western Kansas, cos-
mically speaking, and no witness protection program could have so
successfully hidden us from view. And don't except Earth from the
dim statistical probabilities, either. The odds against our own presence, much less our perpetuity, are unimaginably long. Indeed, if we
were a bet, you wouldn't take us.

Some poets may invoke an instress that guarantees the intactness
of all things, as if every grain, each precious smithereen, were firmly
tucked in the hip pocket of God, but our subatomic burgling tends
to prove the tenacity of nothingness instead. What is the atom if not
an individual instance and symptom of the general nullity: a nucleus
surrounded by vacancy like a baby asleep in its bedroom or a planet
turning and turning through a bad dream of vastness. Break the lock
on any structure and you'll discover it's already been looted. Creation
seems to have been cleaned out before we got there, so it's mostly ransacked atoms you come upon. So are you. Matter's densest concentrate
is mostly hole. And so are you. Think of those diagrams of atomic
squadrons, columns, and stacks your high school textbooks offered to
insinuate the hidden scheme of sine qua non, spread out like so much
bubble wrap. All those containers of unoccupiable space, like those
see-through office buildings in overgrown cities whose economies

have gone bust. In a sense, made up of molecules made up of them, we are more or less already gone.

Run the vacuum as long as you can stand to, and you'll see it's impossible to upholster the universe with poetry. The sky is a catastrophe of blackness, which proves so absolute that writers have been casting every conceivable turn of phrase into it for centuries and never hooked a thing. Mary Oliver writes in *Blue Pastures* that misbegotten forms— badly edited bodies and stillborn prose—are consigned to "the oblivion of the ill-made, nature's dark throat." But deftness fares no better, finally. Welcome to the validation of Wallace Stevens's "Domination of Black," which blots out even *his* images. And if canonical writers can't dissolve their detachment, who can?

What Gertrude Stein said of Oakland—"There is no there there"— in the universe is writ large. Crawl out late at night when nothing but physics is on, and it's only so much Oakland everywhere you look. All poetry can do is "there, there" you back to bed and put another blanket over you against the cold.

In the absence of alternatives, artists consign themselves to nocturnes, banging their imaginations against the wall in the hope of waking some deity who'll tell them to keep it down. Facing vacancy, poets posit themselves by producing poems, just as under the very same conditions potters would produce pots or cobblers shoes. They are all reflexive gestures—stanzas, ceramics, soles. So are Christo's canvas installations, his curtained valleys, battened-down beachfronts, and wrapped woods. So is Alain Arias-Misson's Pamplona text, an extensive deployment of gigantic punctuation marks intended to manifest the city's underlying grammar. So are the sales of stars as birthday gifts, which the purchasers can register in honor of loved ones. (One might buy a nebula to commemorate a nephew's graduation, a constellation for a special cousin's bar mitzvah, or a whole swath of astrology for a twenty-fifth anniversary, as his budget allows.) So is the naming of every rise and declivity on the moon, not to mention every other boulder big enough to detect up there. And so is "Black on Black," a ten-foot-square black canvas painted black, which dominates the west wall in a room of the Chicago Art Institute, where it draws in and spooks the patrons, anticipating by example the announcement of "Lights Out." All craft and supplication pitted against the void, which has all the room in the world and all the time.

And if all that weren't unsettling enough, rumor has it that the universe keeps retreating from us, somewhat the way millions of Russians did from the incursions of would-be conquerors during war, leading them ever deeper into the zero. Science is pretty frank and unforgiving about this, and we don't need all that *much* science to find out how far we fall short in our approximations. Even a layman's appreciation of Einstein is enough to tell us that the clocks and rulers we might carry into subatomic interstices or the endless uttermost prove useless, there where an hour is not an hour after all, and not an inch an inch. Instead of formulating space, we merely alter the terms of our futility. One might say we're down to desperate measures, had that not always been the case.

A monarchy of darkness. An obscure constitution. But no matter.

If all goes according to one current theory, Creation will come down to an omnivorous black hole, the *final* Final Solution and last collapse. There will have been nothing so ecumenical in existence as the end of it, which might be envisioned as an inhalation so complete that even our ghosts will get sucked in. Our holy and unwholesome ghosts, our inconspicuous and colloquial, our silent and sociable ghosts; the abject and the unacknowledged along with the indomitable ghosts; the familiar and the faint, the teasing and the malignant, the availing and the uninvoked, the intimate and the exiled alike; our wistful and forbidding spirits, those that leave spectral evidence behind and those that remove all sign; all the carping, cloying, coy, incorrigible, and unaccounted for ghosts, all at once and all together; the ghosts we were and those we'll become, accumulated and compounded into the one period put to space and time.

In the meantime—which by that implacable definition, it always is—on afternoon television, they are consulting with the dead. Reality may be escaping in every direction every instant, but the premise of this particular show is that dying is centripetal. Our own ghosts return to us like repercussions, and apparently they can be encouraged to do so on cue. It's a comfort—one way of countering the expanding universe by reeling something personal back in. They seize eagerly upon their namesakes to secure themselves, much as etymologists clutch words by their roots. Even if their departed have come back to complain or to punish them, the audience welcomes those possibilities over an eternity of the silent treatment.

Not a single guest judges. It's as Don DeLillo wrote in *Mao II:* "Only shallow people insist on disbelief." Why assume that a television studio is less conducive to rarefied visits than a chapel or a cemetery? Spirits might insinuate themselves anywhere. Consider the portable auras saints wore in old paintings like high collars turned up against the wind. It stands to reason that like everything else in Creation, divinity can come upon us out of nowhere, from behind.

The uniquely accessible host is the only one who's actually occupied by the ghosts, and he translates for the studio audience their queries and talismanic memories, their jokes and concerns, their good wishes and regrets. The posthumous rush he reports occasionally befuddles him, and it occasionally takes him a minute or two for him to connect a given ghost to its family—afterworld traffic is snarled, and entities are crammed like commuters on a subway car. Eventually, though, he is able to home in on one or more idiosyncrasies recognized by selected members of the gallery. And so, this hour's arbitration between incorporeal and carnal Callisons, followed by a reunion of a departed Furillo and some who've arrived in the flesh, is under way.

Tickets to the show are hard to come by. The disappointment and envy of those whose missing familiars do not show up is obvious. Everyone hopes to be summoned (by the host, by the impalpable— there is no discernible difference). Before the program goes to air, their prayers are abstract—customary petitions, more or less equally divided between "Please" and "Please don't." On camera, however, hopes grow as precise as a child's Christmas list. People wish for a little specificity in their immanence, something sensible to fix their awe upon. A little preliminary data and identifying detail—is that too much to ask?

Cynics may quibble, but science is no different, really, when it goes pioneering, trying to snag something unprecedented on a radio frequency or an algorithm. A reassuring density is what everyone is after. A verification of more than we are. "What is the difference between a cathedral and a physics lab?" asks Annie Dillard in *Teaching a Stone to Talk.* "Are not they both saying: Hello?" Mass consciousness is equally on the minds of the forensic and the faithful in the end. In the end, everyone wants to be haunted.

The host of the show tunes in a distant channel and is not amazed. He is never amazed on any other episode, either. He treats his supernatural endowment much the way a professional basketball player might his gift for elevation or a musician his perfect pitch. In an epilogue, he soberly reviews the messages left by the dead. His recap does not vary much from show to show. We are witnessed. We are loved. Even if we feel neglected or ourselves neglect, no one is ever lost or lonely, no one left out or left behind.

"I knew that if anyone would come through the other side, it would be Phil," explains one member of the Callison family. She is tearful but content. "He's the type to, you know, barge to the front of the line." Then four Furillos, representing three generations of descent from their own deceased, congratulate one another on having cajoled Anthony out of the atmosphere like a convict hidden in the woods. "As soon as I heard 'poker chips,' I nudged Connie—didn't I, Con?—and said, 'That's got to be Anthony. Absolutely him.'" It is always a good visit and always too short.

Watching them rejoice over the reemergence of vanished family members, I perversely think of my brother's appointment books. When Jeff completes a task, he doesn't just check it off the calendar, he obliterates it with a vengeance. When he does something that he had not previously noted down as a thing that needed doing, he goes back to the appropriate date, inscribes the assignment, then annihilates it, too. He shrouds September and soaks October in shade; he chars March, eradicates May, wipes July from sight, plunges December in drear. Ultimately, all of his weekends are overcast, his holidays sunk in mourning, his weeks featureless. He refuses even one hour of illumination. What remains is month after month of uninterrupted murk, entire seasons of tar. Eventually, every day is filled in like a grave.

Jeff isn't trying to impress posterity—he trashes his annual record as soon as the new January arrives, when he starts a new book with pristine resolutions. He means only to consummate the year in total gloom, grinding out the hours, the well spent together with the squandered, smothering every circled, underscored, and arrowed errand and dousing every irritating asterisk in black. He leaves no doubt: what's past is past and without horizon. My brother's brutal bookkeeping reminds me of Beckett's Clov, with his dream of ideal proportions and immutable order, which only extinction can guarantee: "A world where all would be silent and still and each thing in its last place,

under the last dust." My brother's Doomsday Books, his yearly install-
ments of shadow, appreciate in much the same way individual days
in nature do: the steady, predictable evacuation of all the world we've
known, until it is inked in to its edges with night.

Maybe he's imitating the kind of timeless sky God sought, too,
showing off His supreme elevation, blowing us away with His perfect
pitch. If that's the case, it's strange that convention has us choose to
celebrate incandescence, however brief and uncertain, when it comes.
We tend to presume that darkness is worthwhile only when it sets off
His disclosures. ("Quiet, please," begs our host, who relies on silence
to help him to find the secret frequency of hospitable sounds.) Against
a solid heaven, it may be easier to see the contrails of God. But space
may be the feature presentation, not merely the screen. "This thing
of darkness I / Acknowledge mine," declared Shakespeare's Prospero, who could not restrict belief to lighter spirits after all. If memory
serves, it would not be long before he cast away his book forever.

6 Reason Not the Need

A telephone, its shorn cord dragging after, a few ripped filaments licking the pavement. A bag of Christmas wrapping. A mobile made entirely of CDs. There is no predicting what someone will rush to salvage from the fire. There is no knowing what an intruder will choose to carry off from an unlocked apartment. A cocker spaniel. Metal chessmen simulating Union and Confederate forces. You'd think they'd think alike, occupant and outlaw, but that's seldom the case. Nor does either one automatically seize what you'd seize. A cabinet that once housed an old-fashioned radio, now nothing but a husk. An ashtray that had been painstakingly shaped by the thumbs of an eight-year-old at sleep-over camp or one that advertises a restaurant an uncle once owned, now, restaurant and uncle alike, gone under. An assonant series sounding like something out of Doctor Seuss—a hat, a bat, a cat, a doll named Pat, and a basketball that's flat—whose rhyme does not guarantee a reason. There is no system to infer from the compulsions that litter the news. A tornado smashes storm doors and storefronts, and the thieves are one step ahead of the Samaritans. The home team blows the pennant or wins it: the host city braces itself for invasion either way. A revolution breaks open the marketplace like a piñata, and the mad scramble is on.

Or not so mad: what seems at street level like chaos and abandon may seem from the distance of sociology understandable. Michael J. Rosenfeld, a Stanford University professor, has inferred an underlying logic from his data on looting. "You get a sense, from what people loot and destroy, of which things they think are legitimate," he discovers. "The things left standing are the parts of society that people feel some solidarity with." Occasionally, the protocol of what gets protected and what gets plundered is obvious, such as when during the Viet Nam War students ransacked the private bookstore on my campus while leaving the Union Bookstore, which gave a superior student discount and funneled money back into the university's general fund, undisturbed. (They also savaged the local phone company outlet and shattered the windows of a bar notorious for carding undergraduates, but the inspiration was not determined to be political in either of these instances.) When the cash register at the dime store remains intact although all the candy bars and gum are gone, the cops rightly forego interrogating suspects from grown-up syndicates in favor of neighborhood kids. Money and jewelry spark obvious motives, and no one wonders about neurosis when they are made off with. Only a handful of culprits might be held accountable for missing vials of anthrax, and while editorialists debate the repercussions, none question the rationale. In a word, thefts tend to make sense.

But just as often, it seems that there is no concept or consistency behind what the violent bear away. Eight mannequins were stripped naked and abducted from a department store in an Ohio suburb. A rack of costumes was filched from a party supply store in the same mall. (A fraternity scavenger hunt? An outbreak of transvestitism? Officials claim that it would be premature to connect the robberies to one another, much less to some eccentric fascination more disturbing than the break-in itself.) All the brass instruments—only the brass instruments—were hauled off from the band room of a community college. In one night a week before Thanksgiving, three cases of Merlot were taken from a Bloomington, Indiana, liquor store and, from a farm less than two miles away, half a dozen baffled, crated turkeys. (Police surmised that the feast would take place somewhere in the same county. Citizens, lock your pantries! Keep your eyes on your pies!) From a barbershop in Pasadena, two electric clippers. From a sports card shop, a baseball signed by Tony Oliva. (Be on the lookout for the only Twins fan in Kansas City, where the robbery was committed.) From an open garage just outside of Nashville, a drill, a weed trimmer, some guttering, and two pair of work gloves, one so worn that it had stiffened permanently into the contours of the guy who'd been using them for so long, so they'd accept no substitute hands. (Credit the criminal with a dedication to home maintenance, despite his other moral lapses, that's undeniable, as well as with a willingness to supervise his own rehabilitation through work detail.) From a dentist's office in Lincolnwood, Illinois, a glittering fistful of picks. The plastic letters from the sign outside the First Presbyterian Church of Jefferson City, Missouri.

When passions surpass understanding, we are left with as much wonder as dismay.

When a Denver felon was asked in court why among the stuff he
burgled from a neighbor's house he bothered to steal a box of empty
jars, jars the man had gathered for recycling, he answered, "It's what
there was."

ABC News publishes an annual "crime blotter" devoted to the
year's weirdest delinquencies, and the competition is always fierce.
There was an outbreak of gumball banditry all over greater metropolitan Newark that was so extensive and so prolonged that only a coordinated gang operation could account for it. During the same week
that a Nebraska man was arrested for stealing garden gnomes, an Iowa
man pleaded guilty to swiping 35,000 toy Hot Wheels cars. There
was a spate of parking meter robberies in Pittsburgh—214 meters be-
headed and absconded with in a span of two months. Then there was
the case of Melvin Hanks, who swiped ninety-six ponytails that had
been donated to a charity for the making of wigs for sick children. He
was brought to justice, but the person or persons behind the theft of
a sixty-five million-year-old dinosaur footprint from Bosque County,
Texas, which had to be chiseled out of the surrounding rock to accomplish the crime, remain at large. So does the Condom Crook of Little Rock, Arkansas, whose pilfering of dozens of cartons of condoms
has lifted him to folk-hero status and suggests a brand of criminality
at once profligate and oddly, in terms of proper sexual precautions,
responsible. In countless as yet undiscovered headquarters, under assorted mattresses and piles of clothes in closet corners, in mud-choked
crawlspaces and in plots dug at night in backyards all over America
lies the enigmatic stash of indecipherable crimes. Presumably, the perpetrators can hardly contain themselves for the thought of the classic
hubcaps, Hummel figurines, or trick handcuffs their respective estates
now secretly contain.

In the film *Arthur,* the amiable alcoholic title character, played by
Dudley Moore, marvels at Liza Minelli's Linda, whom he accidentally
observes stealing a necktie from an upscale men's store. "It's the perfect
crime!" he gasps. "Girls don't wear ties! Well, admittedly some do, but
it's a good crime!" He responds to the pure aesthetic gesture of useless,
inscrutable shoplifting. It is the movie's inceptive moment, too: love at
first crime site.

Although TV cop shows would have us believe otherwise, forensics cannot always track the damage back to a coherent, triggering grudge. Such was the case at the Tri-State Mineral Museum, where a Saturday night's vandalism struck both the museum curator and the detectives assigned to the case as arbitrary and impenetrable. They—for it did appear to have taken more than one crook to accomplish so thorough a trashing in a single visit—had shattered the glass cases where the better pedigreed gems were kept and scattered their lines of ascent all over the floor. They had dislodged the plutonic tools from their wall mounts and toppled the reef of semi-precious stones that had stood for more than half a century against the north wall. They had scattered the sullen plunder of Joplin's founding excavations and spilled the fittings and gears of bygone machinery like the black castings of titanic worms. Displays that had taken the proprietors months to construct and patrons even longer to fund were overturned. Even the reporters on the scene, stepping gingerly through the muddle of base metals, could not restrain themselves from commenting on air about the loss to community history and the shameful conduct of teenagers—for the consensus was that this was the handiwork of teenagers, evidenced in part by the lingering aroma of beer and (a clue discreetly kept off the air) a soiled prophylactic—who had no conscience and no resources for finding something more worthwhile to do on a Saturday night.

Within the year, however, the museum restoration was essentially complete. In a follow-up interview, the curator expressed his relief that almost the entire collection had been recovered piecemeal from the wreckage. Although the place had "looked like West Hell six months ago," he said, he was confident that it would soon reopen to the public "good as new, that is, if you can say that about a history museum."

So robbery was not the point, which was some comfort in the wake of catastrophe. The instigators did not steal the lucre from the filth or load their every rift with irreplaceable ore. It seemed that their sole incentive had been the thrill of trespass itself. Breaking into and breaking down the Tri-State Mineral Museum might have been a logical extension of their alcoholic and sexual transgressions, nothing more.

On that latter subject, wistful citizens definitely had trouble appreciating the appeal of having intercourse in such glum and loveless confines. How plight troth amid the mangle or wrest pleasure in this subterranean context, where thoughts must eventually turn from carnal urgency to the somber way of all flesh? When in *From*

Here to Eternity Burt Lancaster dropped knees first to the sand, paying no heed to military protocol and sharp coastal deposits, millions of women envied what Deborah Kerr was about to succumb to. (Some couples like it rough, they say, and we may remember Howard Nemerov's "The Goose Fish," a poem about another beachfront liaison, whose guilty lovers "had thought to understand / By violence upon the sand / The only way that could be known / To make a world their own.") But Burt and Deborah suffered nothing compared to the injuries the anonymous guilty parties at the Tri-State Mineral Museum must have endured to exercise their desire among the rocky debris. What romance could flower in the dank and gravel there? "If kids are going to risk juvenile records for a little erotic adventure," a neighbor commented to me, "why not break into a furniture store? At least there'd be mattresses. I mean . . . ouch! You know?" To which I could only reply that the course of true love never did run smooth.

The inside dope is that there is still at least one item missing from the museum inventory. They have yet to recover a shard of alexandrite, small enough to fit into a pocket—not the rarest or most expensive loss they might have incurred, but by no means negligible. The single souvenir of an evening's ardor in the dark: perhaps it betokened a birthstone. The police should be advised to focus their investigation on the whereabouts of high school students born in June.

Hoarding can be its own reward. It can be its own indictment as well.

"Well, he left, see. And the secretary went out. I was all alone in the waiting-room. I don't know what came over me, Hap. The next thing I know, I'm in his office—paneled walls, everything. I can't explain it. I—Hap, I took his fountain pen." This is from the testimony of Biff Loman in *Death of a Salesman*. Reduced to feckless, petty revenges for imagined slights against him, he cannot reason his own need. "That was an awful dumb—what did you do that for?" his brother asks. "I don't know. I just—wanted to take something," Biff replies, lost and foundering.

War, retribution, and romance—all come with spoils. But acquisition is not the only means of establishing a relationship between the taker and the taken. Witness the example of Alcee Arobin, that paragon of self-involvement in Kate Chopin's *The Awakening*. When Edna

Pontellier, the novel's heroine and his current paramour, calls his attention to a photograph, surely a memento of their affair, Arobin rejects it without sentiment or ceremony: "What do I want with it? Throw it away." Thus dispossession may be self-possession on another plane.

"It was a part, at once of Mrs. Sparsit's dignity and service, not to lunch. She supervised the meal officially, but implied that in her own stately person she considered lunch a weakness." As an entrenched luncher myself, who for that reason views noon as the zenith of the day in more ways than one, I am stung by the self-righteous abnegation of this Dickens original, who turns up her nose at the very enticement that captivates mine. She maintained her pinched and disdainful manner as others indulged in eating, "looking quite cast down by the popular vices," of which lunching struck her as among the more vulgar.

I can well imagine Mrs. Sparsit wincing as I dig in to my own midday meal, with her minatory expression tightening nearby as though someone had yanked a drawstring on her bag of a face. A world purged of lunch? Hard times, indeed!

The contrast between Mrs. Sparsit and me explains why I'd be the more sympathetic juror in the case of the elderly gentleman who, having never committed so much as a misdemeanor in his whole scrupulous, dutiful life, after the cafeteria he had frequented every day for so many years was scheduled for demolition, managed to unfasten the lock and smuggled his lunch onto the condemned premises. Passersby spied his humped figure through a soaped-over window and contacted the police.

When they arrived, the man was layering his daily bagel with sugar-free strawberry jam (a concession to his doctor's advice about improving his diet). "Five minutes more, please," he said, and they saw no harm in stepping back and allowing him the courtesy of finishing his lunch before taking him into custody.

As I would have. For I, too, customarily protect and prolong my lunch as much as possible and would elevate every lunch to the level of fetish or ritual if the workday permitted. I, too, expend loving attention upon the embellishment of my bagel and find trenchancy in the trifles that accompany the task. Just consider the cunning little tub of jelly that is given free of charge with each day's selection. I find it touching to think that it is someone's job to detach the packets from their frames, the orderly corpuscular networks in which they are shipped from Mason, Ohio (the home of PPI Corporation), and to position them in wire baskets (unless this second procedure is entrusted to a second employee), where they gleam like isolettes in a nursery for the delectation of lucky lunchers like me. Each plump packet has a simultaneous quality of sturdiness and give, a sensation at once agreeable and disquieting, with something of the heft and suppleness of a small toad resting squat in your palm. It makes a shearing sound as its epidermal seal is pulled away, like a rake's screech against pavement or what I imagine the legendary mandrake root would cry if it were abruptly stripped from its bed. The silver underside of the cellophane gleams in the fluorescent light of the lunchroom, and there is always a translucent blood blister of jelly adhering there, a jellied ectoplasm, which gleams, too, and which, like the general experience of the jelly packet, is at once agreeable and disquieting as well. Such sweetness concentrated in a condiment! Such ingenuity and simple grace, free for the taking, for as long as one's lunch allows. (Begging Mrs. Sparsit's pardon for my dilations, but a lunch hurried is a lunch dishonored.) Had police denied that poor, hungry soul, not to mention any given luncher, so little as five minutes' lingering to satisfy so modest and sublime an appetite as that, they'd have committed a crime worse than the one they'd been summoned to interrupt.

Recognizing that age only intensifies our addictions and that custom beds down so deeply in us that not even dementia can extinguish it, the corporation that had bought out the cafeteria decided not to press charges. For if lunch is a weakness, Mrs. Sparsit, lack of compassion is a greater one.

Any upscale store worth its standing recognizes that the first item to be manufactured and sold is desire. Before Sharper Image and other such companies brought esoteric needs into being and focus for us, who knew enough to want to want their products?

Bookended mid-row by a couple of massive, implacable sleepers during a flight from Austin to Tulsa, I paged through my complimentary copy of *Sky Mall*, one of those magazines dedicated to the proposition that passengers are so desperate for means of passing the claustrophobic span of their captivity that they'll not only prolong and savor a bag of pretzels from the snack cart but will also read *any-*

thing, even if it's a magazine that's 100% advertising. But as I thumbed through *Sky Mall,* I found myself authentically absorbed. If the chief quality of a perfect gift is that it is something one would never think to buy for himself, I'd hit the mother lode. I learned that a motorized Turbo-Groomer for trimming nose and ear hair and featuring rotary blades that whirl at over 6000 rpm goes for $59.95. A remote control for paging one's keyrings, memo pads, and other elusive possessions, which the owner would electronically "tag," can be had for $49.95; for that matter, a caddy for holding *all* of one's remote controls (made of solid maple and available in either cherry or mahogany finish) costs $69.00. If that's too dear a price for the coach passenger to afford, an automatic, silver-plated business card dispenser runs $37.95. A canister of Oxygen Shot, for that quick blast of cell-cooling refreshment, is only $29.00 for a three-pack. The same $29.00 will also buy a Lip Enhancer Vacuum for creating fuller, more voluptuous lips, an effect that lasts up to twelve hours per treatment. A fair price? Who can say what the market will bear when the market did not previously exist?

It requires a special sort of genius to ensure that eccentricity does not diminish as budgets tighten. A pair of lawn aerator sandal attachments—you walk your lawn in these special elongated spikes to revitalize your grass and rid it of thatch build-up—is only $12.99. So is a decorative sink strainer / stopper, which comes in white, almond, blue, or gray speckle (this last ideal for a stainless steel sink). And a mere $8.50 buys a Bracelet Buddy, which by helping someone fasten her own bracelet puts an "end to another of life's little frustrations." On the other hand, and at the higher end of the consumer scale, you can replace nearly anything you own, from your showerhead to your hubcaps to your putter to your garden gnomes, with gold. Also, there are countless products that allow you to similarly couch, swaddle, and otherwise pamper your pets, including, for $189.00, a PetStep Ramp to aid arthritis-stricken or injured dogs in getting into and out of the van. And my favorite, for the person so utterly endowed that his possessions seem impregnable to precedent-setting presents, there's the Sparta Watch Winder, which uses a "natural swinging action" to wind any automatic watch. It takes only two D batteries and $225.00 to guarantee that look that says, "You know, I never would have gotten this for myself."

It's like my father's friend Maury once told me: if the customer already wants it, you don't have to sell it to him. "When noon rolls around, you don't have to sell a guy lunch. He comes into the restaurant because he's hungry already—he's ready to buy, right? There's nothing for you to do except maybe get out of his way or refill his coffee. That's not selling. Selling is persuading someone that he has to have something he doesn't know he has to have and maybe really *doesn't* have to have. More important, that he has to have the *one* something *you've* got to sell him."

"I don't get it."

"What is it you don't get?"

"I don't get how you know people want the stuff you're selling."

He leaned in meaningfully. "That is exactly the wrong question. How do *they* know that they *don't* want the stuff I'm selling? That's the right question. That's the last twenty-seven years of my life, from my car to my clothes, from that question." Then the big signature smile of his opened over his cigar. "It's a lot more interesting than taking orders from off a menu, right? And even though it's not such a secret, most of the schmucks out there act like it was. Believe it."

I did. A compelling fellow, Maury, who had the knack of making people feel smart because they listened without contradicting him. Smart the way guys whose pens contain currency translation programs, who travel with laser-sleek leather document organizers, and who store their liquor in massive walnut Old World globes feel smart. Or so I can only suppose, having none of those items and, truthfully, not wanting them either, a fact that does make me feel free, but only when someone like Maury isn't around to dispel my contentment.

Twenty-five volumes constitute the full set of the *American Review*, which ran for ten years, from 1967 to 1976, on the literary journal scene. Twenty-five, plus a special valedictory volume compiled once the extinction of the series had been determined. I happened upon my first volume while I was browsing through a used book bin at a university bookstore. My rule of thumb is that a journal must contain at least two items to which I suspect I might want future access before I buy it, and AR #9 readily passed the test. A week or so later, I happened upon AR #7 in that same bin—the merchandise is fluid, and regular customers have the best crack at securing the treasures—and #5 and #6 showed up later that semester. AR #8 appeared on, of all places, a grocery store close-out rack, idly at swim among the reduced plastic wrap and Graham crackers, the remaindered Grishams and Krantzes.

It is hard to say just when not having shaved for a while turns into deliberately growing a beard—the boundary probably differs from man to man and from face to face—but one day you look in the mirror and you're a guy with a beard. Who knows but that the infamous Collyer brothers, Homer and Langley, whose corpses were unearthed in 1947 from a moraine of newspapers, broken furniture, garden implements, medical equipment, umbrellas, gas chandeliers, rusting guns, and other rubbish—103 tons of junk, all told—heaped in their Harlem mansion, didn't begin innocuously with, say, a few outdated phone books or the jawbone of a horse? (Yes, the phone books and jawbone were part of the booty that the cops shoveled out.) That is to say, I did not consciously covet the series and never characterized myself as a collector. But when I saw AR #1 in a bag of books a colleague was preparing to trade in for cash, a shiver of eagerness ran through my fingers as I snatched it and, with no bargain hunter's pretense toward nonchalance, offered him the full cover price.

Around this time I formally subscribed to the periodical and cleared off a bookshelf to devote to it exclusively. In addition to the growth of my collection through the mail—for a collection it by now had most certainly become—there was the occasional swelling of the shelf due to the odd volume I'd find serendipitously. (This was before the Internet, of course, which has made collecting far easier, more systematic, and, assuming one has sufficient cash flow, dependably predestined to succeed.) As for the red-letter day when out of the blue I received a call from an old friend from graduate school alerting me to his having discovered at his campus bookstore AR #2, #3, and #4 huddled inconspicuously together on a sale table like in-laws kibbitzing over the cold cuts at a family reunion . . . well, the memory of that lucky find and lasting friendship still moves me. With a little effort, I believe I can still feel the texture of the checkbook as I gleefully signed off on his reimbursement.

Novelist Alexander Theroux would grant my small penchant greater profundity than I do. To his way of thinking, collecting is, variously, a quest for adequacy and identity, a disclosure of personality through what one accrues to bolster it, and an aspiration, however scaled down or trivialized, toward the Absolute. Or so he asserts at the conclusion of his essay "Odd Collections," in which he inventories dozens of collectors, from the renowned to the otherwise anonymous, and thereby, in the form of his catalogue, creates an odd collection of his own. "The mere challenge of collecting may generate the impulse," he muses, "the impossibility of success like the inevitability in high-jumping of failure guaranteeing a strange kind of buoyancy, because it is endless." To put it another way, the essence is the process, the collecting rather than the collection the key. Indeed, the futility of ever having it all, the principle of inexhaustibility, ensures the sheer ongoingness of the enterprise, which, Theroux suggests, might be the real point of engaging in collecting in the first place. (Comedian Steven Wright may have hit upon the ideal balance between reach and grasp when he boasts of having the largest seashell collection anywhere. It is so extensive, he says, that he keeps it on beaches all over the world.) Thus to amend Camus' interpretation of the myth of Sisyphus, the eternally condemned man's confrontation with the Absurd would not result solely from his having finally successfully shoved his boulder to the top of the hill. We must also factor in the paralyzing realization that that single component completed his rock collection as well as his curse.

As opposed to accumulations of marbles or Mickey Mouse memorabilia, though, my own collection is relatively unambitious, being so concisely defined and circumscribed. Neither is it unique enough to warrant inclusion among Theroux's chosen ones, since with the termination of the *American Review* in 1976, a comprehensive set could reasonably be had by anyone. As of this writing, I possess twenty-five of the extant paperbacks, AR #11 having eluded me for well over two decades now. As I say, I'm fairly certain that I could scare up a copy of the prodigal volume on Amazon, Alibris, or eBay, but somehow resorting to websites strikes me as not being truly in the spirit of the thing. The prospect rubs against the grain of my idiosyncrasy: in randomness and vague fortune I began, and so I will persist. My compensation for the hole in my holdings parallels that of Thomas Hardy's Tess, whose slightly flawed features made her all the more fetching: "And it was the touch of the imperfect upon the would-be perfect that gave the sweetness, because it was that which gave the humanity." And should my collection forever remain unfinished, I shall content myself with my allegiance to those Native American artisans who purposely leave a flaw in their weavings so as not to offend the gods by competing with their perfection.

On the other hand, I might decide to sell off the lot, renunciation being the other side of the collector's coin. Then I might be the Arobin of the bibliophiles, whom not acquisition but purgation fortifies, whom relinquishment frees.

The American-led war for the liberation of Iraq broke the government's grip on its property as well as its grip on its people. As of this writing, tens of thousands of artifacts are still missing from the National Museum of Antiquities, many dating from the earliest civilizations. Some maintain that this illicit network must have roused to action the moment the bombing of Iraq began, so precise and efficient were the strikes on the museum's most priceless objects. As archaeologist Paul Zimansky dolefully admits, "A whole industry developed after the Gulf War of people going out and digging up things at night. We're talking about organized, armed teams."

Rumors have been as prolific as the looting itself. It is said that pieces are trickling out of the country inside suitcases and spare tires, sewn into collars and cuffs, heading for the elevated netherworld of high-stakes art connoisseurs with an appetite for the forbidden. Because these items are instantly recognizable and because identifying information about them is spreading with unprecedented effectiveness, experts are hopeful of their ultimate recovery. "These things are radioactive from a legal point of view," says William Pearlstein, co-counsel for the National Association of Dealers in Ancient, Oriental and Primitive Art. "They are hot, hot, hot and simply unmarketable." Should anyone try to sell clay tablets bearing the earliest cuneiform writings in existence, the 4,330-year-old bust of an Akkadian king, or the so-called Mona Lisa of Nimrud vase, intelligence agencies throughout the world, not to mention the global offices of the Art Loss Register, are on the alert.

It must be pointed out, however, that the fact that the thieves will never be able to broadcast or cash in such holdings does not necessarily mitigate but may actually intensify the delight of procuring them. Although legitimate dealers would never touch the major pieces, says Jerome Eisenberg, owner of New York's Royal-Athena Gallery, "I could visualize some multimillionaire hiding a piece away and gloating over it." Getting and spending, we lay waste our powers; therefore, by con-

fining ourselves to the getting alone, we keep more of ourselves in
reserve.

For what consolation terminology is worth, it is more accurate to
speak of the artifacts as "missing" or "transplanted" rather than "lost,"
in that certain people undoubtedly do know where most of the objects
are. In all actuality, with the exception of gold artifacts that may have
been melted down to re-enter the bloodstream of international capital,
they are not only intact but better protected in some hidden vault than
they ever had been when their location was both familiar and open to
public view.

Our most acute drives drive us into privacy. From the highest
echelon of corporate embezzlement on down to pickpocketing in the
street, from the tycoon who godfathers the pillaging of Mesopotamian
heritage to the centripetal Collyer brothers holed up in their decaying
freight, we steal to steal away, restricted to what we are surprised to
learn is necessary. To reference Steven Wright once again, you can't
have everything. Where would you put it? So it is always a quirky version of the world that is too much with us, something about the size of
our cellars and obsessions. And even though it may not be exactly or
all we long for, we take it anyway, if only because it's what there is.

7 Taking Pains

The soul is our capacity for pain.

—Marina Tsvetayeva

Going by human testimony alone, one would have to conclude that the chief reason behind alien abductions, the main impetus for their taking the trip and the trouble, is biological. According to the accounts that inspire summer movie fare and dominate the tabloids, aliens are fascinated by what makes us tick—or rather, by what makes us slosh, secrete, and expend ourselves on this out-of-the-way planet of ours. Thus it is principally for scientific intimacies that they snatch, transport, or absorb us aboard. Folks who claim to have been diagnosed and discarded by visitors from other worlds describe abductors that vary in height, hide, and hue. Their captors are as likely to amble as to ooze about their spaceships, whose interiors reportedly range in décor from stark Mondrian geometry to the sumptuousness of the Playboy mansion. Their communicative efforts run the gamut from mental telepathy to barnyard squabble to a din reminiscent of the mingled ring tones of cell users on the floor of the stock exchange. But whether they do their probing with paws, tentacles, or titanium rods, make no mistake: it's our orifices they're after.

Verifying Hamlet's nightmare, things rank and gross in our nature possess them merely. So as to sample our functions and our fluids, they insert and extract, siphon and scrape, filch, defile, and file away the blood, capture the excrescence and possibly the odd gland, upload the physical data, the scruff, the sludge, and the dung. By their reasoning, anatomy is all there is that matters about us. They do not sacrifice light-years to get our takes on the Poincare Conjecture or the designated hitter. They do not travel all this way to clarify foreplay, French cuisine, or *Finnegans Wake*, nor to elucidate punk culture, minimalist

art, or the subjunctive. They have no interest in our sit-coms, our politics, or our gods. As to why we quail in fear or hunker down in love,
forget it. Subtler concerns are for the sublunary—they are content to
analyze our organs and glean our meat. Whatever shape aliens take,
and whatever brilliance you'd infer from their getting to Earth at all,
rumor has it that they are basically buzzards colluding over a carcass.
They are anally fixated, intestinally tracked. When they come, they
come for our guts.

If you want to satisfy alien curiosity about human beings, you
won't have to share corporate secrets or surrender your soul. Their
penetrations are literal, surgical, and will not be stayed by protests
that there is more to you than meets the polygonal eye (if eye it is
that confronts you). In this, more or less everybody who has fallen
afoul of aliens and managed to return from their extraterrestrial incursions concurs. Argue between your agonies that you are altogether
more complex than the gelatinous clinical staff can adduce through
technology copied from the back lot of Industrial Light and Magic.
Protest that people are more profound than their plumbing, that it is
not enough to scoop out our slop to reckon the sum of us, that their
lack of further curiosity about humanity insults us as much as their
instruments do: those cries fall on deaf ears (if ears are what those al-
leged vegetal protuberances are). Say that the body may be the citadel
of the self, but that architecture is hardly the whole. The heart contains a legacy of romantic connotations centuries long; the brain is the
armature of a mind. None of that blather affects their conviction that
you are your body only, and the point of the body is to invert it to get
at its wet meld, much the way you delve past a lobster's shell to get at
the dinner inside. By your prostate, not your poetry, will they know
you. Metabolism, not metaphysics, most deeply intrigues. No need to
bandy philosophies, just bend over.

Essentially, then, aliens are not all that different from Bobby Greene,
my next-door neighbor when I was growing up, whose favorite hobby
was mangling. Bobby was a natural descendant of Mark Twain's citizens of Brickville, Arkansas, in *Adventures of Huckleberry Finn,* who
dealt with boredom by "putting turpentine on a stray dog and setting
fire to him, or tying a tin pan to his tail and see him run himself to
death." Bobby liked to light punks left over from the Fourth of July
and drive their glowing tips through the tops of anthills that battened
on the sidewalk cracks on Christiana Avenue, spewing its inhabitants

like tiny Hawaiians from a volcano. Or he'd flick lit matches into a queue of ants, the heat balling their corpses, shriveling them into ellipses. (Called to dinner by his mother, he'd simply plow through what remained of the colony with the toe of his Converse All-Star.) From the earthworm roils that plugged the gutters after a heavy rain, he would peel out sacrificial individuals like whips of licorice to eviscerate with his Boy Scout knife. (It was the only memento of that brief allegiance he retained and, as was obvious to all but his parents, the only incentive for his joining the Boy Scouts in the first place.) With the toothpick attachment, he'd skewer slower beetles, which oozed goo the color and consistency of spat tobacco. Returning from a friend's birthday party with helium-filled balloons, he would scour the empty lot at the end of the block for grasshoppers. He would pluck their appendages and strip their wings like the insignia of failed pilots being dishonorably discharged; he would then tie the casualties to balloons in order to launch them into unprecedented, unimagined neighborhoods. (Most were solo flights, but occasionally he would knot two of the crippled insects together for a Gemini mission.) Bobby called his assaults on the unwitting "experiments," but what they came down to was damage, torture, and, as Bobby put it, the fun of "just cutting shit up."

I've long since lost track of Bobby Greene. Maybe the one-time sidewalk entomologist ended up like Perry and Dick in *In Cold Blood*—not to suggest that he was bound to target a Clutter family, only that like Capote's killers, he might spend his idle hours deliberately adding to the Midwest's road kill count. And while I do not doubt that Bobby was indigenous to Earth, I would not be shocked to learn that the detached kid who detached the legs of spiders and the supposed alien visitors operated out of the same manual, which tells them that guts are what the Other is most conveniently reduced to. Certainly the neighbor I remember and the aliens I've read about or seen on the screen perform in ways that are equally exacting and equally oblique.

I hesitate to judge the reasons of creatures I cannot understand, whether they're from a far galaxy or, like Bobby Green, just next door. That it turns my stomach to hear about aliens tearing up stomachs may simply mean that I don't sufficiently appreciate the rigors of communication. Filleting some hapless fellow who stumbled upon the wrong Tennessee swamp at the wrong time might be different in degree from an American tourist's performing an impromptu pantomime while trying to get directions from a dozen Calcuttans who have twice as many languages as people among them, none of them intersecting; but it is comparable in kind. Perhaps the aliens' corporeal digs are funded by institutes akin to those on Earth that sponsor scientists to pick through shambles of alphabet in a Minoan ruin, the idea being that our entrails are the most legible part of what we present and leave behind.

The budding sociopaths in Yukio Mishima's *The Sailor Who Fell from Grace with the Sea,* who excavate the body of the family cat they'd killed, may obey the same rough compulsion as outer space creatures do. So, too, may Jerry in Edward Albee's *Zoo Story.* Failing to curry favor with hamburger patties from his landlady's vicious dog, Jerry kneads ground glass into the last offering, and he comes to wonder if both were not equivalent gestures. Indeed, Jerry cannot say for certain whether the dog's trying to bite him (not to mention the uninterpretable red erection the dog sports whenever Jerry comes within range) isn't a clumsy, urgent effort to communicate, too. But the starkest statement of the predicament may be represented by Samuel Beckett's blithering protagonist in *How It Is,* who accelerates his crawling through the muck in order to catch and to score with a can opener his share of conversation into the ass of the crawler before him.

"And so each venture / Is a new beginning, a raid on the inarticulate / With shabby equipment always deteriorating / In the general mess of imprecision of feeling, / Undisciplined squads of emotion." T. S. Eliot's complaint in *East Coker,* while it does not prevent him from producing the poem, does in large measure disavow anything his machinations might reveal. Words or surgical supplies, insistent figuration or hacking of flesh—shadowy motives, shabby means. Couldn't all of these be, in a manner of speaking, a manner of speaking?

Grant this possibility, and you might say that, by extension, practitioners of concerted self-abuse—cutters, branders, piercers, and other more egregious body modifiers—are in fact engaging in interior monologue. I have seen them, sullen and punctured, trundle past like the wounded dragging home after the Civil War. It did not take a Bobby Greene to gouge them or some interstellar sadists to incise them as if marking up suits for alterations. On the contrary, theirs are self-inflicted scars. Some of their cuts are precise and symmetrical, leading me to think that specific principles underlie the masochism. Or, like the vestiges of hooks and hazards overcome by Elizabeth Bishop's titular fish, they could be badges of battles survived and thereby demand our reverence. Other cuts look haphazard, even frenetic, as if the victim, desperate for ventilation, had quickly opened up any airway he could. One neck bolt might be disguising a botched tracheotomy. A spray of rhinestones at the belt line might be tacking up torn gaskets or otherwise plugging leaks. But these are only surmises—the cutters' countenances and suppurations stave off any conversation I might venture. I find myself remembering Toni Morrison's Sula, who scatters a bunch of encroaching boys by taking out a knife and slicing off a piece of her own finger. "If I can do that to myself," she tells the would-be molesters, "what you suppose I'll do to you?" In other words, I'd be dealing with someone who can administer anything that she can endure. My reflex is not to engage her.

And if the severity of pain one accepts correlates with the level of introspection she risks, what discoveries must await those who engage in even more brutal, more exotic rendings of their own flesh. I mean the saline injectors and the tongue splitters, the facial sculptors and the scrotal torturers, the urethral re-routers and the genital stretchers? I have to admit that I find it difficult enough to do the research, much less entertain the practices.

But let us gird ourselves together and more closely consider the example of body suspension. "When you open the flesh, you let something in," confides Alex Binnie, who is one of a small but seriously dedicated "cult" of "suspendees" living in and around Joplin, Missouri. The process features the insertion beneath the skin—typically through the shoulders or the chest—of large metal hooks attached to cables or chains, followed by hoisting. Many suspendees have piercings and tattoos as well, but when compared to suspension, those pursuits seem superficial. "It's definitely painful and shocking at first," says Rick Banks, another local suspendee, but he maintains that this is crucial to the development of personal awareness. "The pain allows you to own the experience." Anesthesia would undermine the impact and the significance of the experience. Pain fends off the dilettantes, who, while they may be genuinely interested in the phenomenon, are not willing to pay the price to see what they are made of. They are captivated by the image, not by any authentic attempt at self-interrogation. The same stigma applies to the posers who, while they do "throw hooks," do so for specious reasons. As Rick Banks explains, "They come to suspend and they just do it to get looks and to be cool and be goth and be something different than what they really are."

There are solo suspendees, dangling couples, and group pullers. There are suspension circles, in which participants, hooked through the belly, breast, or face, yoke and yank together, the tensed central point marking the unification and redistribution of their respective energies. Like the methods of suspension, the motives vary. Some associate suspension with the release of aggression afforded by loud rock music. Others allude to the Native American origins of the practice—a rite called O-Kee-Pa—and some current-day suspendees testify to the connection between seeing visions and ripping skin. There are suspendees who compete to see how long they can hang or how much weight they can haul. In fact, there are as many incentives as there are people who are drawn by the exercise. Some suspendees hang like tarps or slabs of beef in a freezer (which, again, from most accounts of Martian assessments of the specimens they lift into the mother ship, is pretty much what we are); others drag cars with harnesses driven through their hides. But whether one joins a tapestry of fellow suspendees or simply submits to private crucifixion, the basic commitment does seem to be consistent. Every suspendee wants to be raised to a higher state than what being rooted to Earth ordinarily affords him.

Nevertheless, *Body Modification E-Zine* admonishes the novice against any spiritual expectations he may bring to the procedure. (The complete charter on behalf of body modification and manipulation, provided "for the purposes of safety, history, culture, and good will," is available for download from the website.) The range of effects runs from pleasant trances to panic attacks, from numinous intimations to nausea. In response to the question, "What is the experience of suspension like," *BME-Zine* notes,

> As with much of life, you get out of it what you put into [it] and your expectations will often become self-fulfilling prophecies. Some people find it boring, others are changed forever, and some don't even think about it beyond simply performing the act. Many find that good or bad, it is not what they expected.

While it is true that many people feel "intensely at peace" during a suspension, as if they have entered "a state of hyperawareness and deep trust in themselves and the universe," not everyone feels so blissful in the rigging. As to whether one can "meet God" during suspension, *BME-Zine* offers this disclaimer:

> Meeting God would depend primarily on your spiritual views and your personal reality. . . . For some the suspension creates an ecstatic state that is not unlike deep meditation. That combined with an extreme influx of hormones and rapid changes in heart rate and blood pressure, and anything is possible. All of this is of course completely dependent upon your god, you, and how you communicate.

But beyond those factors, if the experience is going to communicate anything other than agony, the Being beyond one's body must keep up his end of the conversation. Otherwise, instead of achieving anything as sophisticated as ecstasy, the suspendee might become stuck at the status of a chunk of sirloin dripping on a spit.

"Exchanging signals with the planet Mars is a task worthy of a lyric poet," muses Osip Mandelstam, but in light of the depositions I've read, either their capacities do not include aesthetic appreciation or we aren't sufficiently lyrical to stay their scalpels. Possibly, human beings would make a superior impression on the next expedition to our planet if instead of setting down next to an unlettered Okie in a swamp, plucking the first poor schmuck who wanders away from the trailer park, or ambushing a Bobby Greene busy with his mutilations, they landed outside the office of the current poet laureate. But for some reason it always seems to be the Brickvillian whose incendiary business they disrupt.

Ultimately, alien itineraries are unpredictable. Good or bad, the aliens are bound to be different from what we expected, just as we will for them.

On the off chance that everything we do becomes us and might better recommend us to others, maybe the most sensible preparation for a close encounter is to work at being as fascinating as we can. Let us make the most uplifting argument for the human race possible. And let that sentiment introduce our charter. Whoever they are, we ask that they hold off with their instruments and their electrodes, to give our essence the benefit of the doubt. In the event that we are made to ascend by this tender flesh, we ask, for the purposes of safety, history, culture, and good will, that judgment against us be suspended as well. To earn that dispensation, we must strive to be worth the trouble of translation. Just in case they come for us, that is. And just in case they don't.

8 From the Notebook of the Human Cannonball

On Trajectory

The model flight path is parabolic, a pure, uninterrupted curve from takeoff to target, like a swoon in outer space. Its perfection suggests the repeal of gravity altogether, and to be sure, some witnesses report just such an experience. But the videotape refutes this. What we typically see—and the word "typically" should be taken under advisement, in that the phenomenon of human cannonballing grows increasingly rare, its attrition proceeding even faster than that of the circus itself— is a rough tumbling toward a rough landing. At the very instant of liftoff the cannonballer begins to succumb to drag coefficients and the natural mandates the ground levies upon all bodies. One cannot long sustain his objection to Sir Isaac Newton's findings, and in the end there is no subduing the Earth. For it is not flying but falling that is the ultimate illustration of the human cannonball, who in his brief excursion through the air does not imitate the carved arc of the diver so often as he turns end over end like a flipped stick. Those who remember the sight otherwise are apparently more susceptible to enchantment than others who are disappointed to realize just how far beneath the floor of the sublime the human cannonball operates.

On Matters of Proper Billing

Among the first edicts handed down by the Human Cannonball Congress (*see below*) was the formal repudiation of the terms "stunt" and "trick" in official documents pertaining to human cannonballing. The preferred terms, including "act," "art," "performance," and "science," each proffered by the Executive Council and ratified by separate votes requiring two-thirds majority of those voting, were adopted in the hope of promoting and sustaining the prestige of the profession. "Stunt" and "trick" imply deception, even incivility, and thereby erode the confidence of audience and cannonballer alike. The authorized options, on the other hand, emphasize characteristics of honesty and fortitude, the camouflaging of the cannon's actual propulsive mechanism notwithstanding (*see* "An Historical Note," *below*), which properly reward the audience while doing justice to the personal qualities of the cannonballer himself.

Otherwise, effective adjectives—rather, effective adjectives that will hold up in court—are harder to come by. "Death-defying," a tried and truism conventionally utilized by lion tamers and trapeze artists, does not really apply here since the prospect of death does not enter into it. On occasion, a performer will bounce off the catching net or misjudge the target and scud against the asphalt. On occasion, a performer will complain of vertigo as he perches on the mouth of the cannon to address the crowd. On occasion, a performer will spin off course like a fisherman's errant cast or get hung up in the catching net like a dazed moth. Of course, he is going to have to deal with the odd concussion. But seldom will he suffer any mishap that outpatient treatment cannot handle. Statistically speaking, smoking and driving downtown on any Saturday night more arrogantly tempt fate than human cannonballing does, and who would buy tickets to watch either of those activities? What the human cannonball most defies is not death but reasonably priced insurance coverage.

As for "uncanny," that descriptor remains exclusively within the jurisdiction of magicians and is inappropriate, anyway, to the exploits of the human cannonball, which, whatever its enticements, does not challenge our belief in physical laws but rather demonstrates their function. Despite the controversial claims made by Donnie "Rocket Man" Trumbull, who during the 1960s tried to unite in the public imagination his act with President Kennedy's space race initiative, the human cannonball does not explore new frontiers; he confirms present boundaries. Likewise, the human cannonball fails to measure up to "amazing," that old standby, in that when he falls, he falls short of the marvels concocted for summer blockbuster films or, for that matter, so-called "reality shows" on television. "Peculiar" comes closer to the mark, but because it is unlikely to sell tickets, it is best avoided. Yet it must be admitted that the charms of the human cannonball compare more precisely to those of the clowns and the animal oddities that for obvious reasons itinerant circuses relegate to the furthest cars on the train.

On Training, Diet, and Exercise

No one starts out as a human cannonball. No one sets out to become one. Even William Hunt, a.k.a. The Great Farini, who is often credited with having originated the human cannonball act in the 1870s, began circus life as a high wire performer. The acrobat with tendinitis, the aging bareback rider, the aerialist gone fat and swollen beyond the capacity of his costume—these are representative recruits for human cannonballing. In this regard, the career is less a goal than a destiny.

Arguably, the human cannonball is less a rigorous athlete than a round of ammunition, and disparaging reviewers have declared that it doesn't require much prowess to be expended, not even for two shows daily. That said, there is general agreement that a diet low in saturated fats and high in fiber, fruits, and vegetables is indicated for maintaining the health and overall well being of the human cannonball. While a muscular physique is desirable, in part because it promotes the notion that the human cannonball is about to grapple with, withstand, or overcome something beyond the powers of ordinary men, it is not mandatory. Fortunately, too, spandex—the fabric of choice among the majority of performers—is very forgiving (*see* "On Uniform and Accoutrements," *below*).

This is not to suggest that human cannonballing requires no art or effort whatsoever to accomplish. As Brian Miser of the George Carden Circus asserts, "It takes nothing short of intelligence and courage." Or as another longtime flyer cheekily puts it, "It's no more dangerous than shaving with a chainsaw." While such advertisements are inflated for effect, they should not be discounted altogether. Nevertheless, the fact remains that because most human cannonballs originally practiced other circus skills, they often share in the sense that in committing to human cannonballing, they have settled for less.

On Related Scientific Concerns

Chief among the components to be heeded when preparing the human cannonball act are the weight of the performer, thrust capacity, wind speed, barometric pressure, humidity, and air resistance. The aerodynamic tendencies of a given cannonballer—does he twist, crumple, or flail in flight?—must also be factored in, and the distance and tension of the catching net or tarpaulin, the launch angle, and so on, should be adjusted accordingly. As a precautionary measure, every site should be checked out with several firings of test dummies so as to estimate as reliably as possible the results of human ballistics in the arena, school playground, or mall parking lot hosting the performance.

An Historical Clarification

The Great Farini's original launching mechanism was not a cannon per se but a system of rubber springs, which was not housed in a gun barrel. In his application for patent in 1871, Farini referred to it simply as a "device" for launching "human projectiles," employing no gun-like encasement whatsoever. A young man known only as "Lulu" undertook the initial flight in 1873, whereby he reached a reported height of forty feet. This became known as the "Lulu Leap," an expression that emphasized the performer's accomplishment, as opposed to "cannonball," which implies passive surrender to the power of technology. (As was noted previously—*see* "On Trajectory," *above*—the propelled performer does not even momentarily resemble a ball at any point during his transit. The most aerodynamic, aesthetically satisfying posture is more on the order of flung knife than tucked fetus.)

Students of space flight may recall with what virulence the Mercury astronauts demanded that the amenities of a jet cockpit (especially a window) be added to their capsules: they wanted to look and feel like pilots instead of specimens. Therefore, the eventual advertising victory of "human cannonball" over all alternative terminology must be viewed with ambivalence. Its intimations of daring are complicated, if not defeated, by connotations of the diminishment of the cargo involved.

In 1875, George Loyal, a member of the Yankee Robinson Circus, became the first person to be fired from a cannon, and within four years entrepreneur William Leonard Smith patented the design. Hence the makeshift cannon enclosure became customary and has remained the act's signature image. Even the earliest version featured an explosion and a burst of smoke set off simultaneously with the expulsion of the human ammunition to reinforce the sense that a massive weapon had been discharged instead of rubber springs released. When in 1929 Ildebrando Zacchini created a new cannon powered by com-

pressed air for John Ringling's circus, he did not abandon the theatri-
cal accompaniment of Sturm und Drang to the rude birth. Today's
state-of-the-art bungee catapult launching units continue to rely on
smoke and explosions for effect. Without those conventional masking
efforts, the launch would sound no more marvelous than an amplified
clearing of one's throat, relegating the dislodged occupant to the status
of a stuck chunk of meat.

On the Continuing Presence of the Human Cannonball in Popular Culture

The romance of the human cannonball retains its purchase on the
popular imagination. This is true despite the fact that the public began
losing interest in human cannonball acts as early as the 1890s, when
other circus thrills like "Diavolo" loop-the-loop bicycle acts supplanted them. More than a century later, audiences have grown increasingly
immune to awe. Indeed, sarcastic social critics contend that given how
far entertainers must ratchet up the action nowadays to get a rise out
of people, we are not far from reaching that utopian realm where no
disease other than jaundice remains. And it must be admitted that the
persistence of the human cannonball is largely a nostalgic throwback.
Sentimentality, not thirst, inspires many adults to patronize a child's
lemonade stand. Those same people may find the human cannonball
more quaint than breathtaking (*see* "On Matters of Proper Billing,"
above).

Spatial limitations render impractical a thorough inventory of appearances of the human cannonball in contemporary popular culture.
Consider three exemplary instances. Before it was swamped by the
flood of competition in the home computer market in the late 1980s
(a flood which has yet to evidence any ebbing at all), Atari put out
a Human Cannonball game, whose player was challenged to compensate for posted changes in wind direction and velocity in order to
precisely deliver an angular little figure to the landing area. Unfortunately, with its reliance on rude pixils and primitive effects, Atari's
Human Cannonball was not even a match for its contemporary Pong,
which in contrast did not sacrifice demands for nimbleness, strategy,
and competitive zeal for the simplicity of its program.

Superior pleasures may be obtained from the Human Cannonball
Science Toy, which affords parents the additional compensation of
prying the child away from the computer screen in favor of a pastime

more akin to what they remember from their own childhoods. Available from Terrific Toy, Inc., of Milton, Delaware, for $20.95, and intended for children ages ten and above, this simple, reusable product vividly proves Newton's Third Law of Motion in a manner "much safer than the circus variety" of the human cannonball "but perhaps even more fun." The "human" counterpart is actually a mustachioed face that the child applies to a soda bottle-type cylinder. The fuel is composed of baking soda and vinegar, and a special pressure-release valve controls the launch. In keeping with the company's avowed commitment to manufacturing "toys of superior caliber and intelligence," the Human Cannonball Science Toy enables the child to be an engineer, decorator, chemist, physicist, and ringmaster all at once. At the same time, he learns fun facts about the history of the human cannonball and the basic science behind it. (The kit includes a one-liter bottle, a plastic human figure, a six-inch plastic tube, an eleven and one quarter-inch launching howitzer, a pre-assembled fueling module, and detailed instructions. Mom must provide baking soda, vinegar, tape, scissors, and a ruler.)

Last, let us not neglect the song "The Human Cannonball" by the rock group Hell Mach Four, whose refrain, "Embrace today," not only neatly encapsulates a primary incentive for human cannonballs past and present but also reminds audiences of a philosophy that might usefully inform careerists of every stripe.

On the Advisability and Content of Meditation

Should the incipient cannonballer dream? Readers of Melville will undoubtedly remember the perils attending the lookout in the crow's nest, for whom even a momentary lapse of concentration could spell disaster. In the case of the human cannonball, however, plummeting is half the act. Furthermore, his maintaining the appropriate posture requires neither equilibrium nor vigilance, so the analogy to an Ishmael is at the very least misleading. On the contrary, intrepidness is confined to maximum stillness in confinement. The human cannonball's task is to keep his blood pressure down and the natural inclination to squirm in check. To accomplish this, he must trust in the mechanism and the immutable laws of motion he's at the mercy of. If possible, he should empty his mind entirely of obstacles, much as he himself represents an obstacle to be emptied. The accomplished human cannonball relinquishes his anxieties to the black interior of the cannon as if it were a sensory deprivation tank.

Barring this enviable, Zen-like resolve, which may only be achieved, if it is achieved at all, after years of capitulation to the cannon, the cannonballer should concentrate on coziness rather than on the expulsion to come. A fetus does not fret about the evanescence of the comforts of the womb but attunes itself for the length of its stay to the soothing sounds of the heartbeat of the mother and the soft tides of her digestion. So, too, should the incarcerated performer strive to become snug in the bore. Girding himself against a potential misfiring or musing on the likelihood that the contract to build the apparatus he's stuffed himself into was granted to the lowest bidder will cause him to chafe and struggle, and that can only jeopardize the successful completion of his performance. Who hasn't cringed at videos of human cannonballs whose pre-flight distractions or mid-air misgivings—Did I close the garage door? Did I give up too soon on that correspondence course in computer repair? Why didn't Maria pick up the phone last night?—led to tragic, or at least inelegant, conclusions? Better to realize that once he's sunk into the gun, the logistical Rubicon has already been crossed, and there is now nothing to be done but endure while he's down there. Thus if the Buddhist is ideally suited to conduct himself effectively as a human cannonball, the existentialist is next best.

On Uniform and Accoutrements

Streamers, decoupage, epaulets, baubles, and other dangling or protruding paraphernalia should be kept to a minimum or simply dispensed with so as to guarantee unobstructed emission from the gun and, to the extent that the cannonballer might contribute to it, an untrammeled delivery to the target area. Imitating the liberty in costuming enjoyed by the sharpshooter, the trick cyclist, or the bareback rider is therefore not only undignified but hazardous since the exploits of the human cannonball's colleagues are not so fraught with aerodynamic complications.

This is not to say that the human cannonball must forego gaudiness completely. Braids, spangles, and colored cords affixed tightly to the jacket, martial stripes and stars (he is a flyer, after all!), iron-on chevrons and filigrees—these are regularly employed accents to the basic jumpsuit and do not interfere with the general streamlining sought by the human cannonball. Lush brocades, expensive freckling, eruptions of paisley, eccentric arrangements of rhinestones, stitchings, and studs—these are often prominently featured and threaten neither the smoothness of the flight nor the sensibilities of the spectators. Helmets—usually shaped like the noses of bombs or made to resemble what World War I aviators wore into battle—are also frequent additions to the wardrobe, even though it must be said that they have less to do with safety than with the general spectacle. When it comes to color, too, the human cannonball is welcome to give his artistic taste free rein. It does bear mentioning, however, that some variation on the fundamental palette of American patriotism—red, white, and blue—is the norm, and one should weigh carefully what he perceives to be the advantages of departing from it. Also, given the unpredictability of his precise position at touchdown, clasps and pins should be avoided.

THE FIRST FAMILY OF HUMAN CANNONBALLING

Meet the Smiths, the foremost modern-day heirs and avant garde of the art. There is David Smith Sr., who is the reigning distance record holder (with a shot of one hundred eighty-five feet, ten inches in 1998, breaking the record set by Mario and Emanual Zacchini—yes, two of the seven performing sons of the innovative Ildebrando Zacchini). There is David Smith Jr., a.k.a. "The Bullet," who keeps up a friendly rivalry with his father in regular "Dueling Cannons" events. And there are Rebecca, Jennifer, and Kimberly Smith, whose sister-daughter tandems have shattered the human cannonball gender barrier once and for all. (Frankly, it is only routine usage that encourages us to refer to the "human cannonball" as "he." There are in all probability sufficient votes on the Executive Council of the Human Cannonball Congress [*see below*] to ensure that an enlightened revision of such usage will soon prevail.)

Whether a genetic predisposition among daredevils is in evidence here, or whether this is just one more example of the tenacity of the same economic realities that send the children of attorneys to law school while shopkeepers' kids keep on in their fathers' shops, is a subject best left to the sociologists. What is clear, however, and what can never be stated too often, is that the Smiths testify to the inherent solidarity and wholesomeness of the human cannonball enterprise. There is an unfortunate, widespread myth that human cannonballers are especially prone to domestic violence, recreational drug use, and the purchase of pornography. Those who perpetrate or worry about such rumored malfeasances and discontentment should study the Smiths and be comforted. There are working mothers who find time to bake and fathers who coach Little League baseball instead of stopping for drinks with the boys from the office, and they do not know where their stubbornly alienated teenagers are. Meanwhile, here are the Smiths: parents who once tucked their children in at night and wished them sweet dreams of angels soaring along perfect vectors are today openly and easily discussing new maneuvers with them. Make no mistake: wayward cannonballers are the exception; the Smiths, the rule.

THE HUMAN CANNONBALL CONGRESS

The Human Cannonball Congress, or HCC, was established in 1939, which was also the year that Mario and Emanuel Zacchini left the Ringling Circus to found their own traveling carnival, in whose climactic exhibition both brothers were blasted over the top of twin Ferris wheels. For nearly three quarters of a century, the HCC has been recognized throughout the world as the principal informational, legislative, and organizational body of practitioners of the art of human cannonballing. Among the privileges afforded members (who, according to the latest HCC Directory, currently number over fourteen hundred) are the right to vote for officers and on possible alterations in statutes and bylaws, as well as on international social and political stances taken in the name and on behalf of the HCC (for instance, the position paper composed on calling for protection of the status of human cannonballs in the former Yugoslavia); participation in an HCC-sponsored credit union; the right to run for election to standing committees or, in the case of special exigency, to be appointed to serve on said committees; discounted registration and hotel rates at the annual convention; and password access to the on-line newsletter, *The Launch Pad*. Other concerns of the HCC include but are not limited to questions of public dress, gestures, flourishes, and general decorum; improvement of consortium rates for health, life, and dental insurance, as well as COBRA extensions of benefits; evaluation and provision of cafeteria-style retirement packages and perquisites; investigation and protection of the status of minority cannonballers; and evaluation and provision of counseling services for members and members' families.

On the Resistance to Obsolescence
of Human Cannonballing

Although there are many explanations for the perseverance of the phenomenon, a task force of the HCC expressly created to investigate the
matter has deemed the following five causes pre-eminent:

1. Because gravity is the answer to almost everything, we need to
   contradict the ground as best and as often as possible.
2. Because it is crucial to be reminded of a more dauntless definition of all we are, from time to time we need to react to thunder
   with thunder.
3. Because transcending our scale is a job that cannot be dependably left to politicians and movie stars alone, we need to turn to
   something in life that isn't life-sized.
4. Because even if it is only for a second or so, even if it is only
   pretend, we need to take a punch at the sun, or urge on the sur-
   rogate who takes the punch on our behalf when circumstances
   prevent our doing so on our own.
5. Because even if it is only by example, we need to get the air
   under us for a change.

"For what is a field of vision if there's nothing visionary moving
through it?" So spoke Donnie "Rocket Man" Trumbull in 1961, and
these words, issuing from the still center of the cannon he would inhabit for upwards of three decades, resounded there and still resound.

9 The Obligations of the Harp

When you tapped me on the shoulder,
O light, unsayable in your splendor
A lot of good you did to me. . . .

—Charles Simic, "My Quarrel with the Infinite"

Dazzled into adoring monologue by his initial glimpse of Juliet, Romeo decks her out in metaphor—in Shakespeare, passion is tropical fruit—and during his inventory of her attractions deems her "beauty too rich for use." In the centuries succeeding their eloquent demises, the question of whether authentic beauty was ever otherwise has absorbed immoderate lovers and aesthetic scholars alike. Obviously, no one contends that you should reference Shakespeare the same way you reach for a soldering iron. But for Beauty's accountability you are as likely to be directed to the Bursar's Office as to the Dean of Humanities nowadays. Whether or not Beauty must accomplish something other than its own burnished enthronement, as well as whether that accomplishment might be verified by the wholesome wake its achievements leave, may be discussed in terms of a debate between schools: the Transitive and the Intransitive.

Camped among the Transitives are school superintendents who, though they cannot budge their budgets by even one more dollar, raid the discretionary fund to ensure that students will be bused to a concert or an art museum before they graduate into video games and TV movies exclusively. There is the Core Curriculum Committee at my own college, which designated Using the Arts as the catch-all category for requirements in art, theater, literature, music, and philosophy. (The phrase was undoubtedly coined to mollify those Jack Spratt rationalists on our staff who'd outlaw all but the narrowly practical from the undergraduate menu. Still, "Using the Arts" makes it sound as though we are producing America's future hair stylists, plastic surgeons, and cosmetics demonstrators.) There is Cynthia Ozick, who in "What Is Poetry About?" assails the suspensive tendencies of Beauty, declaring, "Always and everywhere, art attaches itself to the utilitarian."

There are Martha Nussbaum and Elaine Scarry, who in *Poetic Justice: The Literary Imagination and Public Life* and *On Beauty and Being Just,* respectively, offer manifestos for putting beauty to work. Nussbaum champions a responsible fancy, "creative and veridical," to inspire the "judicious spectatorship" necessary to ethical public action and, by extension, societal rehabilitation: "[Fancy] nourishes a generous construal of the world. This construal is not only . . . more adequate as an explanation of the totality of human behavior as we experience it, but also a cause of better ways of living." Nussbaum's Beauty charms us to challenge us; it is, above all, *applicable.* (One again recalls Ozick, whose fictional Ruth Puttermesser animates a golem to carry out her dictates as mayor of New York.) Scarry likewise envisions an active role for beauty in her administration. Indeed, her argument abjures the passive voice: in her diction, beauty sponsors, perpetuates, enacts, begets, generates, installs, and compels relation, all of which suggests the essentially centrifugal nature of the aesthetic. For Scarry, Beauty "ignites moral urgency" through "instrumental perception," not only representing but inciting honorable practice beyond the constraints of the frame, page, or compact disk.

In a sense, the Transitives charge Wallace Stevens's "motive for metaphor" with ambition that exceeds contemplative pleasure. Instead of "shrinking from / The weight of primary noon, / The A B C of being," figures must make their way into the public forum, where noon's incisive light is conducive to illuminating humane policy. Conceits must conceive worldlier issues. After all, if a dose of poetry cannot provide what a dose of penicillin can, why prescribe it?

Thus, in order to impress the coordinating board of the Transitive School, Beauty must handle tasks and modify behavior; it must *conduct* us. Save the school referendum for replacing the roof. Presumptions of self-evident value are not enough to warrant revamping a curriculum, much less guarantee the National Endowment for the Arts. Aesthetics must be as directly and practically answerable to our needs as bypass surgery. Art must do more than increase the sum of wonders: Mozart must catalyze the mastery of differential equations and Shakespeare bring out the vote. (Let's see Sinatra operate a forklift before we feature him. Let's convince the current poet laureate to pick up a course in air-conditioning repair to make himself employable.) Good music and good literature must perform more than their own memorable passages, just as a good car must do more than gleam on the lot. In short, Beauty must be a function of *function*. Beauty must be Beauty *for*.

So let us arouse Aurora from the fabled bed she's kept to for a century without so much as a shrug to show for her slumber. Hitch up the plow, Sweetheart, or at least make some headway on the dishes that are brimming in the sink. For "Sleeping Beauty" is a contradiction in terms the forces of Beauty For cannot brook. While dwarfs conjecture over the coffin of Snow White, lying chaste as baby clothes in a drawer—how ideal that incarceration! how supple that untried skin!—true princes are industrious and committed to agency. One will come to revive his beloved, yield to a succinct honeymoon, then get back to business at the castle. Even the lowliest factotum must in some way contribute to corporate growth; surely Beauty must have beefed up her vita to earn promotion. What sort of example are transcendent sleepers setting, anyway? Elysian languor is merely goldbricking by another name. As the poet Dean Young puts it, "Even / a harp has obligations." Psalms notwithstanding, unless the lilies of the field earn their keep, don't expect civic fathers to build the highway around them.

Meanwhile, there are those who think that trying to make a discipline out of Beauty is like trying to legislate a rainbow or shoving butterflies down your throat. When seen from outside the professoriate, tenured aestheticians, that pale cast of Thought, come to seem like E. E. Cummings's prurient philosophers, all thumbs in their fondling, as they prod the earth for understanding, only to be answered by lovely, unintelligible spring. Cummings also warns that people who concern themselves too exclusively with the syntax of things will never wholly kiss you, a caveat that in this context implies that anatomizing Beauty threatens to sterilize it. It isn't that attending to Beauty is barking up the wrong tree, but that barking is the wrong way to go about it, given that the tree's fundamental pleasures might be better appreciated when, carrying no ground axe, we peacefully take to the shade.

Regarding Beauty in this regard recalls Auden's contention that "poetry makes nothing happen: it survives / In the valley of its making." That valley, an inviolable Brigadoon, is thereby imagined as an aesthetic free space, a privileged reprieve, which must be cultivated

gently instead of scheduled for strip mining. And if Beauty is only con-
ditionally permeable by ulterior urges, the opposite might likewise be
the case: what occurs within its confines is confined to them. Here we
may speculate, test, and transgress with impunity; here all operations
are pre-consequential, in the sense that, as George Levine writes in
Aesthetics and Ideology, "the immediate pressures of ethical and political decisions are deferred." Agreed, the aesthetic may tutor our behavior beyond that suspended realm, but it should not be misconstrued *as*
that behavior nor have to answer for causing whatever behavior follows
exposure to it.

Maybe it's a mistake to look for judicial rigor in the midst of rhap-
sody or, for that matter, to suppose that Beauty is supposed to *do* something if it wants to earn its welfare check. And if you accept the notion
that a poem is more of a prayer than a program, much less a prosecut-
able offense, you may be ready to enroll in the Intransitive School of
Beauty. Looming largest among the faculty is Harold Bloom, in whose
magisterial study, *The Western Canon,* he bemoans the betrayal of aesthetic priorities for the sake of adulterous ideological interests. Bloom
champions those literary works whose sheer stylistic originality, depth,
and power overwhelm and disqualify—"scandalize," in Bloom's estimation—any presumptive ideological reduction. The preeminent
texts of Western literary tradition deserve that status not because they
can be coerced into "the service of any social aims, however morally
admirable" but precisely because they cannot. In other words, Beauty
cannot save us; its value inheres in its capacity to enable us to "over-
hear ourselves," which is to say, our most intriguing, worthy, human
selves.

Depending on in which of his books he is at the moment extolling
the aesthetically gifted and gift-giving, Bloom calls them Geniuses,
Masters, or Angels. All of these grand titles absolve artists so endowed
from sins and responsibilities that encumber the rest of us. True, a
writer may be violent, treasonous, or uncharitable, stingy with his affections yet excessive with drugs and alcohol, but if his stanzas enchant, he shall remain securely anthologized. Sedition, sacrilege, and
suicide are excusable so long as his sentences sing. For it is the poems,
not the poet, we allow our daughters to fumble with behind closed
doors; it is the novel, not the novelist, we let our wives take to bed.
And so Bloom rates writers by the brick-by-brick solidity of their imagery. Just run your hands over a paragraph of Faulkner or Beckett or

Woolf: not a splinter anywhere in the planking, not a crack anywhere in the hull. Hence a self-sufficient Beauty is the only criterion the Intransitives castigate or canonize an author for. Reason not the rest of the resume.

And yet, if in arguing that Beauty is an instrument of ethical improvement the Transitives presume too much, in generally repudiating any ethical task or impact for Beauty, the Intransitives may be presuming too little. For example, what of those writers who apply themselves to vileness and cry "Beauty" at the circumstances? When in *Blood Meridian* Cormac McCarthy lingers over a massacre with greater resolve and greater relish than even the buzzards do; when in *The Tunnel* William Gass sets a Holocaust-inspired murder scene as lavishly as if he were laying out a feast; or when in *The Book of Daniel* E. L. Doctorow has his narrator execute his parents on the page as systematically as the State did them in, does craftsmanship convert the horror or consecrate it? One remembers the relish with which Baudelaire spoke of Beauty's inclusive empire, not all of whose provinces would inspire tourism among the Puritans: "You walk on corpses, Beauty, mocking as you go; / Of all your jewels, Horror's not the least entrancing; / And Murder, certainly your dearest cameo, / Is on your proud abdomen amorously dancing." Again, it doesn't take a Philistine to worry that Beauty may be complicit in the crimes it embroiders. To simply ignore accusations of aesthetic opportunism is unconscionable, even if you ultimately decide that the artist's decision to pitch intent in the place of excrement is not.

Imagine that the most melodic harp were strung with the guts of murdered girls because those especially tender tissues were most conducive to music. Would we then content ourselves with the sufficiency of Beauty? Would we assuage their memory by playing Beethoven over their graves?

In fact, we needn't invent the premise. Aesthetic philosopher Denis Dutton asks us to consider the carvings of the Sepik peoples of New Guinea. The decline in quality of those carvings, he maintains, is directly related to the elimination of the headhunting society in which they originated. As it happens, the art of carving continues to flourish among the Sepik (fostered in large part by the tourist industry), but the contemporary products are "bland, vapid, kitschy," a result which

Dutton ascribes to the eradication of the dreadful commitments and deadly faith that had once been their inspiration and context. "Making an indisputably better world can entail losses," he concludes. "Head-hunting is terrible, but so is the disappearance of headhunting arts. Nevertheless, the colonial powers knew what they had to do for the sake of New Guineans, and the loss of the arts is tragic."

In other words, the price of saving the natives from their own prac-tices has been necessary but not negligible. Beauty must not jeopardize social amelioration. (Faulkner might have hesitated before asserting that "Ode on a Grecian Urn" is worth any number of old ladies if it were his own grandmother instead of a lump of mud that had been baked for art. And for saying that World War I was worth the sacrifice of millions for the sake of enabling him to produce *Ulysses,* many think Joyce should have been pummeled with a hardcover edition.) But isn't it troubling to the Transitives that the carvings did nothing to improve the conditions that necessitated cultural renovation in the first place? Conversely, what can the Intransitives say to excuse the sponsorship of slaughter, as though Beauty were a pampered princess blithely presid-ing over debauchery from her splendid, elevated seat?

We are doing definition in Freshman Composition. It is one of the mandatory modes of development, but I've always balked at the way it is typically handled in the handbooks: a predictable campaign for the importance of definition as a way of clueing the audience in to what you're on about, followed by a list of abstract nouns—intelligence, evil, equality, happiness, love—serving as essay prompts. Support your argument with examples. Be specific.

When it comes from deduction, definition is a bitch.

"You've all heard the saying, I don't know what art is, but I know it when I see it. Let's see what you see when you see it," I say. I pass out a list of possible candidates for the label "work of art" and ask them to check off however many of them they believe qualify. A child's finger-painting fares very well with the class (their rogue fashion and dismis-sive posture to the contrary, they are sentimentalists at heart), as do a spider's web, a seashell, a woman's makeup, a photograph of a wed-ding party, and a newborn baby. When it comes to the collage made by the food I toss in the trash, the frame around the "Mona Lisa," a photocopy of that consensual masterpiece taken off a magazine cover, a stone that looks like a duck after I accidentally drop and break it, a light switch on the wall of the Museum of Modern Art, or a dime, they begin to equivocate. Then there's a monkey's scratchings in the dirt with a stick, which I dare them to differentiate from little Lisa's fingerpainting that's taped to the refrigerator door. A house of cards. A mathematical formula. John Hancock's signature. A fifty-story-tall Mickey Mouse balloon wafting through a New York City street. A slam dunk.

Criteria blear. What about a scientifically engineered microorganism or the Thanksgiving meal your mother made? What about a corpse the cops chalked around in an alley, its face an impasto of blood, or the chalk outline that remains after the corpse has been carried off? We are in embattled territory, and no one feels confident enough to bear the standard. Is the atomic bomb, which made the mushroom cloud that captivates us as much as any other image ever has, a work of art, the military its artist, and the war that made them the muse?

Once the dust of exploded deductions clears, we see if anything's stable enough to rebuild a definition with. "Life-affirming" is under too much rubble. "Original" is badly damaged, as are "man-made," "permanent," "good," and "honest." And where is Beauty after the blast? Is it still sound enough to sustain your footing and your belief?

Strangely, "useless" is more or less intact. The general opinion as the period ends is that a work of art is fundamentally useless. What separates a chair from a museum piece is a ring of velvet ropes. "If I thought enough of a rug to have to git hit all the way from France, I wouldn't keep hit where folks coming in would have to tromp on it," moans one of Faulkner's hopeless Snopes daughters, recognizing even better than its wealthy owner did the distinction between what her reckless father ruined and any other rug. In short, my students conclude, a plate is a plate until it's stuck in the collector's hutch or fractures on the floor; after that, art is all it's good for and Beauty all it's still fit to serve. And now they're off to Economics, armed with that sole induction: art doesn't do them any good—doesn't, despite the Area One requirement and the tuition spent, do much of anything at all.

It was on one of those field trips to Chicago's Field Museum of Natural History that we took in junior high that we saw the Toys through the

Ages exhibit, the sole sensation apart from ransacked mastodons sufficient to rouse the kids from the stupefaction of obligatory culture. What a holiday haul: Ethiopian toys, Persian toys, Etruscan toys; toys taken from the Tigris and raided from the Euphrates; toys delicately stripped from Polynesian swamp beds, Chinese ravines, and Egyptian tombs; toys stolen from tar pits and swiped from children five thousand years dead—all of it now art, the rude wagons and twig-and-nut animals of almost unrecognizable species and intention too fragile, and all too precious to play with. There was nothing that wound up or plugged in, of course, yet we gazed enviously at them, crowding the glass cases that kept them uncontaminated by our savor. Treasures no one could win by doing chores, reaching birthdays, or being good. Pleasures no one could have and, because of that, though they would have bored us faster than any item Mattel ever advertised and broken in less than a day anyway, beautiful.

The obverse of the obsolete—the reverse side of the coin removed from currency—is antique. With unprecedented speed, our methods and machinery are superseded nowadays, and the landfills brim with outmoded toasters, telephones, and television sets that would have cost more to repair than to replace. On the other hand, nostalgia has picked up its pace, too. The epochs it once took for objects to trump Auden's definition of poems and transcend the cry of their occasions were reduced to generations and then to a few years only. I know this by my visit to a local antique store, which featured, among those fustier items with a respectable age obviously upon them, toys I myself had played with as a child. It is not any dementia of mine that declares that my childhood was not all that long ago at all. But there they were: the Spiderman comics I pored over, the army soldiers I conscripted and sent in for the kill, the Lionel engine I heedlessly skidded along the basement linoleum after the tracks got bent or lost, even the cereal boxes I rooted through for the prizes inside, never dreaming that the boxes themselves would one day—a day not all that far off, it turns out—be worth more than the treats they contained. Like one of those ancient generals they dust off and mount for local Founding Day ceremonies, here was my salvaged and retrofitted past, rendered trendy and (my God!) expensive. Going by the price tags, it was as if I'd teethed on emeralds and drooled on a dresser made entirely of dollars. Who knew that I was growing up with art back then, art I could have kept and cherished? Who knew it was beautiful?

Kids are more sophisticated collectors nowadays, I suppose. My nephews consult the Beckett price guide before inserting their new baseball cards into plastic sleeves, to be filed away with other protected investments. My daughter will not snip the manufacturers' tags from the ears of her stuffed animals for fear of depreciating them. Bad enough they will have to weather her affections. Bad enough she exposes them to dust and girlish endearments, to the treacheries of light and love. Some day, the children promise, they'll be *worth* something.

After that afternoon's instruction at the antique store, I decided to rummage through my own premises for riches I'd missed. Because the criteria were mysterious—there is no telling the crucial bloom in the bud nor the genius from the fetal reading of his genes—I got sloppy, my inductive process devolving amid a random scatter of greeting cards, worn-out wallets, keys whose locks I'd forgotten, and other oddities on end, bereft of incentive and about as purposeful as ballast after the balloon has flown.

And finally, of all things, a Xerox copy of my lover's hand, fingers wide, palm up, which she had given me when the relationship was first under way and every gesture was significant, unique, and saved. It meant supplication, consolation, openness, or perhaps, as a show of hands does in class, just the desire to be called on, a way to say "Here." I've had it so long that the nimbus of urgency has worn away, to be replaced by something I choose to call, for want of a better word, beautiful. Which is always for want of a better word and which, I'm delighted to find, does everything I need it to do.

10 Name-Dropping

During my sophomore year of high school, without announcement, I decided to change my signature. Since then, my signature has represented my secret identity, the intrepid self disguised by the lockstep typography my computer spits out. My memos, resume, and formal drafts, blocky and consistent as Clark Kent, never disclose the capacities the handwritten Art Saltzman displays. Know me, know my script.

Like everyone else my age, I was trained in the Palmer Method of cursive writing, that exacting, persnickety system designed to instill in us such unwavering respect for unwavering forms that no teacher need ever look twice to decipher any student's writing. Correct penmanship was extolled like civic responsibility. The Americans we would become lay dormant and inevitable in the larval letters we produced. Accordingly, all of us learned to shape constant consonants and inviolable vowels, which would link only at designated locations on respective letters, with the easy fealty of Campfire Girls holding hands at the jamboree. (The Palmer Method has since been displaced: now grade schoolers are weaned on D'Nealian Handwriting, a slightly altered but equally uncompromising set of prescriptions to manacle the next generation.) Second-grade teachers across the country supervised a sort of manual ballet among their consternated charges, seeing to it that our Number Two pencils were properly pinched and propelled. Each of us submitted to the imposed posture of morphology, as dictated by people like Miss Mazurek, who stalked the rows and slapped a ruler into her hand, glaring over our shoulders the way that the more renowned Palmer studied his putts. In every class children crafted their ABC's with martial coordination: thirty hands simultaneously contorted over their pages like mantises contemplating their meals.

Just a few months earlier, Jeff Diamond and I had been blissfully walking back from another undemanding day of first grade, when we happened to catch up to Myra Osheff, a neighbor girl three years our senior and, therefore, doubly deserving of disdain. Jeff spilled her notebook from behind, and as she retrieved her papers, I noticed one that was covered with indiscernible scribbles. "That's cursive writing," she said. Then, in a voice so rife with doom it sounded almost parental, she added, "You'll have to do that next year."

At that juncture, of course, we dismissed her like grasshoppers ignoring Aesop's dour ant. After all, we still inhabited the relatively unlettered fellowship of first grade, whose greatest traumas, if there were any, resulted from the rough diplomacy governing recess. Otherwise, all of our rituals, games, goads, and mockeries were effectively accommodated by oral tradition. We figured Myra was just retaliating with what little ammunition she had at her disposal. Let her blather about the ambiguous future if she wanted, we silently agreed. It wouldn't prevent us from getting her again tomorrow.

Then after one final uncursive summer, we entered second grade, and Myra's prophecy and revenge came to pass. Jeff Diamond and I and all the rest of us were sentenced to hard labor at the refinery. We kept at our *o*'s until they could be used as fittings for Titan rockets. We perfected our *p*'s until Plato himself wouldn't purge them from heaven. We machined the alphabet into symbols of consistent size and shape until we were sick with precision.

I don't remember whether or not I did so specifically to commemorate my having reached fifteen, but I determined that after eight years of servitude it was time to take my handwriting into my own hands. Admittedly, this was hardly a newsworthy revolution in the tumultuous 1960s, no doubt of no great account to the counterculture. Yet it seemed to me that this subtle apostasy would affect me more intimately than the numbing, routine savageries that made the paper (always heralded, by the way, in the same unalterable font). Furthermore, such an essential change might prove the source from which all future anti-establishment activities would spring. What I envisioned was a profounder signature, an inscription to reckon with. Why not make my *m* momentous instead of matter-of-fact? What about an *a* that quelled mobs or an *r* that broke hearts? With my *z* I might redefine the zeitgeist; with my *s,* bring peace to the Middle East. It was time to resign standard notation and mature into a unique, plenipotentiary self, made manifest in a freshly willed signature. It was time to engi-

neer a discipline all my own. It was time, that is, to give my name a
good name.

For a couple of weeks at least, like a producer casting his musi-
cal, I held tryouts for my name's sake. One would-be Art Saltzman
swashbuckled about the page with flourishes worthy of Errol Flynn.
Carving out my capitals and slashing my *t*'s as if dueling a bumbling
band of pirates, this alias implied more derring-do than the actual Art
Saltzman had ever dared or done, either at fifteen or in all the years
since. Would that I had an *i* to show off a customized thrust, much the
way that after toying with the dastardly Basil Rathbone, Errol Flynn
finally rammed his point home; but, alas, I hadn't an *i* to my name.
(And again, alas, in high school I had never been nearly so dauntless,
and "dastardly" far outstripped the injuries anyone had ever done me
there.)

A second claimant to my name plied me with rococo, tonsuring
tufts, whorls, and filigrees wherever a letter angled or tailed off. This
so-called Art Saltzman practiced paraphs involuted as ganglia, as if
cultivating the ego's own root system until it overwhelmed the trees.
My name came all in costume, sporting cowlicks, frills, and flounces,
its components secured with subtle knots. Flags unfurled from the
upper-case *S* to celebrate the liberation of the country of myself. From
the upper-case *A* rippled ribbons; there was also the occasional epaulet
worn or the odd sconce depending. Retrospect revealed this pretender
to be too fey a decorator to employ, but I confess that at the time I was
charmed.

A third potential autograph reversed this strategy, negating elab-
oration with Spartan resolve. My redoubtable capitals competed for
prominence with Washington and Moscow; the supporting cast, sturdy consonants and invincible vowels, was cast iron. Or I perceived the
l and *t* that centered my surname to be solid masts, aptly suited to sustain me through the unpredictable seas of my teens. For life at fifteen
was already hard and threatened to get harder. Let the most durably
designed Art Saltzman precede me.

Lying in bed at night, I saw my signature as a cityscape undergoing renovation. I would level the old and obsolete Art, with its predictable initial looking like a wobbly almond, needing support; down
would go the bulbous *S,* like an unstrung lyre uselessly trying to herald the mute, conformist Saltzman second grade had laid upon me.
Soon an improved skyline would loom over my papers, with a gestalt

(nearly asleep at this point, surely) familiar and adamant as New York. Already susceptible to a writer's wishes, I dreamed of the flyleaves I might land on, the libraries I might reside in, my name hobnobbing with the other eminent citations in the card catalog.

I ultimately settled on a compromise Art Saltzman of sorts, a hybrid whose genetic debts to all of the autographs petitioning for paternity could be inferred by anyone who'd ever gotten a good look at its lineage. Its most apparent upgrade was the severing of the capital letters from the lower-case followers that bunched and cowered behind them like sycophants trailing their sovereigns. As if anticipating their ascension to monogram status or their self-sufficient denotation of me one day on copies of contracts, I granted my aspiring *A* and stalwart *S* the singularity of being printed out, commemorating the uncorrupted days before I'd incurred cursive writing. Furthermore, I granted my *A* the distinction of a few centimeters' distance from pack, much as any monument is set off from the street. My *S,* meanwhile, held fast the seven letters it dwarfed by a line that cinched its middle as though *S* were the anchor in a tug of war. As for the remainder of my troops, I patrolled their ranks with care, demanding that no one slouch in my outfit and that every single kern was neatly kept.

Once I had the design down, I drilled until I could sign myself naturally, reproducing my name with the scrutiny of a Hindu pronouncing his mantra. Thus I repudiated Palmer and the chains of enforced penmanship. Thus I constructed a signature which I believed to be resilient enough to sustain me well into the next millennium. And thus it was in December of 1968 that as part of the heading of my English essay exam on *A Tale of Two Cities* I debuted the all-new model Art Saltzman. My immaculate inscription, ready for indelibility, beneath which the test I was taking seemed almost incidental.

And I imagined that I'd entered a venerable place, a vast hallway of renown, an endless stretch of accomplishments emblazoned with my imprint, bearing my lately minted name. And I thought: Look on my Works, ye Mazurek, and despair!

Nevertheless, I have discovered, not without regret, not without shame, that it is not only our bellies and our beliefs that slacken as we age. Looking back over old documents that have unaccountably clung to me over the past three or four decades, I realize how faint the trace of that assiduous signature has become. Unconsciously, I kept easing the tolerances. Especially after a long day's signing on and signing off—professors shuffle and stain more papers than most—one Art is too hard to master. And so my once-regal *A* often looks as if it were slopped onto the page by Jackson Pollack; the rigor has gone out of my *r,* which slumps like a doddering boxer who got out of the game too late; and my *t* is about as bracing as a ragged cross whose claim on its nameless plot the next stiff wind will erase. I have now and then opted for "Arthur" to assert some wherewithal on checks and other formal public appearances; but the discriminating reader will find less of the legendary British king than of Boo Radley, that shy and blighted Arthur who haunted *To Kill a Mockingbird,* who inspired compassion, yes, but never emulation from anyone.

As for my last name's fate, one by one the letters have slurred, starting from the outermost reaches and collapsing backward. My own private Domino Theory, as it were, is inexorably at work. By 1988, I had all but lost the "man" in "Saltzman," my name's diminishment not only undoing but symbolically emasculating me. A decade later, the clutch of consonants in the middle of my name, that very copse where my Eastern European roots were planted, had been more or less plowed under. And today, when I sign in a hurry (and how long has it been since I've signed in any other fashion?), Saltzman is essentially an *S* dragging its train like a diva after a protracted dinner party or a fisherman reeling in his unresistant line, coming up empty except for the thinnest drizzle of ink. More direly, it is a memento mori. Although those particular letters never actually intrude upon my name, I recognize this as the Saltzman EKG, which has nearly flat-lined. The fuse is burning up behind me, and I won't outlive it: when the last of the letters disappears, I'll be utterly ground down, anonymous amid the rest of the wordless majority.

Too easy—dismayingly so—to portend the old man I'll be, complaining: "Once I was richly syllabled, chock-full of promise, consonants, and vowels. Once I signed with a steady hand. I have the receipts somewhere to prove it." I foresee the day my *A* disintegrates into two vast and trunkless legs of stone standing in the desert, which will themselves disappear in time. I foresee the day my *S* lets go, much as my organs must ultimately give out. When I consider how my last signature is spent, with all remaining artifice subdued, all conceit and eccentricity bled out, until nothing is left to pronounce me but dead, I crave a namesake to carry Art Saltzman on in some recognizable condition.

I hereby authorize my proxy. May He of a thousand names one dare not name, Who signs Himself everywhere, in continents, physics, and fire, inscribe me for a blessing in the Book of Life.

11 On the Blink

Three boys are gathered before the wall of aquariums at the pet store. They have already been scolded for throwing wood chips at the guinea pigs. They have already been chased away from the parrot cage for poking at the bird and urging it to imitate their curses. But at the back of the store they have escaped the gaze of the store manager, and here the most interesting occupation is tormenting the fish. One of the boys pokes at a pump hose to interrupt the bubbles. Another swirls a finger, whirlpool-fashion, above a school of baffled mollies. But it is the third whose intrigue trumps what his companions have come up with. "Guys, watch this!" He sweeps his hand before a tank of a hundred or so swordtails. When he moves to the right, the fish all glide left; when he moves (almost balletically) left again, the fish drift back right again. The boys are amazed by the unanimity of the swordtails. One inaudible quake moves through the school; one thrum simultaneously quickens a hundred hearts. "Let me try it!" says a second boy, the one who had deserted the mollies he'd been trying to dizzy. He shoves past his companions and begins swishing his hand rapidly in front of the tank. The faster he does it, the faster consensus is transmitted among the fish, which as the boy whips his hand back and forth seem to ripple like an orange flag in a crazy wind. There is something paradoxically martial about the way they mass for withdrawal as, like Robert Frost's shore patrol in "Neither Out Far nor In Deep," they "all turn and look one way." Now all three of the boys are ducking and dashing about, testing the limits of instinct. They laugh and collide, bumping a couple of the closely packed tanks, instigating tides. The manager finally hears the noise, and his approach scatters them. He regards the damage—nothing that a mop and the laws of physics can't repair. He regards me, too, with a look that says either "Boys like that . . . they're like walking birth control, you know?" or "Couldn't *you* have said something to them?" I can't tell which, but his look is sufficient to force me to drop my eyes and turn away.

But the hundred swordtails still compel. Something about the way that at a moment's notice they could be magically conscripted into a failed battalion, or so it seems because they always drag their weapons behind them, in retreat. By now the fish have already recovered the few atoms of individuality they'd enjoyed and have resumed their oblivion. I leave them to their meantime, which for fish in a tank is simply the interval between intrusions. Feedings, cleanings, captures—from their point of view, all advances imperil. Already they are once again separately and otherwise engaged: some nuzzle the glass, some mouth and discard the artificial pink and blue sediment, some guzzle nearly invisible nutrients, some drift without incident or aim. And yet, I know how the very next human approach, the next gesture that invades their transparent, water-tight perimeter, will unionize them into a gang recoil.

I submit that flinching is one fundamental way in which our two species coincide.

The proof is how much painstaking training goes into learning to put oneself in harm's way. So said Terry Sawchuck, who should have known. A Hall of Fame hockey goalie, Sawchuck once told an interviewer that the hardest thing about learning his trade was overcoming his natural reluctance to deliberately put himself in front of the speeding puck. *Anyone's* natural reluctance, he might have said. Something there is that doesn't love a welt, much less the black blur it will derive from, but every mark on Sawchuck was the mark of a successful save. Every nerve and pretty much every other experience tells you that if you can't escape a projectile, minimizing the impact is the best alternative. Blocking it with your body refutes every principle of good health and common sense. (A rising slap shot knows no diplomacy.) Ignoring your own best interests: that's what training is for.

During practice, on the coach's signal, rookie goalies get peppered by a flock of wingers assaulting from all directions at once. Let them subsist on a crash diet of hard rubber. Let them know death by a thousand pucks. Sometimes, imitating a fraternity initiation ritual, teammates will skate by and poke, whack, and stab at their own goalie just to toughen up his tender meat. The goalie's goal is to instill in himself the very opposite of the matador's mentality, whereby the bull may be teased or coaxed near but never intercepted. According to Sawchuck,

the goalie conceives of the rink as a funnel tilting and narrowing toward him. Thus the goalie's integrity and creed: the puck stops here.

One look at my nose—it is shaped like a shillelagh that's been left
out in the weather for a couple of winters at least—suggests that I
have mastered this aptitude for brass tactics myself. To the dismay of
photographers, I don't have enough consistency in my countenance to
provide one wholly good side so much as more and less viable facets
to my face. (The camera generally proves me fractious, what with my
nose being permanently out of joint.) And indeed, thanks to the combination of years of contact sports, questionable reflexes, and plain bad
luck, I have had my nose broken four times, making shaving a delicate
negotiation and shopping for sunglasses, which always sit askew, exas-
perating altogether. You might go so far as to mistake me for a goalie,
in other words, granting me a goalie's unstinting commitment and
lacquered attitude, fitted with the regular mechanism of a goalie's flut-
terless heart. However, my visage to the contrary, I confess that I am a
flincher, a chronic sufferer of winces and twinges, who still has uneasy
dreams about the bad-hop grounder or the weak-side rebound that,
should I try to corral it, I will have to pay for in blood. Opponents figure it out quickly enough—flinching is a weakness more glaring than
any addiction—and, according to the given sport, take advantage. For
I am the batter who incessantly steps in the bucket and gives away the
inside of the plate, my face having gone white as the impending ball.
(Discretion is the better part of pallor.) I am the midfielder who twists
away from the impending header. I am the receiver who gets alligator
arms when he senses the predatory linebacker homing in from behind.
I am the human version of the horse that pulls up short of the steeple.
There goes the fumble squirting to the turf. It's all yours. It is too late
for me.

I sometimes believe that the unflinching, anomalous as they are,
are born, not made. How else can I account for those uncautious
young girls who nowadays populate the gym? "Box out, Bekka!" "Kill
it, Lynette!" Title IX and televised women's basketball alone cannot
account for their willingness to forego a legacy of daintiness centuries
old and enter the fray face first. Of course, there are still plenty of girls
who drift back to shoot their jumpers from beyond the arc and squeal
and shy from the tussle that breaks out under the rim. They have my
commiseration, but not my heart, which I reserve for the girls who
are game enough to choke the lane. That they may have inherited
their propensities from fathers who stepped between the weaklings

and the bullies on the playground, who themselves descended from men who charged first from the landing craft at Normandy beach, does not in the least temper my appreciation. I have seen girls launch themselves after loose balls as if there were nothing especially fragile about their physiology, much less the social history of their gender. I have watched them show off new bruises and heedlessly stream blood after a victory. I have heard them laugh experience-rich, pain-defying, debt-canceling laughter, the sort of laughter that resounds in professional locker rooms, the sort brought up from deeper down than you'd have imagined a teenaged girl's reserves could go. Earned laughter, I mean. Laughter paid for gamely by players who did not cringe. Laughter justly won.

But again, I want to emphasize how abnormal it is to take having a nose for the ball so literally. It is no accident that one of the principal strategies of the martial arts program known as American Defense is that you preface whatever foray or retreat you have planned with a flick of your fingers at your opponent's eyes. Unless he's synthetic or stoned, either of which possibility would disqualify him as a threat to your physical well-being anyway, he will startle, squint, hesitate, or shrink back the least little bit, which will give you an opening to proceed with your retaliation or, better yet, run for it.

I remember seeing a videotaped demonstration of how a baby learns to trust her mother so completely that she will ignore all other instincts except that one. A psychologist situated a ten-month-old girl on a platform across from her mother. Between them stretched about six feet of solid, transparent plastic. Using familiar cooing and less cajoling than you might have thought the stunt required, the mother managed to convince her baby to disregard what must have seemed to her like a lethal ravine and to crawl happily into her arms. Not every baby tested the air so boldly, the psychologist confessed, but many scooted eagerly across the way this little girl did. A born power forward, that one.

I also remember watching Ronald Reagan being shot by the deluded John Hinckley, a sight made indelible by the ghoulish insistence of every channel to replay it over and over while our wounded president was going under the knife. What most impressed me was the image of Timothy McCarthy, the Secret Service agent who responded to the first shot by launching himself between the shooter and the president and taking a bullet in the abdomen himself. It was his automatic willingness to sacrifice his body—and quite possibly his life—that has stayed with me ever since. I thought, How remarkable, how courageous, and how thoroughly unnatural of him. Several days later, a special ceremony was conducted in the hospital as McCarthy convalesced. Obviously uncomfortable before the reporters—Secret Service agents are as committed to secrecy as to service, and the sudden notoriety appeared to bother him more than the gunfire did—he said that he had only been doing his job. Furthermore, he didn't really consider what he was doing when he did it—he simply reacted. Viewers in living rooms all across the country shook their heads in wonder. Here was a real hero, a man as untroubled by ambivalence as a hawk by *Hamlet*.

Can the agency test for that propensity? Is there a kind of SAT that detects the ideal intersection of reflex and duty? Surely you don't pick up disregard for impending personal injury in a handbook. There are no courses in undistractibility. McCarthy's demurrals to the contrary, "just doing my job" doesn't do justice to the job he does.

Can you imagine Prufrock clapping you on the shoulder with the assurance "I've got your back"? What about counting on Quentin Compson to step between you and the bully in the schoolyard or, let's face it, any character in the last volume of the Norton anthology to stand his ground? As an English professor, who confers upon his American literature students every semester a whole syllabus's worth of ticks and inhibitions, I am often taken by examples of those who go for the jugular or, more amazing still, expose their own jugulars without hesitation. As I say, this goes well beyond goalies and bodyguards—people who intercept professionally. Just as wondrous to me is the young private who discovers in himself a caution-be-damned capacity that triggers his charge out of the foxhole in the direction of enemy fire. That's the stuff they make martyrs and movies out of. That's the sort of daring that merits theme music. Or consider the 112-pound mother whose athletic prowess has otherwise been confined to twice-weekly hours on the treadmill, but who when she glimpses her child about to be flattened by a van instantly transforms into Batgirl to save him from what the kid's own comic books call "certain doom." "What were you thinking?" asks her husband or the local newscaster, depending on which astonished party arrives on the scene first. "I didn't think. I didn't realize what I was doing, really. All I knew was that Jason was in danger." I'd wager that neither Reagan's nor Jason's respective saviors ever suspected that an alter ego waited within.

Nor does the potential for casualty have to be that extreme to separate the forged from the feathered. Therapists and scout leaders will sometimes encourage their charges to demonstrate their faith in one another by taking turns crossing their arms over their chests and falling backwards, relying on their partners to catch them. The object is to surrender absolutely to trust and gravity. To ball up, put out a hand to absorb the shock, or even so much as sneak a peek during the procedure, however understandable an instinct, is an insult. What you want is the sort of clean swoon a magician's assistant might submit to. In this way, the risk is doubled: you will find out not only what you are made of but also what the person who presumably will take your weight is made of as well. Also doubled is the eventual satisfaction or dismay, depending.

We reserve our greatest respect for the effort that is not in our nature to produce. At a museum of contemporary art, who hasn't shaken his head in bewilderment before some minimalist piece—for instance, "Portrait of a Square," which is merely, precisely what the title proclaims—and wanted to levy a fraud charge against the artist? The argument that this is a democratic redefinition of art gets shouted down by "Hell, *I* could have done that!" or "I *did* do that when I was six, and it may have made the refrigerator door but not a museum wall!" However memorable William Carlos Williams's "Red Wheelbarrow," for most readers it doesn't hold water. "This Is Just to Say" is the title of another of his poems, a dashed-off apology for swiping plums: one could contend that the "just" of his title is an appeal for legitimacy, but students dismiss it as meaning "merely," and whatever poetry might be, there shouldn't be anything mere about it. It should be something they can't do. It should be *hard.* They might not like Eliot or Stevens or want to emulate their activities, but they respect the effort. There is nothing ordinary about *An Ordinary Evening in New Haven,* and for sheer accomplishment, composing the *Four Quartets* favorably compares to taking four of seven in the Stanley Cup Finals. Once we recognize our own capacities in an athlete, he should be dropped from the squad. Whatever his province, a professional's reach should exceed our grasp. Heaven is not heaven on the first floor.

At first glance, it appears that literary intrepidness is competitive with other sorts of storming the breach, as if putting down a seemingly indomitable concept with a deft sentence were comparable to taking down a charging bull with one thrust of a sword. From another perspective, however, the most celebrated makers of metaphor are not matadors, staunch and sneering from inflexible stances, but doubting and floutable flinchers through and through. With apologies to Robert Frost, with whom I showed brief allegiance above, there are few things more fickle than a symbol. Don't look to creativity if it's constancy you're after. It is the very model of mitigation, all edgings and inchings, in the phrase of Wallace Stevens (a phrase no doubt arrived at only after a long evening's editing and shuffling at the foot of Parnassus). A discipline hardly worthy of the steadiness "discipline" denotes, literature is adamant about nothing so much as its own disclaimers. Specific policies lie well outside its purview. At most, literature lobbies to win and retain some innocuous post in the current administration of each reader's consciousness. Rarely will a poem secure a thesis like some melodrama damsel tied to the tracks. Instead, each successful simile is another slipped jab. Even William Carlos Williams, who for a poet is relatively fond of straightforwardness, can describe his findings only as "a fiery light, too fiery for logical statement." "We catch a glimpse of something, from time to time, which shows us that a presence has just brushed past us," he says, "some rare thing—just when the smiling little Italian woman has left us. For a moment we are dazzled. What was that? We can't name it; we know it never gets into any recognizable avenue of expression; men will be long dead before they can have so much as ever approached it." Who'd bother to depose such a witness when sentencing is at hand? The artist's insights flash as fleetingly as semaphore, whose messages, often as not, are refuted by the sun. It is more defensible to view poetic figures as the verbal equivalents of deflecting the brunt, turning into the skid, or rolling with the blow. They are flicks to the eyes of brutal circumstance that upset its balance just enough to let the writer get away through the gate.

By this reasoning, the writer really connects with everyone else that cowers throughout the animal kingdom. I mean not only the aforementioned swordtails, genetically predisposed to cover their collective rears, but also the tangs that sport false eyes on their tail fins to tease predators with misdirection. Writers might also ally with octopuses, which similarly employ their ink in the service of subterfuge, and spiders, which likewise weave their intricacies out of exhaust. We are talking about career opportunities in risk management. We are talking about the cautionary sublime. Everywhere you look, creatures are making their livelihoods from running variations on Three-Card Monty. (At the very least, they look at their hole cards before plunging in after the pot.) Whether they nest in jungle canopies like toucans or commute through subways like prairie dogs ever on the lookout for the next inevitable daunting, no matter what chrysalis, covert, or grotto they keep to, they do not take up residence without knowing where the exits are located. So too are authors, secreted away in communes and corner offices, anxiously redrafting.

Emerson said in "Self-Reliance" that to be great is to be misunderstood, or something to that effect. Were he more forthcoming about his profession, he might have said that to be great is to cultivate immunity to understanding. Whereas the impolitic writer, whose book contains an argument oversized and obvious as a shotgun under the coat, will be accosted at customs, the canny writer, who has only potentialities, glimmers, and inclinations to declare, goes on his way unapprehended. Not argument but guile gets him by.

When it comes to survival, let us not underestimate the value of a stylish manner and a noble, metrical gait. Like the elegant burglar who insinuates himself into the cocktail party for drinks before stealing off to the bedroom where the jewelry is kept, the writers we most admire are the Cary Grants of the canon, who prosper through urbane talk and formalwear. Grace Kelly fell for the debonair feint, and so do we.

But this is only to keep from falling further. Writers shy from finality like a yawning ravine. Admiring the elasticity of birch trees that are bowed before him like respectful subjects before their liege, Frost realizes that their condition is undoubtedly due to ice storms, for only that unremitting weight could have "bent them so low for long." However, Frost decides to exploit their limberness further by twisting the image to comply with his own past and his own purposes: "But I should prefer to have some boy bend them," he says, for that would confirm and consecrate his own youth. "So was I once myself a swinger of birches. / And so I dream of going back to be." Facts are fastballs under the chin. Who wouldn't lean away in the direction of his ideals? Because the poet's boyhood lies on the other side of nostalgia, there is no telling to what extent his conception of his past has been altered anyway. The same goes for us: most readers, years after having encountered "Birches," will remember it as being not about tree limbs that storms distorted but about ones ridden into permanent submission by boys "too far from town to learn baseball."

Frost's flinches are memorable but by no means unique. Every figure of speech proceeds from a comparable instinct. From Emily Dickinson's "tell it slant" to Howard Nemerov's "beautiful inexact" to Richard Wilbur's "mad instead," ingenuity comes down to finding ways of turning what you regard into what you'd rather. These examples all come from esteemed artful dodgers, it is true, but you don't have to be a poet to live by this practice. It is enough to look back on when you were young. Once young people seem to you enviably, insufferably young, insultingly, unforgivably younger than you remember ever having been—now that you use the term "young people," that is, before realizing all that saying that saying says about you—it becomes harder and harder to recall when you yourself used to crowd the plate that way, if you ever did. Or perhaps, now that you subsist on a chalky, unwholesome diet of rue, imagining it is as close as you get.

Leave it to the poet to promise compensation beyond what we, grown queasy, grown up, deserve. In "The City Limits," A. R. Ammons cannot withhold his appreciation for our daily ration of radiance, which does not withhold itself. Instead, "it will look into the guiltiest / swerving of the weaving heart and bear itself upon them, / not flinching into disguise or darkening." At the heart of the lyric is a vision of Nature that can take a punch.

I don't know what alternative entertainment those apprentice hoodlums went in for after they'd been shooed from the pet store. (The manager had thought it prudent to usher them all the way out the door, after which he shouted after them not to come back without some legitimate business. This because he knew that young toughs tend to hover. Conversely, adults are the only flight risks in any community.) Possibly they next went in for some vague and minor vandalism, perhaps a makeshift game whose potential for injury was sufficient to absorb them for an hour. Possibly they merely settled for a staring tournament, in which the winner was the one who kept from blinking longest. Whatever they decided on, it is safe to say that it wasn't anything so dodgy and squeamish, so insistent on its own inability to insist, so bait-and switchy and intrinsically flinchy as literature. I feel fairly confident about this. Still, I am willing to admit that I may be being too harsh on them and unfair to sensibilities the manager wasn't swayed by and I simply didn't happen to see. If that's the case, let me claim the writer's reflex and prerogative. I take it back.

12 Chapter Thirty-Four, in Which Our Hero Cuts to the Chase

The efficiency experts descend in force. They come with rulers and levels, protractors and T-squares, calipers and razored pleats and engineering degrees. They come with blotters that double as calendars and desk caddies that double as classifiers for unpaid bills. They come to bag our clutter, to cleanse the office of every offending obstacle and adjective, to assert their carpenters' rule. To pave and to purify, to angle the cubicles and cure the askew, to purge our binges and blue pencil our urges, they come.

They are Wallace Stevens's square-hatted rationalists, who'd jar every sloppy Tennessee into orthodoxy if they had their way. Given the chance, they would organize every landfill's contents alphabetically and consolidate the surf. They are the Jack Spratts of business and industry, who'd ruthlessly subdue the devil's excesses and exalt alacrity, leanness, and "let's get to it." Scourges of surplus, they worship the streamlined and the spartan; they endorse the trimmer sail and the tighter ship. Their implicit motto, with apologies to Rogers and Hammerstein: You've got to be carefully taut.

What endeavor nowadays has escaped their discipline? Whole industries are devoted to the contemporary attack on slackness. More insidious than any partisan politics, their doctrine has conquered our library shelves and grocery aisles, our laundromats and condominiums. It is all so stunningly . . . functional. They heap and multitask us like updated Ahabs. In our burnished kitchens, every technological upgrade shaves another ten seconds from the cycle of consumption. In the consoles of our cars, our maps, snacks, cigarettes, and coins are ideally distributed for ready access, while gauges, CD players, cell phones, and global positioning units are planted in the dash as the latest advances in logical deployment dictate. Doctors adjust our spines and our medications, policing our postures and our moods, our circuits and sensibilities. Dieticians calibrate our proteins and carbs with the promise that our bodies will run as reliably as Mussolini's trains. Personal trainers instruct us to pare away any adulteration of muscle. We wake in our scientifically sculptured beds, whose frames hide our socks, underwear, and extra linens in drawers that shut back flush; and we ready ourselves for sleep by setting our clock radios, coffeemakers, and climate controls, and restoring the computer-designed tools of personal hygiene to vanities so ingeniously concentrated that they'd turn a Japanese landscaper green. Our entire day's endowments are aerodynamic.

Wouldn't they idolize Temple Grandin, an animal scientist featured by Dr. Oliver Sacks in his book *An Anthropologist on Mars.* Dr. Grandin is a renowned designer of slaughterhouses. What makes them special is the way she has arranged the chutes and pens to prevent the livestock from recognizing what is about to happen to them. What makes Temple Grandin special is that she has Asperger Syndrome, a mysterious disorder marked by weird obsessions and often described as a sort of functional autism. Thanks to her lethal expertise, the condemned animals remain more or less tractable and composed.

Moo.

I sometimes wonder what the efficiency experts might make of my own willful incongruities. My office, for instance, is set in the most intemperate mental climate. Check out my desk, a longstanding site of defects indulged. The surface is spattered with ink and sauces from sandwiches past, covered by castings of a worming imagination, decorated by vague drizzles, secretions, pigments, and stains you'd expect to find on a housepainter's dropcloth, not a professor's workplace. Any area that is not covered by Heraclitean piles of paper—I can't step in the same reverie twice—lies under dust. So does my computer, which purrs like a cat content with clutter and mange; its housing is pasted with notes, as if that cat had gotten loose in a closet full of wrapping paper. I will not pretend to speak for the damage done by the plate tectonics that must be going on inside the drawers, except to say that it's a sight best reserved for the hardened medical examiner. It is posed and it is posed, mocks Stevens, but in my nature it merely grows, you know? In sum, my office is the record of my many years of standard deviation. I'm sure that the scene would insult the clarity and shake the determination of *any* efficiency expert, whose sole consolation might be the notion that pretty much all of it will burn.

Actually, however, the field marshals of linearity and calculated inhibition do not harass me. I may not believe that the eternal may be readily extrapolated from efficiency, but I am no Luddite, either. I do not always join with William James, who wondered, "Why should anywhere the world be absolutely fixed and finished?" If I do not pledge allegiance to every way of cutting against "the black inane," I have been known to prize accomplishments of sanitation and exactitude. When errands overwhelm and correspondence, rough drafts, and appointments pile, who wouldn't want to do more with less effort? I am not above appreciating the stemmed tide and the momentary stay against confusion. I can admire responsibilities strategically staggered, memos deftly edited, and little worlds made cunningly. I'm not above downing the day's minimum daily nutritional requirements from a can as I drive to class. To my mind, the retractable appendages of a Swiss Army knife admirably compete with any physiological advancement the animal kingdom has managed through evolution. Even if I don't always emulate them, I often crave the tapered and respect the tucked.

But when efficiency's incursions spread to those appropriately untucked and untaperable areas of the imagination, I rise from the intrinsic disarray to object. I am speaking of the bowdlerization and abridgment of literary works in deference to Mrs. Grundy's Guide to Grooming. I mean the reduction of rich discourse to shrink rap. I refer to the not-so-subtle shoving of ambiguous, bristling, and stubbornly untidy texts over the brink of Cliff's Notes. These are the efficiencies that offend me most because they scrape too near the wood and closest to home.

Take speed-reading, that staple of self-improvement gurus and convenience evangelists. Students hastening to have it all, sick of time and with it, briskly ski down the pages of *The Magic Mountain* or race across the daunting terrain of *War and Peace* more impetuously than Napoleon ever did in the book. When it comes to passages that defy the "ready to serve" aesthetic, they complain that "if the writer wants to say something, why doesn't he just *say* it, then?" Truth should need no paraphrase, they claim. Meaning should move as dependably as a grade school fire drill or a funeral cortege. Why beat around the bush when you can sooner uproot it and move on?

Poems, in particular, offend their sense of propriety because poems are essentially played hunches. What with all of their figuration and maneuvering, poems are like so many hostile witnesses fidgeting in the box. But readers weaned on speed would seal up stanzas like packages from UPS. They would consign obstreperous verses to corners, where they'd be forced to sit until they learned to behave. They would comb out the stylistic tics, iron out the ironies, raze the byzantine in favor of the Shaker and severe. They would force the dreamer out of bed and shoo nuance out the door. And whenever a poet's subject knuckled under undue stress and ornament, they would threaten to stop the conversation—that is, until the poet adopted a normal tone of voice and a civil tongue. Ezra Pound counsels that poetry is "news that stays news," but we are talking about folks who want their news scrutable and delivered directly to their front doors.

I name Emily Dickinson my co-counsel—"Tell all the Truth but tell it slant—/ Success in Circuit lies," she advises—but Dickinson is herself one of those pokey poets, a dyed-in-the-wool 'round-the-busher, and she does not always compel the unconverted. Literature is a nut only critics crack at. But the analogy to sex . . . well, sex, they get. If regimen reigned over intercourse the way it seems to do everywhere else, I suggest, sex would be performed as succinctly as a flu shot. But where are the lavish tactics of affection and assault, the worship of unique and intimate curves, the intricate approaches and the gorging of *every* organ involved? Where's the craft and cadence? If it's really lovemaking, where's the *love?* "I know you can make love in two minutes. Let's see you do it in two *hours,*" I charge. So, too, does literature require and reward readers with stamina and ingenuity. Like any desire, it will not be easily reduced to a rigid, digital alternative—not if it's done right. A poem that gives itself up immediately, eyes on the clock as its customer comes to it, is a whore you might wrest easy pleasure from but never take home with you, much less want to husband. Put another way—a writer's compulsion, if not his prerogative, is to put things another way, then another yet—opposing a poet's antic attachments is like balking when a lover bothers to fondle or breaks out in song.

Why must everything in life get down exclusively to business and brass tacks? There is plenty of proof that nature has little patience with straight lines. On some level, it makes sense to grant the poet her slant on the world, especially when it appears that, more often than not, the world is so inclined. Robert Frost, another treacherous, wrench-in-the-works writer, said, "All our ingenuity is lavished on getting into danger legitimately so that we may be genuinely rescued." Readers who contend that if we avoided the mountains and swamps in the first place we wouldn't *need* the picks and ropes have to be seduced into literature's lovely muddles if they are ever going to value the loveliness at all, much less learn to long for the distraction as much as they do for the directions out.

I like to think that in teaching literature I'm offering a *slow*-reading course. Although we do plow unwaveringly through pages on occasion, my class allows for plasmic activity as well. We dilate, allude, loop, flirt, hint, submit, brood, fiddle, tinker, tickle, and redirect our attentions—we have a whole thesaurus for farting around—exercising all those darting, squirty verbs, which flicker and efface themselves throughout their unplottable progresses. We browse and linger over texts, contemplate and tongue them. We redefine "purposefulness" and "quality time." Art doesn't expedite awareness for us—this isn't a matter of stamping out dimes in a factory. It pays to remember that the saving grace of free association is that it's *free.*

What I'm suggesting about efficiency is that, basically, human beings aren't built for it. Certainly our very bodies must consternate the experts, what with the ungainly way our heads totter and bobble about so whenever we stick our necks out, which is itself not the most efficient decision to make. To be truly adept, we would have to be totally supplanted by a better-regulated idea of mankind. What a rattletrap anatomy we are! How we blotch and sag. Which of our organs doesn't deserve to be returned to committee? Every jerk and nerve-splash begs another adjustment. Our senses, such as they are, are slight and don't endure. Our hands and feet are breakables thinly knit, whose components are cramped together like breakfast cereal in boxes, and as easily crushed. Needless yards of large intestine are only so much waste. And on and on—the evidence is irrefutable that other animals have it all over us in terms of agility, power, prolificacy, and physical grace. Who would presume to order our pores and hone our bones? Who could re-align the body's gnarled roots and rake the sand trap of personality? Brains are made for vagrancy. They can't be shaped and aimed like bullets. The fact is that there's execution and there's execution: too methodical an implementation can murder creativity in the cradle. Yes, brains are the trump humans usually play, but whatever advantages those lumpy, subtle seats of intuition, wonder, and doubt provide, efficiency is definitely not among them.

The same seems true of the entire planet. If the Earth is an engine, it has less in common with anything the Lockheed people have produced than with Fluxus artist Jean Tinguely's *Homage to New York,* a wacky-looking contraption whose operation caused it to spew stink gas and flames as it destroyed itself. Annie Dillard has suggested that the Earth could be seen as a massive device principally designed not for the sustenance of the human species but for the production of sand. (Or possibly termites. As Dillard notes in *For the Time Being,* there's half a ton of them for every single person alive.) It requires a pretty narrow, unbending anthrocentric perspective to even begin to argue that our world is efficient and that its hypothetical foreman knows what he's doing.

Efficiency promises to fix us, but there's fixed like a toaster and fixed like a dog, isn't there? Yes, I want my accountant's ledgers to follow the straight and narrow and to have the snarls untangled from city traffic so it doesn't jam, but I'd just as soon keep the experts' eager, hygienic hands off our poems and stories. I can't speak for all writers, but when I'm at hard at it, the efficiency-minded would be hard-pressed to find very much potential for solid geometry about me. My pockets are flowing with notes to myself about where the latest pages have gone or might fruitfully go. I keep leafleting myself with comments, phrases, queries, and corrections, making a kiosk of my clothing. I tend to glaze over, fall to mumbling, pull off the road, or not—I'll sometimes prop a scrap of paper against the steering wheel and jot a line down while driving, once in a while setting off the horn. Family members worry over me. Friends shake their heads. Cops stop me to ask if I'm lost. This is when it's going *well,* mind you. Fine-tune my system, if "system" doesn't overrate the rickety bridge-making from sentence to sentence I sentence myself to, and it could all collapse into a vain stability, like a frozen cord of wood.

Robert Frost tells us in "The Constant Symbol" that the way of the mind "will be zigzag, but it will be a straight crookedness like the walking stick [one] cuts himself in the bushes for an emblem." Well, there's constancy, and then there's constancy. Be forewarned: as I said, Frost is yet another one of those writers who has a penchant for taking the long way around the barn. It's a hit-and-miss aesthetic, you might say, tricked out with disclaimers and compensations. We're moved by zigs and zags; by zigs and zags, we move our stubborn length along.

13 Blown Away

While I hasten to confirm that I have no plans to begin writing poetry, a decision sure to relieve as many as a dozen likely readers, I confess that one possible perk in particular causes me some ambivalence in that determination to abstain from producing any. I am speaking of the prospect of becoming Poet Laureate. This incentive has nothing to do with any remuneration, university residency, or fan support associated with the post. Like Dylan Thomas, I would not labor "for ambition or bread / Or the strut and trade of charms / On the ivory stages"; in fact, I'd extend my indifference beyond the "towering dead" Thomas dismisses to include the heedless lovers he hopes to court as well. No, the really enticing benefit, to my mind anyway, is the opportunity to supervise a national project on behalf of the art.

As Poet Laureate, Robert Pinsky spearheaded what has arguably been the most celebrated of these efforts, the "favorite poem" data bank. His interviews with Americans from all across the country and representing all walks of life have spawned an on-line resource, a videotape library, and at least one hardback anthology. A noble effort, to be sure, if a bit predictable: so many literary palates have been schooled to prefer the same Frosting, and it is no surprise to learn that so much of the Dickinson read into high school classrooms reads out years after graduation. Joseph Brodsky took a different tack during his reign, announcing his wish to have a poetry anthology placed in every hotel room in America, snuggled right up against the requisite Bible and the local telephone book, thereby adding a third form of "directory" to every guest's stash. Unfortunately, Brodsky had no budget to put his brainstorm into practice. When we consider the potential impact upon the transient businessman, adulterer, or suicide who could have happened upon the latest edition of the Norton, the failure to enact this program seems most unfortunate.

To be honest, even if I did win the appointment, my own pet project has even less chance of being funded than Brodsky's did. In a dramatic escalation of the concept represented by Magnetic Poetry, I would propose that sufficient turtles be acquired, bred, or otherwise rounded up—surely there are turtle wranglers who've been languishing, just waiting for this dream opportunity—and each inscribed with a different English word. They would then be released en masse as a kind of organic randomizer program to jostle, separate, and recombine without preconception all over the nation, the result being the infestation of America with found poetry. I favor turtles for this operation for a variety of reasons. Salient among these: they are already plentiful, inexpensive, and comparatively durable creatures; their shells can be etched without significant threat to the animals; and they move slowly enough to allow readers to linger over new passages—a tanka arrived upon a log, a stanza sunning itself on a river bank—as the most satisfying poetic interpretation warrants.

Through this operation, poetry's subtlest infiltrations would inflect the landscape, making America legible in unprecedented, unpredictable ways. Imagine happening upon a ballad basking in a field in Athens, Georgia. In Lima, Ohio, a line is discovered scrabbling over the natural punctuation of pebbles and twigs. Near Concord, New Hampshire, wakened syllables lift and wiggle their delicate, variable feet.

I have considered insects in the alternative because of their sheer abundance—a decent-sized college dictionary would not exhaust more than a couple of colonies—but the practical difficulties of writing and reading scotched that idea. (Indeed, imagine the fate of ants innocently yet fatally placed under the magnifying glass for the sake of clarity. Contemporary poetry is already a sufficiently frail enterprise without our alienating the ASPCA along with a majority of today's students.) Birds occurred to me, too, due to the lyrical capital they've earned over centuries of attention. None would question their poetic heritage and their totemic claims to beauty, freedom, and sublimity. However, any method of imprinting them that I could come up with would to some degree inhibit their capacity for flight, which is, of course, their principal claim to lyrical ascendancy among the beasts. In "The Blue Swallows," Howard Nemerov temporarily fancied that those birds were carving the sky into hieroglyphs, their "tails as nibs / Dipped in invisible ink, writing. . . ." I'm an admirer of his—himself a past Poet Laureate, Nemerov is my hypothetical colleague in that regard—and I'd love to do him the favor of reifying his image for him if I could. But birds will not sit still to be signed up for this project, and even if we could capture them for art's sake, they might be grounded permanently by our devices. ("Poor mind," Nemerov chides himself anyway, "what would you have them write?") Finally, even if they did manage to rise again, each flock forming its rough draft in the newly worded atmosphere, they'd fly too high for us to appreciate. Viewless wings of poesy, indeed! So, if it's ever to be anything under my jurisdiction, it'll be turtles doing the random bidding of inspiration, performing the gradual but irrepressible display of the language dispersing, reforming, rediscovering itself.

I cannot say whether or not the spectacle increases car sales, but there's no denying it stalls the local traffic. I am referring to the annual raising of the Stovepipe Man during Independence Day week by the auto dealership at Tenth and Range Line. His name applies to his having been built of cylinders, not to any stiffness in him. Actually, it's his limberness that enchants us. Twin blowers attached to his columnar legs shoot him to his full height of twenty feet. Because he is too tall and ungainly to sustain that altitude, he keeps slumping toward the blacktop. Then the continuous current snaps him back to attention again like a gigantic bed sheet—he is barely more than that: a simple tubular concoction of red parachute material—whereupon he exhausts himself once more and repeats the cycle of filling and foundering. I think of trees coursing with xylem and phloem, and I wonder if trees are likewise ravaged by that dependency though to the untrained eye they seem perfectly stolid about it. The channeled gasps shoot through the whole of him, the infusion brutalizing him through every visible dimension.

Not that he appears especially tormented by this ordeal. He rather dreamily accepts and expels the ongoing jolt of air. A literal inspiration, I think, but Jean Cocteau's corrective bears remembering: "It is not *in*spiration; it is expiration." Cocteau focuses on "the gaunt, fine hands on the thorax; evacuation of the chest; a great breathing out from himself," and so emphasizes what each "Eureka!" costs him. So it is a paroxysm of insight the Stovepipe Man suffers. But for the subterranean hum of the fans, the scene is oddly soundless in spite of the agitation we are witnessing.

Emily Dickinson maintained that she recognized poetry because it took the top of her head off, and here is a blatant manifestation of that figure: the gust rushes through his torso of fitted linens and escapes out the hole at the top of his exhaust pipe of a skull. As he flails lazily before the discounted cars, streamers fringing his head shiver in the breeze, showing in spite of his equanimity what a hair-raising experience this is. Certainly it wrings everything out of him. So must Zeus, thrusting Athena out of his thoughts as if spawning a squall, have momentarily collapsed from the involuntary effort. Then the great god lifted himself erect once more to encounter his latest brainstorm and legacy, as it were, head on.

If a poet shows humility by appealing to a muse to move through him to certify and sustain his talent, he shows arrogance by suggesting that a muse would enhance her resume by sharing the bill with him. Like an entrepreneur who impresses his banker with the size of the loan he asks for, John Milton launches into *Paradise Lost* by plying the Oracle of God with his own press clippings: "I thence / Invoke thy aid to my adventurous Song, / That with no middle flight intend to soar / Above th' AEONIAN Mount, while it pursues / Things unattempted yet in Prose or Rhime." Milton's petition mentions a desire to be illuminated, raised up, and supported in his endeavor, but it comes off as advertising. Thus does the daredevil preface his stunt, showing off the scope of his risk by begging the indulgence of the crowd he says he hopes he won't disappoint by crashing in the attempt. It is a talent in itself to grovel and strut simultaneously. Remember the Stovepipe Man, anchored and ascending at the same time.

After such altitude and assumption, what would it be like to lose that rapturous dimension than which there was no other? After such exponential serenity, what would it feel like to fall from grace? I am not referring to Lucifer's unfathomable plummet per se or Adam and Eve's own version of it when with a single misstep they spoiled Paradise, sacrificing staunchly metrical, full-blown Eden for our world of "grosser sleep." I am referring to the epic poet's deflation when the last draft was done, which might have felt like something on the order of Adam and Eve's own demise: "naked thus, of Honour void, / Of Innocence,

of Faith, of Puritie, / Our wonted Ornaments now soil'd and stain'd."
But if Milton remained in God's hands, he could have come down
gently to the conditions he'd spent twelve books justifying, maybe the
way that one becomes supernaturally buoyant in a dream and can leap
from any height. Falling like a soufflé, falling through a generously attending atmosphere, to the unaccountably forgiving concrete.

Other artists envy and forgive the illusion of sponsorship. Robert
Frost trusted in a lump in the throat to betoken a growing poem. A
desperate E. L. Doctorow faced the blank wall of his house in New
Rochelle and found *Ragtime* like a palimpsest waiting for him. Tennessee Williams discovered two plays in a pair of deserted women: *The
Glass Menagerie* inherent in one waiting by a telephone, *A Streetcar
Named Desire* in another waiting by a window. Of all the things one
might spy up the dress of a little girl in a pear tree, William Faulkner
found *The Sound and the Fury.* So many authors reminisce about how
winning alliterations or seminal lines seem to find them rather than
the other way around, so that like unwitting beneficiaries they rely on
investments they can't really understand and on the statements that
come to them through the mail. A rural writer's reverie is ignited by
the double spank of the screen door against the jam or the morning's regular cargo of light delivered directly from the Lord's atelier.
An urban poet, inured to the sound of the subway train like chains
dragged daily across a cell floor, suddenly hears new and necessary
music in it and scopes out a space on the wall between the gang insig-
nias and the plighted troths where he might rough out a verse. Who
knows but that the next ingested morsel won't be the madeleine that
initiates a novel sequence? Who can say that the nail clippings in the
ashtray won't suddenly seem like a gathering of little grins suggesting
positive reviews, instead of the useless jettison of yet another unpro-
ductive month?

A tune issues from the tree, and the imbued author is gratified that
it's a robin, only ordinary and dependably so. Meanwhile, the blocked
author and the barren author, attending from the other end of the
field, are castigated by the same song and think themselves birds of the
same drab feather, who are forever stuck with the sharp end.

For every draught that acknowledged a completed poem, Dylan
Thomas needed two to compensate for blanker days. More acutely
than his reviewers and acolytes, Thomas recognized that drinking
did not guarantee the artist he was so much as it helped disguise his

discouragement over the artist he might not have been. It's a no-win proposition, evaluating how much redemptive bang you've been getting out of your inspirational buck. As Lorrie Moore cautions in "How to Become a Writer," you need to deliberately, severely limit how much time you devote to thoughts of your own legitimacy: "like sit-ups, they can make you thin." Tell yourself that if this is not as good as it gets, it is, at any rate and undeniably, as good as it's gotten, and get back to that relentlessly insufficiently lighted place you work in.

Volcano prediction, like any science, is not an exact science. So it was as close to epiphany as science tends to get when the eruption of Mt. St. Helen's in 1980 occurred within eight weeks of major predictions. Lightning bolts shot thousands of meters high. Douglas firs were flattened over an area of over two hundred square miles, and some of the airborne debris made it from the Washington blast zone all the way to the East Coast three days later. Some of the ash continues to circle the Earth today. Some was gathered and sealed into commemorative paperweights. Set atop their desks, they offer writers critical perspective, reminding them of the ultimate fate of all paper, no matter its employment, content, or bond.

Measurements taken later that year confirmed that the main blast had removed the whole summit, reducing the mountain's overall height by more than thirteen hundred feet. What would Dickinson, who defined poetry as a random scalping, have made of *that* massive decapitation, one wonders. She might well have envied so prodigious a visitation. Nothing uncertain about explosives, certainly. Any impulse to analyze the derangement of the senses was probably overwhelmed by the noise. No negative capability required under such insurmountable conditions.

Back when the *Tonight Show* ran ninety minutes and could therefore spare the last seven or so for an artist or author, Johnny Carson would ask about how his guest went about his work. What color of ink, time of day, or mood is most conducive? Under what conditions does your muse drop in, and how does she take her coffee? Basically, how is it done, and when it's done, how do you know when it's done, and how well? Instead of fumbling for a more compelling metaphor than the cartoon light bulb over a cartoon head, wouldn't it have been gratifying for the evening's artist to have demonstrated with a detonation on the order of Mt. St. Helen's and, surveying the devastation with the thunderstruck viewing audience, simply said "See?"

The media feast on large-scale conflagrations, so subtler, ratings-defiant moments of transformation don't get sponsored. But I recall as a boy honing my amazement before the twice-a-day conjuration of TV weatherman P. J. Hoff. He would close each forecast by drawing the next day's expected high temperature in Magic Marker—he could talk and draw simultaneously, showing the same genial aplomb as dancers in the movies who carry on intricate, plot-worthy conversations while waltzing. Then, as if the numerals were stem cells amenable to any meteorological caprice, in no more than twenty seconds he'd sketch out a caricature or scene around them. If he projected 67 degrees at 5:30, say, the 6 might serve as the snout of a pig hard at his dinner and the 7 the corner of the trough he snuffled at; if the same prediction held at 10:00, the 6 might then be employed as part of a child's antiquated nightcap and the 7 part of the pillow's border—the weatherman's gentle admonition to younger viewers that it was time for bed.

Whatever the temperature, we could count on P. J. Hoff to find a way to bend it in the direction of an impending holiday. On Valentine's Day, he could soften sharp-edged numbers into adoring hearts. Conversely, in July, although the heat inevitably forced him to work with recalcitrant 8's and scything 9's, he somehow managed to overcome their curvature and fashion a sturdy flag appropriate to Independence Day. In winter, he would return to his snowman series, which rivaled Monet's haystacks for variations on a theme. He conjured snowmen at play and in repose, ranging in morphology from bulbous to svelte and from antic to subdued in mood. He revealed them reading, driving, dining, surfing, and dreaming. Then, at year's end, he might deliver a week's worth of Santa hybrids from a seemingly unyielding string of sub-zero forecasts. Thus in a couple of hundred ways each year, P. J. Hoff winsomely assailed the seasons. No matter what was doing outside, from his little window the weather was always accommodating.

Now I won't say that our local weatherman wowed me—even as a child I knew enough about real awe not to use the word half so liberally as kids do today—but he did provide quiet delight and drew us on. In his modest yet unfailing way, he demonstrated that there was more give than you might expect to the given world. There were shapes that stayed with me, shapes that might be made almost out of next to nothing, transient like the messages outlined by Nemerov's swallows, perhaps, but in their own ambiguous way, arresting still. And if there really isn't any absolute connection between any future aesthetic of mine and whatever images came my way out of thin air, that doesn't disqualify creation at either end of the synapse. Not every revelation bursts skulls, I suppose, but might manifest simply as a minist'ring spirit to regulate the breathing. Fortunately, sometimes that is all one needs: an abiding breeze, sufficient to keep him going and his spirits up.

14 An Elegy for Eureka

Thus it remains, and the remainder thus. Perpend.

—Polonius, in *Hamlet,* by William Shakespeare

I can sense it not coming. I want to recall the name of the actress in that movie, the one about the suffering singer, the one with "love" in the title. Her face comes through the mist, but unlabeled, just after the premonition that that's all I'll get of her. Maybe bits of her figure, like wreckage for the forensic specialists to sort through, but not enough evidence yet to notify the family.

It happens with people I know, too, or that I know in every way I ever did apart from their names. A student will approach me from down the hall, and I have about twenty seconds, give or take, to personalize my "How's it going?" I might muster the number of syllables and the first letter of his first name. I might even have the meter down: it's Duh-duh, Duh-duh. And as he makes his nameless way toward me, I can't pin him down any better than "trochaic dimeter" does, which is not what his parents have assigned him, surely, and not nearly enough to count as amicable. He will never think twice about my lapse; he will never guess that in simply greeting him I've exhausted my store. But I will work him over in my mind in bed that night like a bit of undigested dinner. I will pan through the ellipses left by his and so many other student names that have been subject to the erosion of semesters. More often than not, however, like that inaccessible actress, he'll keep his unattributable distance throughout the night and leave me no richer.

Absent-mindedness is arguably not only one of the chief maladies afflicting college professors but also one of his top prerogatives. Which of us in the midst of holding forth from the front of the class hasn't suddenly sensed the tug of something withheld? Who while rattling off something he's known by rote hasn't gotten rattled? One trots out his trusty Tennyson—"It little profits that an idle king, / By this still hearth, among these something crags, / Match'd with an aged wife, I mete and dole"—and then can dole out nothing but wordless meter, which ables off on five indiscernible feet. I pound the beat like a cop routinely checking locked doors, counting on cadence alone to maintain my aim and occupation. "That something something feed, and know not me." And haply our lapsed professor is back on track again, perhaps with his grip on the lectern somewhat moister and tighter than the regular, rhythmic trip through Tennyson should require.

Ironically, this predicament shields me to some degree from potential accusation in the classroom. Were a given student to complain that I had it in for him, that I'd graded him down because his personality rather than anything in his paper per se rubbed me the wrong way, I'd defend myself by saying that any prejudice would depend on who the heck he is. I'd have to be able to place him in order to put him down properly, in other words. "You'll have to forgive me," I'd say, "but before we go any further, could you point yourself out on my roster?" It's the professor's ploy, his strategic shrug and stumbler's trump—the academic equivalent of how, on advice of counsel, the indicted continually rely on the statement "I'm sorry, Senator, but I don't recall." It doesn't win the fuzzyheaded much respect, but it does keep them out of prison.

Another upside of befuddlement, I suppose, is that if Ezra Pound is right when he says that poetry is news that stays news, going blank transforms everything it steals from you into a poem—an elegy, to be more accurate, since absence is its most prominent quality. You can perpetually relive the wonder of European capitals if your travel plans always have to begin with a trip to the atlas. Thanks to senility, you can pare your library down to the few books that will fit into the sanitized confinement of the nursing home since every volume slips away the minute you return it to the shelf. Hypothetically speaking, with your short-term memory sufficiently whittled down, every bite of steak might surprise you several times during the chewing, making every meal astonishing throughout the process. Marvel at the manifestation on the plate, the shock in the mouth.

Unfortunately, in the end, poetry cannot soften the loss from which all other losses derive. Hence Robert Frost's old man, who "stood with barrels round him—at a loss," iambically implodes: "A light he was to no one but himself / Where now he sat, concerned with he knew what,

/ A quiet light, and then not even that." Imagine, while imagination affords you the capacity, such fundamental deprivation. Surveys tell us that Americans now rank Alzheimer's disease as high as blindness and cancer among the most terrifying diseases. Next to dementia, trendier forms of identity theft, like the types that computer users guard against, are only meager depletions. The on-line brochure provided by my server—"Identity Theft: What Can You Do About It?"—is designed to inspire paranoia and an additional monthly outlay, but when there's progressively less of you to do the doing about it, jeopardized credit is the least of my concerns.

Yet although the onset of Alzheimer's is becoming increasingly common in our country as the mean age increases and my own generation of boomers starts to go bust, doctors encourage us to keep from leaping to the direst conclusion. By no means is every lapse symptomatic of some multi-syllabic syndrome, they assure us. Not being able to remember Peru's principal exports from eighth-grade social studies may be frustrating, but it is not catastrophic; not being able to remember the names of your grandchildren is a bomb going off.

The trick is to maintain your sense of proportion when other senses seem fickle. If one day the elisions on designer license plates strike you as conspiring in a code you can't decipher, do not phone the media or the medical team: it is nothing more than a suspicious mood that's thrown you for a loss, and it will pass. Remind yourself that there is a difference between not remembering where you put the scissors and not remembering what a scissors is. Having to resort at times to terms like "doohickey" and "thingamajig" when the whisk eludes you or the remote's remote should not be cause for alarm. Just because some of your words seem to have to be hauled out of their origins like coal from a mine or because they seem to leach their painstaking way through their entire etymology before they make it to your mouth isn't by itself clinically interesting. You are not in the same calamitous league as the grandfather who can't live in his own house any longer because everything domestic lurks and tasks him: his kitchen utensils have grown treacherous, his pipes prevaricate and deceive, his dead wife's bobby pins collude against him in their box. (They are secretly allying with the mugs in the cupboard.) Note the general defection of his faculties, which leaves him incapable of noting it for himself. Note the abandonment of ordinary words, the first lieutenants of common sense deserting under fire. At the door of the nursing home, the grandfather surrenders his last transitive verbs along with his pocketknife, now that he can claim no better than an indirect connection to objects, now that he can only hurt himself. Here he is reduced to essentials, then abbreviated even beyond that. (Contraction is in the contract, in the fine print he finds illegible. Like all of the papers his family signs for him, impenetrable as leather.)

I am talking about the wholesale erosion of explicitness here. When the colloquial goes south on you and your vocabulary gets impounded, when all fluency feels dubious, unattainable, or at your expense, when once-familiar surfaces lose their nap, go bald, or abate at your approach, then you can claim your place in the ward. Imagine, while you can, being robbed of your accomplishments and cheated of your griefs like that. Imagine while you can. Obviously, occasionally losing the nomination is different in kind as well as degree from joining the ranks of the thwarted, the pillaged, and the culled. It is crucial to keep this distinction in mind when you can retain little else. No doubt your doctor would make the same diagnosis, dismissing you with something Latinate that not twenty steps from his office door you'd lose anyway.

While the care workers cluck and cajole Grandpa, feel free to investigate the cost of long-term care for yourself. But rest assured, the whitecoats aren't coming for you yet.

Nevertheless, when people reach a certain age, even casual uncertainties—the evaporation of song titles, the absconding of Canadian provinces and the starting line-up of the 1969 Chicago Cubs, the digit-by-digit attrition of telephone numbers like campers being picked off one at a time in a teen slasher flick—feel more forbidding than they did a couple of decades ago. It's hard to be philosophical about any burglary, however petty the theft, when it takes place on your own premises.

Against that possibility, I find unwavering certainty in any of its forms offensive. Thunder from the pulpit represents a rough, unwelcome reign. The politician's pat stances and practiced affect, though the senator may happen to be serving my interests at the time, repel me; the playfully smug disgust of the quiz show host toward contestants because he holds all the cards grates. I've read enough mythology to remember how heaven answers hubris: lightning strikes the podium.

Angela Bassett, by the way. All right. A minor "aha!" moment, but a relief nonetheless. Little epiphanies are not inconsequential or less precious because of their relative size. It's the surprise gift that's redeemable. Angela Basset opens a momentary crack in my agnosticism. You never know what benedictory fragment is going to find its way out of the general mass of imprecision, which is a line somewhere by someone, I'm sure. Yet for every bit like "Angela Bassett" or "binomial" or "tungsten" that materializes, for every occasional "Ezzard Charles" that gets up off the canvas or "phlogiston" that appears out of thin air, there are several that go down with the mental ship. (Not *Titanic* or *Lusitania*. The other one.) And the breakthrough isn't as satisfying as, say, the unblocking of a sinus or the initial shit after constipation, much less the first solid column of light to reach victims of a cave-in. It's more akin to a little neural flicker or flutter in the stomach, as if you'd learned that the protagonist of the novel you're reading shares your birthday. An invitation and an implication at the same time. And a muscle somewhere obscure but, you sense, essential goes slack from the subtle but undeniable corruption of what you used to know you knew. "We cross our bridges when we come to them and burn them behind us, with nothing to show for our progress except a memory of the smell of smoke, and a presumption that once our eyes watered," mused Guildenstern in Tom Stoppard's *Rosencrantz and Guildenstern Are Dead*. Unless it was Rosencrantz. To be fair, even the cast can't keep the cast straight.

Finding once-familiar facts and faces evasive is so common a malady that there are upwards of twenty memory manuals currently in print, which provide everything from training regimens to strategies of compensation to diets designed to stimulate and sustain critical brain functions. (Fish and whole grains reportedly make for especially memorable meals.) The guides all promote the same incentives. Better memorizers are likelier to achieve in business than their less retentive competitors. They appreciate what they read longer and in greater depth. They are less diffident at family reunions. In short, they possess the world more effectively than the muddled rest of us.

Who knows but that the diligent student of memory might one day achieve the rank of Grand Master. To be eligible, one must memorize 1,000 digits in less than an hour, the order of ten decks of cards (that's 520 cards), also in under an hour, and the order of one shuffled deck in under two minutes. There are at present only thirty-six grand masters of memory worldwide. They are the most intimidating contestants at the annual national and world championships, each of which mandates different feats of memory. For example, the United States Memory Championship consists of a mental pentathlon, which features timed memorizations of ninety-nine names and faces, a fifty-line poem, a series of numbers, a list of words, and a shuffled deck of cards. According to Joshua Foer, who covered the 2005 U.S. Championship, "the best memorizers in the world—who almost all hail from Europe—can memorize a pack of cards in less than a minute. A few have begun to approach the 30-second mark, considered the 'four-minute mile of memory.'"

One of the principal tricks of "encoding" is association. For instance, to commit a shuffled deck of cards to memory, the competitors might assign each card a person, an action, or an object, which would enable them to turn three-card sets into simple sentences. Thus, explains Joshua Foer, when English grand master Edward Cooke "sees a three of clubs, a nine of hearts, and a nine of spades, he immediately conjures up an image of Brazilian lingerie model Adriana Lima in a Biggles biplane shooting at his old public-school headmaster in a suit of armor." Figuration, then, is the order of the day. So we might double up Ezra Pound's paradox: if poetry protects news from obsolescence, it also ensures us precedents. Just suppose that all numbers greeted you like close friends or were as instantly recognizable to you as the contents of your pockets. "When he sees 342102," Foer writes, "Cooke imagines Frank Sinatra crooning the Britney Spears song ' . . . Baby One More Time' to an obelisk." It is a surreal scene that Cooke inhabits, to be sure. It speaks to him in unforgettable sentences.

Samuel Johnson—I think it was Samuel Johnson, unless it was Ben, who had a somewhat different spelling and, I suspect, a somewhat different sentiment—said that there are two kinds of knowledge: having the facts and knowing where to find them. Or an aphorism to that effect, anyway, assuming that it was Samuel Johnson who offered it. His implication was that these are equally valid forms of purchase on the truth, which may deflate folks with photographic memories somewhat but will hearten those who can manage to produce a library card or can access the Internet. But while Johnson's argument recognizes one or the other form of knowledge *as* knowledge, it may be more accurate to think of them as causally related. In other words, we know facts *because* we know where to find them. "Long ago you kissed the names of the nine Muses goodbye, / and watched the quadratic equation pack its bag, and even now as you memorize the order of the planets, // something else is slipping away, a state flower perhaps, / the address of an uncle, the capital of Paraguay," writes Billy Collins. But by Doctor Johnson's logic, as he adds these subtractions together, the poet can take heart because facts that can't be found on the tip of his tongue can still be located in the index of the almanac or the mental collective of the World Wide Web. And yet, unless we can locate the right book on the shelf or the right cell in the brain, it is as if we don't know what we know, for all the good our protests of knowledge do us. "Officer, I'm afraid I can't find my license, but I know that I have it somewhere." Try that finesse next time you're pulled over, and I predict that you'll be taken into custody, not taken for granted.

In my case, as it happens, the onset of the problem often does occur when I'm driving. In the midst of the trip, I realize that for a moment or so I can't remember where I've set out for or why. I have to go by the scenery to decide why I'm going by that scenery. On longer drives, I'll zone out for miles at a time, trusting in muscle memory to keep me on course because for certain ten-minute stretches what memory I can muster is invested below the neck. If I'm traveling with family, it might be the repetition of a question that snaps me back, and I hope that no one sees any daze lingering on my face. So there is another reason besides keeping the kids busy that I suggest a game of State License Plates or I Spy or Four Fourths of a Ghost, which is to stave off the hypnosis induced by I-44. That the kids wiggle and whine otherwise is annoying; that I tend to drift off the topic and, once in a while, off the highway, is rather more unsettling.

John Updike devoted an entire story to this kind of gamesmanship. In "Walter Briggs," finding themselves incarcerated together for the duration of a car trip home, Jack and Clare entertain their two-year-old daughter by testing her on snatches of children's songs or devising a single-elimination tournament out of who the most likeable guests were at the party. Once she drifts off, her parents reminisce about the people whom they knew at a Y.M.C.A. family camp where they'd spent the first months of their married life. The mutual reclamation project develops into a gentle contest between them, which, as identities blear, turns into a test of the foundation of their relationship. Particularly niggling is the name that titles the story, which the reader sees hovering over the frustrated couple. They can locate him on the shuffleboard court and nail down his profession, pastimes, and physiognomy, but they cannot read his signature. (Had Edward Cooke been in the back seat, he might have suggested that prisons on ships are "brigs," and ships travel on water, so "water brigs" would be a reliable route by which to return to him.) And Jack needs the points: having "made an unsatisfactory showing" so far, he is "anxious to put in something for himself." It is not until well into the night, with everyone else asleep, that Jack manages to recover "Walter Briggs" from the morass of memory. He does not rouse his wife to win the game, but he is tempted. Instead, he simply whispers "Walter Briggs," a minor comeback and recovery, perhaps, but as much as he can provide. Clare cannot know that she will awaken to learn she's lost after all.

I also sometimes feel as though by falling asleep I'm falling behind. Whatever the variations, it's always the same dream at the core that I succumb to. I am late. There's an appointment or a test or a train, and I'm late. I'm losing ground, or rather, the ground won't let me loose, in that mud is sucking me down, or cement is softening to envelop me, or the sidewalk has begun to billow beneath me like a flag to buck me softly but inexorably off, or the grass is swallowing my legs, and I feel, with what feelings the dream cedes me, like the grizzled Quint in *Jaws* sliding down the crippled deck of the *Orca* into the gullet of the shark. I go from running blindly to being balked by blind alleys, and if I do meet a guide, he's grudging or German or altogether deaf, so that does me no good. And I'm too tired to keep running, or my knees are locking, and in a torturous, steady declension of my capacity to progress, I have to hoist myself leg by leg through an atmosphere gone wickedly arthritic, until I'm literally down to a crawl, then to a Marine's arm-over-arm worming through whatever relentless element the dream has steeped me in, then to being extruded like a stubborn turd or having to roll like some Samuel Beckett catastrophe through tar. When I collapse, or all my joints lock, or I turn to stone on the unforgiving tarmac, the labyrinthine terminal, or the insatiable lawn, it is with the mortifying awareness that I would never have made it on time to whatever ticket office I hadn't the money to deal with or to the midterm in a subject I hadn't studied for anyway. Like the boy who, having committed some child-sized crime, rushes home to get his punishment over with because prolonging the interim is worse than any whipping he'll receive, I am trying to hurry, except that I can't rush, I can't find home, and I can't recall for the life of me (and it does feel as if the life of me is at issue) what I've done that's wrong enough to merit the repeal of physical law at my expense. And when I shudder awake, it's with my blankets in a twist and my body torqued and tingling from the way my neck's been bent or my elbows are pinned. Because I realize that no cash, confession, or calculus is expected of me, my relief is palpable, considerably more palpable than my seized, sleep-stuck limbs, but the dream keeps clutching at me, and it will not forget me even as I forget its particulars, and it will not forgive.

For although the true morning is now fully upon me, although I have clawed all the way back to consciousness, I am still within reach of the dream's conditions. The unnamed woman who had been tugging me toward something urgent and inexplicable has vanished, or the evangelist has, who did his declaiming entirely in vowels, along with any potential significance or dignity. "It could have been—a bird out of season, dropping bright-feathered on my shoulder. . . . It could have been a tongueless dwarf standing by the road to point the way . . . I was prepared. But it's this, is it?" complained Rosencrantz . . . although it could well have been Guildenstern. The room has regathered its atoms and the sleep scene has silted back into the actual, but I still find the results unconvincing. A grudging half-recognition, the sort of trammeled familiarity a child brings to the middle of the street where his dog, or what's left of his dog, as best he can identify it out of the doggy debris, has been run down. I can't help but wonder if the world is out to get me—worse, that it already has gotten me and is toying with me the way a cat plays with the mouse he's nabbed, letting it squirm or inch its way away from the paws that have it pinned, then biting down to dessert on a brain made tender by the primitive thought that, at the last, it could actually escape. In life as in checkers, it's get the jump on things or get passed over flat—this, or a facsimile of Pac-Man, where one dashes gobbling through a maze to keep from being gobbled, ridiculously delaying the inevitable impasse and game-ending gulp.

And the main way that the world gets me is by becoming increasingly as incognito as it is in a dream. Some days, like an infielder who knocks down a grounder but can't find the handle, I can't grasp one particular, particularly mercurial, word, and that's troubling enough. On my worst days, though, it's as if I've contracted forgetfulness like a fever. Then I envision my verbal rations being ransacked, or my parts of speech departing en masse, much the way thousands of gulls will lift from a lake like a blanket shaken from a bed. Even if it is only a trickle, an incremental diminishment it would take a top-flight linguist to pick up on, it is unsettling enough to think of it, that shedding of irreclaimable cells, that insistent nibbling away at me akin to what Emily Dickinson saw as sabotage against her soul. (That was in her poem #501. Mike Singletary, middle linebacker for the Chicago Bears, wore number 50, and the 1 stands for the slender, unprotected quarterback he bears down on. Dickinson's soul is under a similar siege, which presumably makes it easier to hold onto.) A quotation evades me, members of the House of Representatives recess, the Great Lakes dry up as like Tantalus I hopelessly approach—each is added to my growing quota of annihilation.

"Half of what he said meant something else, and the other half didn't mean anything at all." Guildencrantz. Rosenstern.

So I come to rely on devices and with deliberation anchor myself more firmly in the day. Compensation is key. I've depended on bookmarks, post-it notes, crib sheets, and adhesive labels the way toddlers do their dolls. I check my itinerary when I leave the house and my fly when I emerge from the public restroom with all the rigor of an aphasic monk. And to carry the religious figure to the point of pun, I commit to habits as devotedly as any nun. For ritual is at once the gist and the guarantee of my beliefs. Toward this end, I have seen the wide receiver who, having been spun clockwise by a cornerback, rewinds himself before returning to the huddle. I have seen the librarian who, whenever she passes the massive dictionary, returns it to its original position, butterflying it into equal halves: *marimba* marking the west gate, *mezuzah* hung on the east. There are housewives who cannot sleep knowing that their husbands with best intentions have done the dishes but stacked them wrong; they wait until the snoring starts to sneak out of bed and correct the kitchen. All day long the assaults on equilibrium continue; all day long, the insults to kilter must be borne.

Out of private desperation, I make jingles out of errands, mantras out of weekly committee meetings, and more lists than Santa and St. Peter combined. I reflexively double-save my computer documents a dozen times during each composing session, just in case. And when, inevitably, I can't retrieve a piece I've consigned to the hard drive, our campus computer technician, Stan, unflappably finds it for me. He believes that nothing is lost entirely or forever: there's a vestige of my effort interred in the circuitry, an undisintegrated glimmer in the works, an outlinable absence that, like a phantom limb, still pulses, still pains. Stan walks me back from my accident and, more often than not, delivers the document intact the way any fireman might scoop a pet cat out of a tree. Nothing miraculous about that from his perspective, since Stan was born into an Internetted universe, confident of memory's common market, the collective unconscious of our linked and uploaded race, trusting in the equivalent of billions of strings knotted onto as many billion fingers. For not every dream is as dire as the ones in which I'm losing time or trustworthiness or traction on reality. There are dreams like the one described in Marilynne Robinson's *Gilead* "where you're filled with some extravagant feeling you might never have in life . . . and you learn from it what an amazing instrument you are, so to speak, what a power you have to experience beyond anything you might ever actually need." And it is a comfort to consider just how unencompassable the Internet is, how even eternity isn't long enough for the angels lodging in the library in *Wings of Desire* to take it all in, and how maybe God has hit "Save" on Creation on our behalf (His print is too fine for us to read for ourselves), meaning that we need only wait for some serenely messianic Stan for restoration.

Yesterday I read that a local church has deployed its congregation to clean out the oldest cemetery in town. They are removing the leaves and debris. They are straightening the monuments and fortifying the spaces where the ground has given way. When they scrub the grime from the oldest tombstones, they discover that several of the names have worn away. They can barely be read at all. (Auden likened this to poetic activity: brushing off tombstones to see what is written there. If it was tombstones and poetry he had in mind. If it was Auden in whose mind the comparison occurred.) The church is looking to county historians, archivists, and the oldest members of the community to try to bring the names back. The city council has voted unanimously to commission a local stonecutter to approximate the letters' initial shape and groove, undoing the mutable, inscrutable operations of time. But I do wonder if it's identification and not the elements that violated the landscape, as if awareness itself were the wound, and the stones had healed from scars of our commemoration. Perhaps it is nature's way to return the place to its original anonymity. What was Paradise but Paradise before Adam interfered with his designations? Maybe only the nameless get to rest altogether. Maybe before heaven can be breached, the world must be properly forgotten.

Meanwhile, on the other side of town, there is an electronic bill-board that I pass each day on my way to work that advertises the friendliness and prolificacy of the Freeman Hospital Birth Center by displaying the names and birth weights of the latest newborns to arrive into their care. Baby names bubble up and dissolve, their appearance bright, ceaseless, fleeting. One by one, they see the light and surrender to the next. Six pounds eight ounces, eight pounds ten ounces, nine pounds two ounces, five pounds five ounces, seven pounds four and one-half ounces meticulously docketed and dissolving. Minutes after I've passed, all of them are as good as gone. The names and numbers change, but it is the same message showing every day: disappearance is the only revelation that matters and all that lasts.

And Rosencrantz and Guildenstern are dead, mingled in a final aside, who never existed other than in an afterthought, as who does not. To keep them straight, you might make one a flower sprout-ing from a crack in a wall (let a rose in a cranny carry Rosencrantz's scent); the other, the severe visage of a president on a coin (Guilden-stern cashed in for a stern guilder, if you will). Set them down in a sentence—I plucked a rose from a crack in a wall and sold it for a ven-erable penny—the better to furnish a memento mori for them both. But figures can't alter the destiny they are sentenced to. Nobler poetry won't hold us together.

"Cataract that this world is, it is remarkable to consider what does abide in it." Luckily for me, a small part of what abides is this second reference to Robinson's novel, which I admit having had to look up, but which, as Samuel Johnson promises, is an acceptable compromise with the void and, I suppose, still counts against the cataract. And don't the faithful say that the world is the dream, whose fading makes way for the indelibly divine? The question contributes to the mystery we find and lose ourselves in all our lives. It is worth remembering that someone said that somewhere. It is worth writing down, word for word.

15 The Art of Getting By

There is an art to getting by, and they taught it to us early, inadvertently, in school.

Because there was no knowing in 1962 when the bomb would hit, setting ablaze the only atmosphere we'd ever known and whiting every last eye like exposed film less than a second before it turned us all into broth, we took precautions. In fruitless unison we cowered under our desks, aspiring on command to the prescribed fetal posture as completely as possible, for the length of a fire drill disappearing into ourselves before the bomb's fatal physics found us out and we disappeared forever. In short, we rehearsed what to do when there was nothing to be done. We practiced that process of elimination until it became as automatic as raising our hands to be excused. (Ah, the innocence of youth.) For what it was worth, we grew good at it.

Well, Kruschev never found us, never even sought us out. Yet as if the missile crisis had never subsided, for many of us, too many to count, cowering became its own justification and reward. Though the Communists, stared down by Kennedy, stood down four decades ago, there were those who have never stood back up again.

You recognize their descendants today as those whom you'd never know any other way than under cover. They are the ones who ebb from questions as if what issued from any mouth were toxic or, when urged to participate, subside into a silence more habitual and ruinous than any drug the government sponsors commercials to abjure. Genuine attempts at engagement offend them; a glance is sufficient to stare them down. In the wake of the gentlest provocation, I have seen them sink into themselves as though their necks held headstones instead of heads and their shoulders were made of sand that would never support them. Imagine a self-effacement so efficient as to leave its practitioners nearly featureless. Undone by their own design, they do not need any Red Menace anymore to do them in. In a cruel mood, you would wonder if death would not be a redundancy for them. Despite assurances that the latest malevolence has lifted and the skies are clear, they survive in hiding.

I speak of those who notwithstanding the thawing of the Cold War remain undefrosted. Take a closer look at them, but be quick about it—they scatter before the light. They do not exercise their curiosity, much less editorialize. (For such a pittance they would not presume to waste paper.) They make a virtue of constipation so complete that you can barely encourage the smallest opinion to squeeze through. (For such a pittance they would not presume to waste paper.) Indeed, they pretend to be as viewless as Keats's wings of Poesy and, like them, invisible. No, not even literature will lift them or even coax them out of their recoil. Cummings may contend that the world at large, writ large, can be puddle-wonderful, but they still prefer to stay inside parentheses, where it's safe and dry. Williams may warn that they are starving for lack of poetry and do not know it, but they think being force-fed a bother at best, an assault at worst, and keep the lesson hidden in their cheeks to spit out after class. Strange and useless to praise Whitman's barbaric yawp before people who have their responses permanently set at Peep.

No reliable study has been done to verify just how many are so brutally brought low as this, but some days you encounter enough of them to make you forget there could be an alternative. In my capacity as an English professor, however, I feel that I'm as qualified as any lay interpreter to try. Early every semester, I indulge the fantasy that I can correctly discern the birthstone of each of my students. I admit that the trick is made simpler by my collapsing the options into the same three general categories I learned years ago in earth science: igneous, metamorphic, and sedimentary. According to my experience and peculiar bias, a typical class breaks down in the following manner. Cast in fire, the igneous among them appear ready to combust at a moment's notice. Constituting perhaps ten percent of the class, they are balky and belligerent, contentious about everything from the opening day's explanation of your syllabus to the review for the final exam. (Ah, the insolence of youth.) It would be a mistake to confuse their occasional moments of reduced heat with serenity; just a nudge will stoke their coals to life again. Perhaps another ten percent—that dependable, talented tenth, the cherished tithe that Fortune cedes to teachers to keep them devoted when their fortunes are otherwise low—are metamorphic. Much like the rocks their category calls to mind, metamorphic men and women wear best. They adapt to pressure instead of crumbling under it. Moreover, they realize that from pressure comes the incentive—indeed, the opportunity—to change. "You must change your life," counseled Rilke, channeling for the mute, transmuting statue in "Archaic Torso of Apollo," delivering his monumental directive to that marble effigy's metamorphic kin. But as I suggest, the top top out at ten percent.

The remaining eighty percent or so are sedimentary, who gather into themselves in that same seabed where Eliot's Prufrock speculated that a pair of ragged claws scuttled through an enviable and everlasting remove. Sedimentary fellows settle and cling. Mobs are mostly sedimentary, to be sure, and it would not be surprising to find that sports bars and men's clubs (where Masons are mortared and Elks persist with herd mentality) contain a higher quotient than the average sample might provide. All adherents are sedimentary after a fashion, for fashion is what they're after.

The sedimentary scrabble about, if they move much at all, mostly to readjust their covers. (And what is the grit the dedicated sedimentarist digs out of his eyes each morning but what his sluggish blood has washed up from his chest cavity after the heart's gone out of it?) They move through airports with more impunity than you can imagine, if you imagine that the metal detectors were really *mettle* detectors, in which case they'd never trip an alarm.

Surely the sedimentary are made, not born. After all, I remind myself when they react to direct address by diving into their books like moles nosing for cover, not so very many grades ago these were elementary school kids who positively frothed from what they had to offer, often overflowing their seats with eagerness. Consider the urgent, aimless activity of children, ever on the boil and decades away from what their lives will boil down to. It is futile to try to interest in board games those who've been weaned on GameBoy, useless to try to make them contain their twitches when they've spent the school day endesked and forced to adopt that unnatural position for seven hours or so. But it's nearing five o'clock, with dinner distant and still undefined, and so Mom begs or threatens them anyway for ten minutes for just ten minutes to be good. Not "good" as in the promise on the package of Pop Tarts she's ashamed to rely on so often to staunch them—THEY'RE FRESH, SO YOU KNOW THEY'RE GOOD—

but "Good dog" good, "Grant me peace" good, "Stop me before I kill or keel over" good. Mom wants them quiet and settled, but she'll settle for coiled. For the time being, even if it's only ten minutes' time, and only as long as they're this young, this counts as restraint, on her part as well as theirs.

These same kids—eighty per cent of them sedimentarists in the making, mind you—managed to find occupation anywhere their parents dragged them. In the doctor's waiting room their thumb wrestling was conducted as intensely as any procedure Dad was undergoing on the other side of the door. While Mom was bearing off to the dressing room multiple sizes of four different outfits, they were finalizing plans for the obstacle course they would run the moment she closed the curtain behind her. At the supermarket they would clown for the surveillance cameras or hop relentlessly about on the black mats in front of the automatic doors, reveling in the discovery that they had sufficient presence to engage them. (Ah, the inner sense of youth.) But, to adduce Cummings once more, "down they forgot as up they grew"—a line that escapes them as surely as the lesson it laments. Docile to the point of disappearance, wearing and worn down by the wan introversion of ascetics who abstain out of faintness of heart rather than faith, the stricken eighty per cent seem to think that mum's the word, and even that syllable goes unspoken.

In that selfsame sea where Prufrock's metaphor of withdrawal takes shape resides the pearl fish. Or so oceanographers would have us believe, so furtive is that creature that it resists discovery. Tiny and vulnerable, the pearl fish always lurks near the sea cucumber. When it senses danger—which, given the edgy propensities of the pearl fish, is more or less continually—it stimulates the anus of the sea cucumber with its tail fin, whereupon the sea cucumber eases open that aperture and allows the pearl fish to back its way in. It stays put in that superhumid glove until it senses that it's safe to emerge again—which, given the aforementioned propensities, is a rare and temporary event.

I tell my students about Prufrock and the pearl fish, about Williams's promise of personal renaissance and radiant gist, both ubiquitous, and Cummings's wonderful puddles and lovely muddles. I tell the sedimentarists that there are better rocks to build upon than theirs. Seek to establish yourself beyond a satisfactory grade point average and a viable credit rating, I say. Cultivate something stronger than complacency before driving your stakes. Take on nuance, association, ambiguity, complexity, debate, and wonder though they're nowhere mandated on the syllabus. Blake got that much right, surely: it is not only possible but more rewarding to see a world in a grain of sand than to complain that there's too much beach to cross before you reach the water.

Why sit there pinched like snuff in a tin, snuffed and snuffling as far down as your collars let you drop? It isn't discretion, surely, that makes passion a sin.

Perhaps they squirm in their seats because they recognize the rightness of what I propose. Or perhaps they are just tickling a nearby fissure, hoping to slip in.

Still, there is an art to getting by, and one might fashion several chapters for the manual just from the skills we practiced, diligently, in school.

For instance, in social studies class, when he is asked to name a country's major exports and realizes that the almanac is too distant to consult, the insightful student learns to say, "Primarily foodstuffs, textiles, and small manufacturing." "Primarily" is a risky fillip, I suppose, but once you grow confident of your moxie, it's a fillip you'll risk. By virtue of their sublimely ambiguous qualities, these three categories are universally applicable, or at least applicable as far as civilization has progressed, and, thus, unassailable, even given the standards of the most rigorous, retentive seventh grade social studies teacher. "Foodstuffs" is broad enough to cover anything edible; the term will take root in even the most alien, inhospitable terrain. In short, if Ghanaians are still generating little Ghanaians, if Filipinos are still prolific, if Afghans are filling up on anything at all, you can safely figure that foodstuffs are somewhere on their menus and, furthermore, that they're producing enough of them to send off the extras.

"Textiles" wears the nimbus of textbook diction—no one outside of the editorial staff of *Our World: Cultures, Conflicts, and Challenges* ever uses the term, and I suspect that anyone actually involved in the textile industry would question the credentials of someone who tried to, much as drug dealers would be wary of the undercover cop who asked where he could "score some prime weed." But teachers eat up "textiles" as if they were . . . well, foodstuffs. Moreover, unless the country in question is an overgrown nudist colony—a possibility that, given the typically pinched nature of school boards, the politic politics of textbook editors, and the militant wholesomeness of PTA's, you can safely bet against—some textile touches them, and what they can't wear they cast off, much as your older brother bequeathed his surplus clothing to you.

As for "small manufacturing," who can say what goes on in those far-flung, abstract factories, those mills no one visits and villages no missionary has witnessed or PBS filmmaker documented? It could be beaded necklaces or bar glasses, broom handles or bazooka shells, but whatever they're making up there, down there, or over there, it must be handled and shipped, and "small manufacturing" is ideally suited to the task.

I am talking about brazening your way through. These are the countermeasures that will deceive teachers who would otherwise sooner or later stumble over your limitations. They constitute the flip side of going stony and undetectable, so that questions sent in your direction will eddy harmlessly around your head.

Take philosophy—that is, if philosophy is a subject you are required to take. In philosophical discussions of any sort, assuming evasive tactics fail and you must hole up somewhere, it pays to occupy middle ground. Realize that with just a slip of the tongue, abstractions turn into obstructions. Put too much weight upon it and any argumentative buoy becomes an anchor eventually. So split the difference whatever the difference is. My advice is to follow the example of a graduate professor I knew who wore a T-shirt with the legend "In a sense, you're both right!" resolutely proclaiming his ambivalence in all matters theoretical. Since there is precious little danger that any topic that might arise on the humanities half of the Quad would ever materialize to permanently decide debates over moral absolutes, the Lord's essence, or heaven's true décor, it stands to reason that the fence sitter has the privileged view over combatants who hunker down in any entrenched position. Accordingly, "In a sense, you're both right!" does not dissolve your impact but doubles your chances of having one. Furthermore, the statement carries with it the aura of achieved equanimity, the absence of which is, quite frankly, a chief reason why folks engage in philosophical struggles in the first place. Hold only with Hegel or exclusively with Hume, invite Aquinas to your party while omitting Augustine from the guest list, remember the Pragmatists on holidays while assuming the Transcendentalists won't feel the slight, and you can just wait for the mood of the room to darken no matter how tasty the hors d'oeuvres. Or perhaps not—opponents have a point, too.

You'd rather not shift your position or drop some of your bags to get by, you say? Making yourself smaller for the sake of matriculating through a clogged curriculum insults you, does it? Fine. Stand up straight in a line that barely moves and console yourself with your excellent posture.

Are you with me still? In music, labor to prove yourself a bass. Cultivate head colds and practice allergies as assiduously as you would any instrument. More simply, mumble down the front of your shirt at the moment any song is launched. You'll be deemed a bass soon enough. There in the lower regions of the vocals, the Hades of the scales, no elevation is expected of you. Like the ground crew at Cape Kennedy, you get to stand clear before the blast off, leaving the soaring to the astronauts who, incredibly, choose to ride atop the detonation.

In my case, I lucked into the bass section at an early age. When we were commanded by our seventh-grade music teacher to start singing "Wade in the Water," I let my finger slip in the songbook. As I fumbled for the right page, I murmured my way through, hoping to catch hold of the flow, as it were, a few measures down river. Miss Simpson alertly stopped the class to single me out. "What are you doing with the tenors?" she asked, accusingly. "You told me to stand here last time," I replied, my voice breaking a bit. (With her fissiony hairstyle and her bust line fortified like a bunker, Miss Simpson was a formidable defender of the way a song should be sung.) "Well," she reasoned, "you're at the age when children's voices change." And so, having decided that puberty had ambushed me just as I'd begun to wade in the water, much as Zeus had brought the heedless Leda down, she wrested me from the tenor section and deposited me among the other basses. There we had only to sustain our changeless undercurrent of "Water, water, wade in the water / Water, water, wade in the water," going more or less unnoticed (and better yet, uncorrected) for the length of the song.

It was, if possible, even less demanding to handle the bass responsibility for "Goober Peas," for which we merely rolled up and down the gentle hill of "Peas, peas, peas, peas / Peas, peas, peas, peas" like pleading toddlers trying to wear their mothers down to get an extra dessert. As for the zenith of our underachievement, that must have been our rendition of "Roll On, Columbia," during which we were directed just to hum. Thus while sopranos sweated their more demanding and public parts and tenors had to perfect five times as many words and notes as we did for every song assigned, the seventh-grade basses, each of us presumably imbued by a throat-clutching rush of testosterone, never needed to study the repertoire, which freed us up to focus our attentions on, say, some suddenly luscious altos, whose own beguiling attributes were recently under way as well. Had I summoned a lovelier and more limber voice, like the featured singers, who were expected to flutter about their octaves like birds too fickle to fix on one branch, I would never have been afforded the luxury of letting my interests drift. Better by far to be a bass sawing his one slack string, and dream.

While patrolling the bass line spared me grief in music, collage saved me in art. Tempera paints proved temperamental in my hands and depicted nothing other than my futility. Where others daintily, deftly etched and feathered, I pawed; where they evidenced strategy, I left only spillage. Nothing figural could come from the hopeless scumble of colors that, regardless of the pains I took to deploy them, never evolved beyond the amoebic for me. I could press and implore it for hours, but my assigned lump of clay remained lumpish and un-impressed, so that the few semi-human figures I could accomplish seemed to suffer from an interminable case of cramps. Oils eluded me, slipping away from any design I might have invented for them; my sketches in India ink never stained the paper half as interestingly as it did the artist, as my medium often accidentally ran like a vari-cose outbreak over my arms. Forget life drawings, which I couldn't draw to save my life. The blasted anatomies and glandular disasters I managed to render, with their imploded chests and spavined backs, had more give to them than boiled chickens. Well aware of the vain, inorganic shapes I'd been smelting together all semester, none of my classmates was willing to be paired with me for portrait drawing, for nothing could be derived from the mauled features and mugged mugs I made but offense. Even a still life wouldn't stay put on my page, as undefined blights corrupted bowl after barely discernible bowl of fruit. So that was basically my portfolio: a record of stifled intentions and swollen parts.

But collage freed me from these humiliations because it required no talent other than stooping. From the beginning I showed myself to be a Titian of neighborhood trash, a Gaugin of the garbage can, a Rembrandt lighting lovingly upon rummage and the near-at-hand. I could hunt and gather better than Frost's oven bird, nesting out of a different but no less urgent aesthetic. Wreckage was my metier. Bending my efforts to the discarded, I loitered near empty lots and haunted alleys for promising debris. The forgotten vaudeville team of flotsam and jetsam earned top billing in my book. I scavenged suggestive bits of paper, coils of metal, and plastic shards; I swept up bottle caps, nubbed pencils, and sucked bones. I ravaged the backs of local factories—those bastions of small manufacturing whose anonymous products sustained me in social studies class across the hall—and combed the empty lots. I recognized that the vagrancy of art and the art of vagrancy were congruent. The way that any buzzard battens on carrion, I took my fill of the ambient crap.

And so, preempting the official garbage collectors each week, smuggling the most provocative, portable refuse into Mrs. Vance's art class, I became suddenly productive. As my mood or supply of rubbish dictated, my creations were sometimes as cluttered as a subway, sometimes as minimalist as a plate of nouvelle cuisine. Mrs. Vance, grown heady from having found an idiom I might operate in without insulting the history of the discipline or alienating the other kids, actually commended me on my unwitting intersections with artists of the past. She called them "homages," seeing in my arbitrary mixtures mucky imitations of Masters I'd never heard of, much less intended to honor. For if she discovered a Monet in a blotch of condiments, located Van Gogh in a slur of moldy pasta, or made out Mondrian from the rude topography of toothpicks, paper clips, and dental floss I committed to construction paper, her talents were to be congratulated, not mine.

Even more astonishing, you skeptical patrons of the arts, I was displayed: for three weeks a piece of mine that was composed mostly of chewing gum wrappers, fragments from a Coke bottle, some baseball cards the rain had ruined, and pepper (united by liberal applications of open-mindedness and rubber cement and coyly entitled "Construction #4") was prominently shown in the glass case just outside the door of the principal's office. You could look it up: I not only passed, I prospered.

My experience is meant to be exemplary. Who doesn't dream of Houdini and his great escapes when teachers lean in and tests impend? I am offering you a field guide to the closest exits, the escape artist's index of concealments, flourishes, and distractions, false bottoms and false fronts.

If only every subject were as amenable to deflection. Geography, for instance, defies dissembling. This is in spite of the fact that borders are largely arbitrary and regularly susceptible to the vicissitudes of congressional districting and war. No matter that the particular corrugations of any coastline follow the idiosyncrasies of the cartographer in question. (His broken concentration or palsied hand has undoubtedly endowed a given Maryland with additional square mileage or done in a dozen ancient Irish claims.) Face it: with the possible exception of the stock exchange, maps are the biggest fraud going. Gertrude Stein's notorious incredulity over Oakland ("There is no there there") extends for me like a weather front up and down that entire nebulous coast. I long ago ceased to believe in Bulgaria and have always found the country of Chile unconvincing. I bet that you, too, will find more than a few discrepancies between the atlas and your own convictions. Nevertheless, from the time your teachers first insisted you memorize the catechism of state capitals, it should have dawned on you that when it comes to geography, nowhere from Augusta, Maine, to Sacramento, California, will you find any wiggle room. Statistics are strict, wicked, convincing. Square mileage is inflexible; the city census, vindictive. No, you might flee, but in the end you cannot evade geography.

Speaking statistically, mathematicians are also notoriously obstinate about their subject matter. I readily confess to harboring a long-standing suspicion of mathematics. This is not to say that I have no respect whatsoever for mathematics, a fact evidenced, I expect, by my referring to "mathematics" rather than "math," which is at once too familiar and patronizing, the sort of diminutive one generally reserves for a nephew in ball cap and braces. But distrust is my initial and, let it be said, defining response to mathematics. I also have healthy, abiding forms of disrespect for other disciplines littering the typical college catalog. But while my attitudes toward sociology, education, and so on may rise and fall from time to time, surfing the Dow Jones of my esteem, my disrespect for mathematics is unmatched, robust and perdurable.

In what regard do I regard mathematics so slightingly? That's a mathematician's pissy reaction, to be sure, on the order of "show your work." I could resort to the comedian's cheeky suggestion that any body of knowledge infected by improper fractions and irrational numbers, any system presuming to matter whose posited contents orbit a zero, any understanding dependent upon variables and unknowns for its extrapolations should not be trusted as far as you could throw it—certainly not with mathematicians doing the measuring. But let's fix instead on probability. For example, mathematics asserts—without blushing, mind you—that in a room of thirty students the probability that two share a birthday is greater than fifty per cent. The notion, improbable to all but probability itself, may be proven on the board for all to gaze at and glaze over. My objection, obviously, is that the probability and its proof alike are only mathematics. Using mathematics to validate mathematical propositions is comparable to naming a committee of generals to investigate disbursements at the Pentagon, and comparably unconvincing. Let two April 27's come to their feet in the ten o'clock class of my own choosing, both of them wide-eyed with amazement and willing to sign affidavits claiming they'd never met before the first day of the semester, much less concocted the co-incidence of the respective labors of their respective mothers (Julie's in Cedar Rapids, Nathan's in Dubuque), and I won't budge even as much as Julie and Nathan did, much less as much as their respective mothers did when the proof descended. Or maintain that when thir-ty *different* birthdays constitute your class, this fits neatly within the other forty-some per cent of the hypothesis, leaving your premise no less probable and therefore as intact as it had been before the tally, and I'm as unmoved as everyone else who has kept his seat throughout the proceedings. Summing up, then, I submit that every result resulting from mathematics is a false positive.

Call me "innumerate," will you, finding a coinage that correlates to "illiterate" in order to denote my refusal, my stubborn determina-tion to bet against the chalk? So when the chips are down, having fallen according to a parabolic prediction I'm blind to, you turn to words. The last refuge of the aesthete, you know, and of others just as desperate. Yet there is no denying that, statistically speaking, masters of mathematics dominate modern society, from fourth grade forward. Classroom and boardroom alike are run by the numbers.

Of course, there are those who contend that artistic and math-ematical capacities can coexist in the same personality profile just as the right and left hemispheres of the brain can inhabit the same skull. Witness Rita Dove, an exemplary poet, who by her own testimony is as likely to luxuriate in the craftsmanship of a successful equation as in the glow of a new trope. "I prove a theorem and the house ex-pands," she writes in "Geometry." The very windows seem to have freed themselves from their panes for her and taken flight: "They are going to some point true and unproven," where, we are led to suppose, the prodigy will find fresh conquests both poetic and mathematical. But my pains are not eased. Dove's eager feasting on formulas spiced with deltas and her relentless appetite for Pi is so much Greek to me; her celebration, eloquent apple-polishing, is all. Believe me, under the penumbra of numbers, nothing credible grows.

As luck would have it—probability is a business that occasionally functions on the foundering student's behalf—the university I ended up attending did not require either geology or mathematics. Thanks to the forgiving (and to my way of thinking, refreshingly sane) cafeteria-style logic of my undergraduate requirements, I was allowed to opt for alternative courses I can refer to only as "humane." Instead of having to withstand a science that was a stickler for precision—just imagine the threat of chemistry, where the slightest discrepancy in counting a molecule's components could have spelled the difference between safe breathing and suffocation or between a balm and a burn—I finagled my way into Earth Science. (Yes, Earth Science, that blessed plot, that precious stone set in the sequence of Area Three, where I scavenged igneous, metamorphic, and sedimentary rocks and made them my property.) From that poet's outpost, where everything cleaved neatly into solids, liquids and gases and nothing more demanding, we could do no lasting damage, and no chemicals or equations, caustic or complex, could reach us, either. A rudimentary understanding of the distinctions among states of matter sufficed. So long as we passed water and gas differently; so long as we drank liquid without trying to gobble down the ice as well; so long as we remembered that this too, too solid flesh would melt at some temperature we accepted but did not need to memorize, we all got through unscathed.

Similarly, I was able to supplant mathematics with psychology, a science so soft that even professional practitioners did not have to wash their hands before proceeding. Reason not the rationale for storing mathematics and psychology in the same cabinet. Your mother would no sooner put pea soup in your sock drawer or suggest that the Silverman girl go out with her Gentile grocer than consider mixing rigid mathematics with pliant psychology. But there it was, right there in the core curriculum, a loophole large enough to slip thousands of undergraduates annually safely through. It was a natural hospice for the depressed and the lost, to be sure, but psychology offered pretty comfortable digs. (How sweetly agreeable the social sciences, which are, always and above all, sociable.) Secure in psychology's uncertainties, we managed the aftermath of numbers with more aplomb than students who could not circumvent mathematics could muster.

Exercise these finesses and these strategies, and you can gaslight your own way all the way to graduation. Then you can enter that other world those of us tucked away in academe call "the world," backing up, backing in.

And shall we devise a pearl fish flag to lead us in retreat?

For there is an art to getting by, and they teach it, opportunely, in school.

I graduated high school while the war they would not name the war was at full crest, my matriculation roughly bracketed by the Tet Offensive and the dropping of 800,000 tons of bombs by the United States on Laos, Cambodia, and Viet Nam. 800,000 tons. That's 1.6 billion pounds of explosives, an irrational number by any reckoning. As to what cover the quaking ground could provide, it would have required unprecedented art to locate and take advantage of it.

Most of us would not have known how to find these countries on a globe, much less outline a military perimeter or demarcate the DMZ, but ignorance did nothing to mitigate the peril. Graduating high school when we did, about a year after the 2-S deferment had been eliminated for full-time college students, we were captives of the uncanny mathematics of the draft lottery. Radio stations interrupted their rock diet to carry it. Freshmen thronged before television sets in their dormitory lounges to watch the selection process, which was basically a Bingo game conceived in hell. Here we were gathered better than twenty-five centuries since the gods evacuated Mount Olympus (or so we were told in Classical Civilization 101, a notoriously user-friendly choice for Area Two), and what was purportedly the most enlightened nation on Earth had turned to astrology to decide our fates. Basically, your birthday bought you time or brought you down. Those taking courses in statistics could figure their chances of becoming one. (Out of the blithering crowd, two April 27's are simultaneously struck dumb by the announcement that the number chosen for them is four. What were the odds?) Do not ask why—that is a question for philoso-

phy, a malleable discipline that has nothing to do with the imperious-
ness of probability.

You had to stay low to get past the radar. Imploring a family doctor
to invent a disqualifying disease on your behalf, practicing socialism
or sodomy, absconding to Canada—there was an art to getting by. In
my case, however, it was neither art nor craftiness that exempted me,
but a lucky number: 249. High enough even during the high water
mark of the war to keep me dry. They wouldn't be calling me up unless the Viet Cong launched an assault on Morton Grove. So I had a
de facto deferment after all. My official draft status was 1-H, or 1-A
and "holding." I was in abeyance, where, speaking metaphorically, I
continued to be stationed throughout college.

And it is in abeyance I remain, you might say, in that I have never
left college. What is more, I teach literature. So, speaking professionally, I spend my days speaking metaphorically, which suits me right
down to my predilections. I've made such a go of it that I even have to
file taxes—who knew I'd ever manage a pittance worth the paper?—
which I pay someone unshaken by the mathematics involved to contend with for me. As a result, I am more or less freed up to deal with
equally elusive but far more forgiving figures, which Wallace Stevens,
who sold insurance policies no less impenetrable than his poetry, referred to as the "intricate evasions of as." Perhaps one thing on which
insurance salesmen and poets can agree is that loopholes can be snares,
but they can also be escape hatches. For there is an art to getting by,
and I teach it, gratefully, in school.

16 Chump Change

If he stands out at all in school, it is for being in no way outstanding. He has just enough presence to be barely in the way. A cutting comment or a shove into the lockers will dispatch him. He is the Quincy the other kids trip, whose briefcase (that emblem of the outcast state, even more tempting to the other boys than untended cleavage) is almost weekly tossed into the girls' bathroom. He is the Poindexter whose "Ouch! Cut it *out!*" gets him detention while the smirking perpetrator goes free. Decked out in madras shirt, pocket protector, and forbearance, he is by all appearances doomed to be duped, dumped upon, deceived—the class Jack Goff, the inherent Dick Hertz.

Each day when he slinks home, his mother succors him with Oreos and the promise that he is the sort of person who will be worth knowing later in life, one destined to ascend while the bullies and boors he daily has to endure diminish. Even now, they are not worth your notice, she says. Believe me, sweetheart, you won't be saddled with thugs and numbskulls forever. You'll be estimable yet! Until then, have another cookie. There's fresh milk in the fridge.

Unfortunately, her son knows that there are the bathrooms, the playground, and gym class to be navigated first and for several years yet; there are the current scourges to withstand before her mythical future can even be conceived of. For now, there is no getting around the fact that her boy is a boob both backwards and forwards, a Clark Kent coming and going, and bereft of sufficient ego to alter. For all the Mommy homilies laid out for him like the clothes that don't quite fit his body ("You'll grow into them") or the fashion ("The salesman at Sears assured me that *all* the kids wear them"), the nerd knows that neither the coin collection he keeps in his drawer nor the chemical experiments he conducts in the cellar can stay the guys who goad him or offset the disappointment of his wistful, muttering dad. And, indeed, his father would rather his son could master a batting order than figure out computer code or parse quanta. Although he never mentions it to anyone, he would trade twenty points from his son's SAT's for the sound of his solid batcrack sending a baseball through the window that faces their front yard, or for the sight of one legitimate spiral issuing from that square peg of a kid of his.

Nerd. Twerp. Dork. Fag. Spazz. Sounds that the hoggish oink out, his mother says, because they can't manage more. Just avoid the boys you can't vanquish. And if you can't do that, if you can't turn the corner or make the bus before they spot you, keep your eyes on the inevitable, the certain prizes that you're matriculating toward. That way, you'll get through the gauntlet of grunts, snorts, and spitballs shot through the barrels of retrofitted Bics intact.

But until graduation, he wonders, would she have him beat back the boorish with math scores? By college-level vocabulary will they be subdued?

Sympathetic counselors might provide stories to sustain him when, to his chagrin, he strays from the confines of the audio-visual storage room. They could urge him to take heart from John Updike's "A Sense of Shelter," whose protagonist is a twerp, to be sure, but a twerp secure in the knowledge of his coming election. Despite the variety of humiliations that lay in wait for William Young as early as first grade and that have hounded him all the way through high school, he is certain that just by growing up he will grow into eminence:

> The perforated acoustic tiling above his head seemed the lining of a long tube that would go all the way: high school merging into college, college into graduate school, graduate school into teaching at a college—section man, assistant, associate, *full* professor, possessor of a dozen languages and a thousand books, a man brilliant in his forties, wise in his fifties, renowned in his sixties, revered in his seventies, and then retired, sitting in the study lined with acoustical books until the time came for the last transition from silence to silence, and he would die, like Tennyson, with a copy of *Cymbeline* beside him on the moon-drenched bed.

By his reckoning, success is not the grail to be sought but pre-ordained salvation, custom-tailored as a spazz's ensemble has never been and just waiting to be claimed. William's is a vision as precise as it is extensive, and it is able to withstand an adolescence regularly beset by peers who aren't influenced by intimations of his future stature.

Meanwhile, it's been a dozen years of unleavened exile. And frankly, we might assume that going off to college won't necessarily change his fortunes, either. In lieu of popularity, William will likely settle for the Honors Program, that hothouse for the incurably nerdy, whose prize orchids are the awkward. Notwithstanding Updike's eloquence on William's behalf, every mother's son knows that most poets-in-residence, Rhodes Scholars, and Nobel Laureates must carry the stink of always having been picked last for the team. How many presidents and popes still feel the sting of insults or of ice-loaded snowballs against the backs of their necks? It's a fair bet that not one of their resumes mentions a date with a homecoming queen. And what class klutz wouldn't trade a line on his eventual vita for *that?*

But school counselors are nothing if not dauntless. So they might next offer I.B. Singer's "Gimpel the Fool," whose notorious kenning comes at the end of a litany of schoolyard abuses: "I had seven names in all: imbecile, donkey, flax-head, dope, glump, ninny, and fool." (Note that translation from Singer's Yiddish does little to launder the scorn.) What girds Gimpel through a lifetime of being taken in by mischief and double-dealing is the prospect of being taken in forever by a genuine heaven: "When the time comes I will go joyfully. Whatever may be there, it will be real, without complication, without ridicule, without deception. God be praised: there even Gimpel cannot be deceived." Here is a kind of apotheosis of William's fantasy of being protected by mahogany paneling and tenured. Unwitting Gimpel dreams of spending eternity among the vetted and the verifiable.

But once again, for the kid who's besieged the moment he leaves his house, the hope rings hollow: Singer's concluding comfort is one more song of the thwarted. Gimpel is at best an obtuse angel, and he is likely to impress a comparably targeted reader as being more stumbling than sacred. He'll recognize the despair more dependably than he'll believe in the deliverance from it. And how much satisfaction would there be anyway in pledging allegiance to the worst fools in the school?

Having little choice, the schlemiel must console himself however he can, perhaps by ticking off the elements in the Periodic Table to steady his patience. Marooned in the cafeteria from the ordinary masses of other kids, maybe he cobbles acrostics. Maybe, while his cookies are being swiped, he empties his pockets to inventory the smooth pebbles he's scavenged. Maybe, while his ears are being flicked raw or his name is being stretched into meaner and meaner epithets or rhymed with scandalous bodily functions, he muses about plate tectonics, Boolean gates, lines of descent of the English throne, or the way water braids when it falls. Thus do the guilty wait out their days in the penitentiary: reading Russian novels, studying law, improving on one idiosyncratic fluency or another. That the nerd's crime is having been cut out of the herd for being lame and lagging behind the jokes at his expense does not spare him from doing hard time.

On the other hand, shielding his head with a textbook, it might just be their comeuppance he's plotting. They say that living well is the best revenge, but it could be that constructing revenge is living well. At any rate, that is the definite tenor of scores of teen movies infesting the cineplex. Showing in Theatre I, the long-suffering kid becomes a slasher. In Theatre II, the boy who was trampled every afternoon at 3:00 into the wet sand beneath the swings matures into a masked terrorist. The school doofus guns down his persecutors in Theatre III, who die one at a time with incremental awfulness and contrition on their lips. And coming soon, supernaturally endowed by a lab accident and expensive special effects, the one-time dipshit savages his home town, sparing no one except one girl—the one who had retrieved his algebra book for him when he had to rearrange his underpants and his composure after an especially devastating wedgie—who is left to tell the tale. Surely it's easy to believe that there are plenty of former Gimpels among filmmakers. Think of Steven Spielberg pinned and wriggling under the starting right tackle. Imagine George Lucas losing his lunch money to the hoods in the hall. Finally, they have the money to do something spectacular about their grudges.

James Joyce supposedly repaid everyone who'd wronged him by casting them unattractively in *Ulysses*. Such a literary trump may find favor among devotees of Joyce—Bloomsday celebrations all over the world are awash with Williams—but really, it's a geek's strategy, the meager, compensatory prowess and last resort of the routinely rabbit-punched and pink-bellied. They never let poor Rudolph join in any reindeer games, so he mortifies them immortally, by writing them into unforgiving passages, by writing them off. Still, I'd be surprised if even the aesthete, whose eyes when he was a child burned with anguish and anger, and who now bears his chalice safely through a throng of foes, instead of publishing his affronts, wouldn't rather slap some humanity into his attackers. Better yet, in keeping with contemporary film convention, he may just want to wield an axe.

I confess that when I spent a string of recesses being menaced by Brent Fowler and Jay Sax, neither a poetic nor a proportional response was what I had in mind. Face down in the mud and gagging under their combined weight, I prayed for unprecedented strength or lightning strikes, never for straight A's or success in some future profession to prove that they'd misjudged me. The blows I dreamed of were not delivered against their consciences; it wasn't at the chessboard or in debate that I wanted to beat them. And when I had to ask the custodian to interrupt his lunch to help me get down the hat that they'd flung up into a tree—the corduroy hat with the ear flaps that my mother made me wear, the spazzy hat that may have protected me from the cold but that left me vulnerable in the only way that really mattered—I didn't bother God to beef up my bank account or to guarantee my application to Harvard.

If I'm accosted nowadays, of course, it's in a way that's more civil, or at least more subtle, than Fowler and Sax's elementary-school style. My indignities are more sophisticated; my countermeasures are, too. No one gets his suit wrinkled or his briefcase scuffed. Nevertheless, if I ever happen to pass a playground, I'm sure that I can identify the William about to be waylaid, the Gimpel about to be ganged up on by the rest of the group. He has that hunted, haunted look that develops in the back alleys reserved for the furtive to find their way home by.

I don't say anything, but I do wish him encouragement. A parent myself, I wish him what parents instinctively wish their kids: basically, a bright, unbullied fate. I wish him a vantage point to look back and down on his persecutors from some day. Mostly, though, because I remember when I couldn't pass my own playground with impunity, I wish him *big*. And fast.

17 A First Course in Aperture Therapy

Sensory affliction has a complicated and rather sordid place in the annals of medical care. The wise therapist recognizes that sensation is among the hardest habits to break, and the propensity can survive in dormancy long after the practice has been terminated. Relapses are dismayingly frequent. To be sure, even patients who are aware of the perils of awareness may continue to indulge in sensations he knows to be injurious to his mood and constitution. Indeed, the so-called recreational auditor or social seer may have fatally placed his faith in a contradiction in terms. Clinical experience shows that there are no recovered sensors, only recovering ones.

That said, modern science has come a long way in dealing with the onslaught of sensation. What follows is a basic outline of current procedures for stitching up the senses (figuratively speaking, at least when surgery is not an option. More on the controversy over figuration vis-à-vis aperture therapy appears below.)

Note: New patients, particularly patients who have exhibited long-standing susceptibility to sensation, should ready themselves for therapeutic trials via simple preliminary blocking and inversion techniques. The novice may want to employ prosthetic lids and lid fuses, tender buttons, or orifice corks (a.k.a. "butt shuts," in market parlance) to secure what will initially be unfamiliar psycho-physical arrangements, as well as extend and enhance the experience of closure.) Salient among the aforementioned techniques is Cranial Yoga, as described in a case study by Samuel Beckett:

> None of Mr. Knott's gestures could be called characteristic, unless perhaps that which consisted in the simultaneous obturation of the facial cavities, the thumbs in the mouth, the forefingers in the ears, the

little fingers in the nostrils, the third fingers in the
eyes and the second fingers, free in a crisis to promote
intellection, laid along the temples. And this was less
a gesture than an attitude, sustained by Mr. Knott for
long periods of time, without visible discomfort.

The absence of discomfort is prerequisite to guaranteeing the faithful
participation of beginners and their willingness to pursue advanced
therapies.

THE NOSE

Problem Summary: The nose opens indiscriminately upon the world.
Prow of the ship of self, herald of the face and first thing through the
door, it is the body's principal index of arrogance and susceptibility.
The feature was most notoriously featured by Gogol as the title hero of
a story in which, magically liberated from a bureaucrat's otherwise unexceptional countenance and swollen with prominence, it set off on a
considerable, if temporary, political career. For our purposes, however,
the critical moment comes early in the tale, when the nose, poking out
of a loaf of bread, confronts us with the fragility of self-possession. If
the eyes are the windows to the soul, the nose is the vent, which advances beyond those more celebrated entryways by critical millimeters
and, in terms of consequent hazards, must not be neglected.

Threats to the nose are, for the most part, aesthetic, the nose
being exceptionally vulnerable to errant elbows, bad-hop grounders,
and other comparable misfortunes. Facing up to situations and facing
them down equally expose the nose to calamity. Bereft of Cyrano's
scripted wit, most nose-holders rely on other forms of protection. That
said, it should be noted that while the nose is boneless, it is not in-
finitely malleable. Racial inheritance is largely invested in the nose,
and the reprieve from the genes that plastic surgery provides is, on the
whole, illusory.

Preparatory Exercises: The tendency to avoid noxiousness, which
may seem at first sniff to be a reasonable reflex, can in fact damage
nasal elasticity in the long run. Paradoxically, the nose will be able to
transcend these scents only in the wake of systematic confrontation.
(The novice may wish to employ a breathing apparatus or consult a
respiratory therapist before engaging in solo inhalation.) It is therefore
sensible to introduce the nose to the very substances and situations it

will ultimately and successfully eschew. Among the recommendations are animal carcasses, which are conveniently abundant along major highways and retain their tutorial powers for weeks at a time in summer months, several European cheeses, and committee meetings.

Remedial Aids: A range of corks, stopples, and buttresses are available. These will help to ensure that the nose remains in joint and in plumb, able to withstand common assault or harassment. Synthetic mucous has come a long way since its invention; its environmental "friendliness" and its amenability to the patient's sinus contours guarantee that it will continue to perform well on the market. Devotees of the homemade or those who just want to avoid the expense of custom-fitted orthotics may size cylindrical wads of cotton like those ordinarily found in pill bottles; if inserted when damp, these will expand as they dry to form a tight, reliable seal. The practice of stuffing noses that nature has failed to endow with allergies dates back to ancient Egypt: the installation of spice kernels into the nostrils of pharaohs was designed to sustain them sweetly through centuries of interment. But there are homelier validations of the practice, most notably the sedulous efforts of children. Compelled by intuition stronger than the remonstrance of mothers, children will probe and plug their noses with their fingers or, when prohibited from leaving the breakfast table until satisfactory inroads into their meals are made, will insert bits of cereal (with Trix and Sugar Smacks enjoying remarkably durable popularity here). An instructive, if unmannerly, precedent.

Prognosis: Good. Because the cavities are relatively easy to access, antidotes may be quickly and efficiently introduced without professional aid. While the odd whiff may snag upon an unguarded nostril, the impact upon a routinely treated nose will be slight and temporary. Moreover, the inherent human subordination of smelling to the other sensory maladies makes the chance of its subtraction less alarming to the affected party, and the subtlety of its absence promises to speed recovery.

The Ears

Problem Summary: Sounds often vary in tone, pitch, incidence, volume, vibration, duration, resonance, or quality, but seldom in their deleterious outcomes. The ears must be fiercely guarded, for even the least peeps that smuggle in might riot in the chambers.

Carelessly lent or bent over the years, the ears are the rococo door-ways to the sonic brothel, which is scandalously open to unchecked sounds from all quarters, and where all manner of auditory debauchery may be embowered. The promiscuous curl of each aperture, the plump, lascivious drop of the lobule, the egregiously genital contours of the fossa-helix-antihelix-antitragus-tragus-concha complex (not to mention the brazen cleavage of the intertragic notch) all connote the vileness of the invasion of the auditory canal, through which the sludge of all intercourse flows unfiltered to foul the delicate masonry of the ossicles, corrode the tympanic membrane, and generally menace the head.

Preparatory Exercises: Suggested immediate means of confounding sound include packing off the ears with campaign speeches, readings of minutes, or family history from the relatives; baffling them with advertising mantras or rock guitar riffs; or barricading them with cliché. This is a weaning process, whereby, eventually, all words will curdle and clot in the ear canals, actually forming greater protection against future verbal incursions. (Linguists and scientists alike continue to do research in the way words get in the way of themselves. Findings bode well so far.) The goal is to refine sound into something manageable—the monotony of the tide, the om of the dial tone, the static of the dead channel, the blather of laundry writhing in the wash—as precedent to dispensing with it altogether.

Remedial Aids: The ear casket has proved very effective and has the added advantage of being covered by most major health plans. Placed snugly over spackled, grouted, or caulked ear holes—there are several over-the-counter artificial ear waxes available—these gadgets allegedly muffle, mute, or quell up to 98% of all invasive waves and caramelize inklings that do manage to leak through, rendering them harmless. They purportedly leave the user, to borrow from an oft-cited commercial for one such product, "as rapturously empty as a Hindu on diuretics." Warning: Noise occasionally masquerades as silence and may penetrate in that disguise. Even the most secure sound-stanching system or vacuum assembly cannot differentiate between a completely "quietized" environment and one where aural input has merely been disguised in this fashion. The recommendation is not to risk uncovering the ears unless an All Quiet bulletin has been issued.

Prognosis: Ambiguous. Due to the likelihood that patients who have most thoroughly achieved aural insulation are unwilling to jeopardize their achievement by allowing for the infiltration that comprehensive data collection requires, findings are incomplete at present and promise to remain so.

THE EYES

Problem Summary: The difficulty here is easy to see. In the case of eyes, the affliction of witnessing is especially acute, commonplace, and perdurable. Only the operation of the pores is anywhere near as tenacious, but fortunately their constant exudations serve as a natural repellant. The viviparous lizard, which has the capacity to ward off enemies by discharging blood from its eyes, offers an ocular counterpart to the capacity of the pores, but of course there is no way for humans to imitate that enviable mechanism. Indeed, the octopus has its ink to secrete and the skunk has its stench, whereas humans make do with tears, which will blear but not blind us, and hence provide no real cure for vision. Only metaphor might confuse the issue: for instance, by depicting tears as the scalding oil poured from the parapets to keep attackers away from the castle. It must be remembered that all poetic figures are placebos at best, to be used cautiously, if at all. Far wiser to regard any image as an eye infection and take precautionary measures.

Preparatory Exercises: Sentimental attachment to the eyes is often intense. Accordingly, it pays to take an incremental approach to divestiture. The preemptive gougings of Oedipus and Gloucester demonstrate the danger of moving too precipitously against vision. Rather than relieve them of awareness, the treatment sealed their griefs inside them. (Suffice to say, it is not enough to drive the eyes inward, where enlightenment, like elusive cancer cells, may also lurk. Worse, vision can under these conditions escape as rhetoric and redouble the original harm.) Due to the considerable possibility of the recurrence of similarly tragic results, this method is not generally endorsed.

Begin by shading, hooding, and dropping the eyes to help instill the reflex of abjuring light and thereby build a vampire's resolve. Sidelong glances—think of the clerk who dons pince-nez to appraise the latest offering at the pawnshop or the shorebird that halts to evaluate the potential succulence of a wayside seed—will also guide the patient toward undiminished and permanent visual retraction. In stages, he may be expected to progress from "strategies of askance" to full recuperation from sight.

Remedial Aids: The onset of illumination can be disorienting, even terrifying. What is the sand that collects in the corners of the eyes every night but the eyes' own effort to cement themselves against intrusion? Fortunately, there are several products to choose from to fortify the face's involuntary defenses. Prescription sun blunts or, if a given patient's insurance coverage warrants, surgically implanted deflectors (also known as synthetic cataracts), can provide some immediate relief from both coordinated and random strikes of light. Topical solutions, such as twilight salves or gloom balms, may also be applied. (There are many excellent ointments to choose from. A patient should be encouraged to consult with a pharmacist about which one is best suited to the kind and degree of ocular surplus he suffers from.) Used diligently, these devices and medications not only provide statistically significant respite from visual influx, eye spasm, and ocular spall but can also set the patient on a steady course toward the ability to "Cast a cold eye / On life, on death." (Yeats is referenced advisedly here—see *Problem Summary,* above—and only in rare instances should the patient himself be submitted to the allusion. For a prose alternative, which has proved to be no less dependable an inducement, consider using Nabokov, who writes in *Despair,* "Alas, after all that has happened I have come to know the partiality and fallaciousness of human eyesight.")

Prognosis: Uncertain. The existential tundra surrounding the relationship and possible interdependency between being and perception renders the disposition of the "cured" patient as problematical, in a sense, as that of the patient manifesting symptoms. One must proceed with caution and remain alert to the ethical requirement of explaining to the patient the repercussions connected to either living with the disease or undergoing its alleviation. That said, anyone stricken with lucidity should be urged to take heart. As the saying goes, there are none so blind as those who will not see. While most have not been endowed with blindness, a worthy substitute can be accomplished through rigorously applied therapy.

THE MOUTH

Problem Summary: Propensities for hunger and conversation may betray even the most assiduous mouth therapies. Recent research has shown that vestiges of appetite, whispers, and muttered asides may persist in plaguing patients who have presumably been muted, so anyone supervising any and all gagging programs should take care not to terminate therapy prematurely. Another problem is the depth of the cave that the mouth merely implies. Swallowing, salivary activity, and the secretion of gastric juices all conspire to undo the damming of the aperture. Whimpers, regurgitants, sighs, halitosis, and prayers are almost impossible to account for or to suppress completely during the first stages of palate repair. There have also been accounts of gasps and sputters issuing from patients during uvular fusion or sublingual sub-jugation, as if they were engines that had been fed the wrong octane. Typically, these glitches are indecipherable and of brief duration. The experienced therapist interprets them as attempts to encourage him or clumsy notes of gratitude, and he redoubles his efforts accordingly.

Preparatory Exercises: Either glut or deprivation can deaden the mouth. Hence, stuffing or starving the patient, relentlessly harangu-ing him or isolating him from all communication, work equally well so long as one method is adopted exclusively and ruthlessly practiced. Once the mouth is conditioned to "realize" that it can feed forever yet never eliminate the ruinous instinct for food, and that it can talk for-ever yet never satisfy the compulsion to connect, much less to mean something, it will slacken and become amenable to shutting up shop or shutting down operations. (The handbooks defer to the terminol-ogy preferred by individual users here.)

Remedial Aids: The aim is to fill the mouth until it is packed solid as a pocket, so the filler should be viscous or granular and therefore able to be tamped flush into the hidden recesses of the cheeks, gums, and jaws. Molasses and lentils are cheap, easily obtained, and depend-able ingredients; indeed, some therapists urge that they be combined in order that the patient receive the benefits of both. Many of the com-pounds used by dentists to fill tooth cavities can (if procurable in large amounts) be used to fill the cavities that contain them—a method whose symmetry has begun to attract a growing number of aperture therapists. Ball bearings, wheat or white flour, and wood glue are also commonly advocated, as are a variety of foam and latex-related fillers, which can be troweled in and spread about the mouth manually or blown in until it is crammed like a goose with corn. (Speaking of corn, corn meal makes viable filler, too.) Throat thwarts and glottal stoppers are still a few years away, but early experiments with small mammals are heartening.

Prognosis: Outstanding. Whereas all reports suggest that the deprioritization of intake, followed by wholesale relinquishment, is soothing to the patient, the comparable process in regard to speech is positively exhilarating to both the "untongued" patient and their ex-interlocutors, who thanks to the patient's recovery from conversation are themselves spared exposure to the abrasiveness and frequent toxicity of language. When successful, this therapy returns the patient to the characteristic solipsism of the species and a state of contentment indistinguishable from sleep. No wonder, then, that according to surveys, of all aperture therapists, mouth stiflers complain least.

CONCLUSION

In *A Portrait of the Artist as a Young Man,* Joyce's Stephen Dedalus sought to humble his senses, the better to instruct his soul. The greater ambition is to negate the senses altogether. By ridding ourselves of the clamor of phenomena and squelching those insidiously poisonous stimuli that suffuse the atmosphere, we may become pristine. We may finally be free.

Imagine the imagination cordoned off like a crime scene. Imagine a brain whose every breach is healed. A numbing slumber will seal the spirit and compact the self concisely and tightly as fish in a tin. With our mouths immured, ears deafened, noses nullified, and eyes spiked, we would each be a serene genius of intactness.

An idyllic repudiation, perhaps, and at present only a utopian dream. Nevertheless, the combined dedications of medical experts and patients committed to recoil lead us to believe that such a richly wadded, sublimely insulated Eden may become available to the species at large. We have undoubtedly come a long way from the days when men and women were hopelessly beset by the horrors of ingress and issue and were resigned to living out their lives with utterly unamendable heads. Shakespeare's Richard III laid the blame on nature because he was "rudely stamped," and there is no denying that the apparatuses granted us at birth leave considerable room for improvement. Happily, the state of health research and development has never been healthier, and the industry confidently predicts the coming of the long-sought "consummate self." If true sensory midnight is not yet attainable, at this point in the evolution of aperture therapy the prospects do appear— and here we may be excused one last ironic figuration—bright.

18 A Wet Blanket Apology

I am the sober one, the one who stands by the door. I am the narc at the party, or the one who's presumed to be, because I do not partake, at least not convincingly, not entirely, not enough. I am the one who is never stoned and never drunk, whom you count on to change the music when the album ends and to return your records safely to their sleeves. Enlist me to snap your CDs shut in their proper jewel boxes lest they become lost, lest someone accidentally mash an errant disk beneath his heel. Depend on me to stow the coats safely away and to distribute them to their owners accurately when they depart. Leave your keys in my keeping. Give me your cash. When several hours from now you emerge from the ensuing stupor, when the Saturday night miasma lifts and the booze loses its grasp, or you drag yourself out of the drug-induced haze, look to me for your belongings and your bearings. I'll be there with a ready shoulder and a clean handkerchief to accept your slobber and sloppy confidences. I'll steady you—let me take your weight. I'll get you back up and get you back home.

I am the onlooker, insinuating myself only from a distance, looking in from the periphery, looking on. You may think my rectitude would vex the other guests. You worry I'd bum you out like a picture of your lover's parents next to the bed, but that does not mean you need me less. For I am the one who holds you up in the shower as you vomit the rough evening's evidence up, who wipes the gouts and venomous dribble from your chin. Even if you do not know my name, you know my hands supporting your neck, my arms under your arms. I am the teetotaler, perpetually upright though others topple around me, and thus entrusted to do the toting. I am the one who helps you navigate the wreckage you made, who takes your "Fuck you's" and clumsy flails without complaint, who endures the injuries which you do not mean and never remember anyway.

Assuager of the foul-mouthed and the sour-mouthed am I, who hangs over the hung over, cold washcloth at the ready, or postpones a stricken companion's collapse until I can guide him nearer the mattress, only then letting him drop like a whump of snow from a rooftop to the ground. I am the inveterate designated driver, automatically appointed as though by nature, the way that favored and also-ran sons alike are marked by Fortune in fables. So sit back. Rest easy. Have faith. Hold on. In the morning, when you wonder how you got where you got to more or less in one piece, I'm the one who got you there, more or less. When I obliged you, bolstering and manipulating you like a marionette from behind, you don't recall most of it. I'm the one you have to thank you never thank.

A veritable Gibraltar of resolve, I do not make New Year's resolutions, not so much because they'd be redundant, but because compared to everyone else who's counted down the closing seconds of the dying year, I have nothing to give up that is especially infamous. What would you have me disavow that's worth the bother? I do not smoke and never have, not one cigarette, not once. Longstanding allergies have kept me immune to spells cast by leather-bound motorcyclists and detectives fogging passages in Chandler and Hammett. Imprison me, and I would prosper by the barter system on which prison economy is rumored to be based. I would gladly trade away my allotment of smokes, which according to cliché are the highest denomination of craving among the incarcerated, and thereby make my stay as comfortable as forced confinement allowed.

You cannot deprive me of the coffee I do not drink. Not that I do not savor it in the abstract: I have always loved the aroma of fresh-brewed coffee and marvel at the pointillist pleasures of beans brimming their bins in upscale cafes, which intimate a foreign hemisphere so verdant as to seem almost carnal to me. Nevertheless, I have never in my life managed to get even a sip down without choking. The notion of "grounds" alone is sufficient to seal my lips, never mind the slightest hint of grit on my tongue. Even the most exclusive blends— a carafe of Special Kenyan, say, or a cup of rare Ecuadorian AA— are indistinguishable from a gulp of dirt to me. I'll undoubtedly wait until I'm buried before I swallow clods. Until then, I keep the grounds under my feet.

As for alcohol, I occasionally poured a beer for myself at college parties to deflect comment or suspicion, but "nursing" is a term that does not do justice to the long-term care I gave it. A good thirty years has passed since drinking has been a measure of manly fellowship among my friends, so it's been that long since I've imbibed at all. Nothing noble in this—I just never developed the taste for it. Film stars and frat boys amazed me when they gouged holes in their throats with their first gulps and then proceeded to plug them with dozens more. It is clearly a matter of training: subduing the gag reflex and readying the digestive tract for bitters, which are not called "bitters" for nothing. But the difference between acknowledging the knack and mastering it is as great as that between draught and drought. So while half the undergraduates I knew had installed makeshift wet bars in their rooms or fermented beneath their beds any batch of fruit whatsoever they could lay hands on, I matriculated dry and have remained so. So tonight, should the waiter come to our table before I've returned from the men's room, anyone I'm liable to eat with knows not to wait. "He'll just have water." "Just water," as though I were the most maintenance-free of houseplants. Or possibly, if there's a toast impending or if I'm just feeling daring that day, a Diet Coke.

Needless to say, I never tried any of the newsworthy pharmaceuticals that were de rigueur in college dorms either. I forded the Sixties with everyone else who tried his best to forget he was draft eligible, and while doing so I ingested no pill more interesting than aspirin. When the customary reefer made its way around the soporific circle to me, I was the sole Bartleby among the Bogarts, just saying "no" a full generation before that response became an official linchpin of Reagan's administrative policy. (You might say I have always been in my declining years.) Cocaine? Out of the question. I will show you fear in a handful of dust. Acid? you ask. LSD? Get real. The only trips I ever took were to the freezer for ice to bring down tripping friends who'd downed worse or to the local police station to bring the bail money everyone who hadn't been pinched pitched in to spring those who had.

In short, I have never learned to want these things to have to learn not to want them. If the illicit delicacies that pervaded the dorms did not tempt me thirty years ago, the tray of aperitifs rafting past at a friend's wedding or delivered to help christen the latest gallery exhibit does not tempt me today. For foregoing has always been a foregone conclusion for me. That is why there are no New Year's resolutions on my agenda. I'm with you in spirit, but you'll have to toast the happy couple or the artist of the hour without me. Abstinent in so many areas, I abstain there, too.

So what's in it for me? What's the percentage behind being labeled Amish, Republican, or occult because the rest of the crowd is indulging? Why do I come if *only* to come, if only to come so far? Begin with the change in the cushions I'm the only one coherent enough to claim—the salvage after the savagery's passed. (If you can keep your head when all about you are losing theirs, yours are the quarters that fall onto the couch and everything that's in it.) I operate with impunity where everyone else is non compos mentis—I mean, where everyone else's mentis is not as compos as mine. What is more, when all other men are only semi-conscious—when I am the only man at the get-together still together, in other words—coherence can be something of an aphrodisiac, assuming, of course, that there is still a woman left who's sufficiently sober to appreciate it.

In the room the women come and go, came and went. Yes, there's *one* area in which my appetites were never constrained except by circumstance. I never staved off sexual impulses, that is, not when the staving was mine to decide. There's blood in me yet—blood unraised by booze, perhaps, but undiluted by it, too. I have watched them, liquored up and ready to be lost. I have watched them in their languor, clinging each to each. I do not think that they will cling to me.

And yet, there was the time my designs upon an especially fetching sophomore at a biweekly party on the twelfth floor of Oglesby Hall were blunted not by any disdain of hers or obtuseness of mine but because she had succumbed to a beer-soaked slumber I was loath to penetrate. Drawing closer, I was startled to behold her body's prolonged filibuster against the Repose Bill. Positively dainty in her waking hours, she lay there slurping and gurgling like a ship's hull. Hers was a sleep that wasn't solid but fragmented—an indigestible meal of sleep, it seemed. Furthermore, not only did she appear to leak in her sleep from her eyes, nose, ears, and hair, smearing her like a wet painting someone had brushed against, but also (going by the noise alone) her internal night shift was working at full capacity. Some wicked industry belied her rest, something pre-volcanic and uncooperative in the core of her, some laborious dream turning the soil of her insides. It was like being seated too close to the cauldron during the opening act of *Macbeth,* what with the assembled stenches and the threat of discharge. What unwholesome potions was the poor girl producing in there, anyway? Here was a subtle tumult everyone else but me was too distracted or too sleepy to see. Instead of the gentle surf of sleep you'd expect from a sophomore girl, I watched a wracked, ramshackle sleep, which was, to my undulled sensibilities, rather ghastly. A shudder in the loins engendered there, and I withdrew. Oh, I ended up seeing her safely back to her apartment (purity intact and purse in tow—never fear) and even went on to see her socially for a few weeks afterward. Emotionally, however, I had abandoned her at that moment, there on Mark Logan's futon, adding her, with her secret roiling, to my private list of abnegations.

Where I depart from the rest of you who opt for opting out is that you practice abstinence in the hope of returning to some halcyon past. As if perfect health were a novel you put aside and now resolve to return to, certain that in only a few pages you'll pick up the thread of the plot again. As if ideal systoles and diastoles were served in some restaurant from the old neighborhood your family moved away from when your father was transferred to the district office, on the day you have since chosen to mark as the last day of your youth, so that now, although you know it's irrational, the very same dish offered anywhere else does not taste the same and does not do. As if you could pass a referendum to restore your respiratory system, devise a Marshall Plan for your physique, retune your organs and refurbish your nerves. Believe me, you might as well abandon those dreams. (It should be easy enough, what with abandon being more in your nature.)

What I have found is that although abstinence may not necessarily be its own reward, it can, like certain divestitures—shaving, say, or dropping off sloughed clothing at Goodwill—be its own satisfaction. Because the self imposes itself in your every intuition, gesture, and appetite, denying the self is a valuable exercise. The paradox suggested by "self-denial" is that you build your character by resisting it, improving you much the way isometrics does, pitting your muscles against one another, in a room full of stumbling, dashed, and ever-slackening friends adjusting your vertical hold. Basically, if the eschewal fits, wear it.

The point is not to confuse these exercises with striving for moral fitness. Just because I'm up standing doesn't make me upstanding. I look forward to Yom Kippur not primarily for the spiritual purgative atonement promises so much as for the fasting itself. Hunger, even ritualistic hunger, makes me feel virtuous. Hunger delayed, if not hunger subdued, hones my sense of myself, as if I were digesting a whittled rib. So there's exaggeration and pride I have to confess as well, two more sins to swallow, Yom Kippur being the right day for it. It's a proper meal, then, and it will hold me until, indistinguishable from other congregants who have sinned and supplicated more substantially than I, I break the fast.

Inverting volition, reversing the regular direction my blood runs, or taking the long way around a given seduction does me good. True, abstinence may not make the heart grow fonder, but it flushes the system in ways that wantonness cannot match. But again, my predicament is that, having made "I refrain" my refrain, I have a limited assortment of habits and sins to abstain *from*. I cannot return from an annual check-up with a list of increments to base better behaviors on. I cannot cut down or lay off what's already down and off, regulate what's already cut and laid. Face it: once drugs, liquor, cigars, stereo systems, and sports cars are removed from the equation, there's not much left to leave out but calories. Ransack my premises, and you know what you'd find? Maybe a cache of miniature Tootsie Rolls stashed deep in the sock drawer, where more impressively reckless men keep their porn. Maybe a box of Girl Scout Cookies in the garage where months ago I successfully hid them from myself. (Sweets can be as powerful a passion for me as passion. Is there a more transparent deception among all consumer goods than the re-sealable package of M&M's?) When it comes to ingestion, I have never matured much beyond the repertoire I had developed by age twelve. I never made it past smuggled desserts to more depraved, dastardly practices. Sorry to be too sorry to be sorrier.

It isn't will power that has protected me from sophisticated forms of corruption. I'm not puritanical, either, just uninspired and, in the final analysis, unworthy. Don't align me with Gandhi, say, who, legend has it, would bed down with young boys to kindle his lust in order to practice suppressing it, until it vanished altogether, probably in a puff of heightened consciousness. None of that implicit reproach from the lotus from me. I'm more on the order of Kafka's hunger artist, whose protracted fasting was due not so much to aesthetic dedication as to his failure to find any food that he much cared for. I abstain because in the case of high-profile vice, I have no urges to control. And this confession comes from someone who puts a high premium on control. Whenever anxieties descend from their free floating to roost in my gutters (the onset is not seasonal or even era-specific), if there is even an atom of control available, I cherish it the way a battered child curls up with her kitten in the corner. But there's only so much comfort to be had there. Bare cupboards may be easier to keep clean, but one doesn't much look forward to dinner.

Hamlet imagined shutting himself up in a nutshell and counting himself king of a cloistered universe, but he realized that his dreams would chafe. The air in there would go bad soon enough, too. In contrast to Hamlet's withdrawal, there is the calculated involvement of his Uncle Claudius, who, having risen to eminence on the rotten pile his crimes made, wondered whether there were rain enough in all of heaven to purge his hands. Meanwhile, there's me, with my meager filth and transgressions that stain my resume no more formidably than the washable tattoos that come in packs of gum. Drunks dispel and lords propound from loftier climes; I drag my ragged cause across the floors of my disease. If my recoil is not in Hamlet's class, neither would my little lapses distract a Claudius from considering his majestically wretched state.

As a child I avoided feigning fevers in order to stay in when it came time for outings. Carnivals, picnics, birthday parties, ballgames— these were assaults on my precious equanimity. When I could not escape enlistment into the fun, I found myself going through the motions like a soldier during close-order drill or simply marking time and marveling at what seemed the innate capacity of the other kids to relish what threatened me. It was as though there were a membrane between me and the crowd; their aggregate rustle made it hum. An invisible tympanum, you might say, attuned yet exclusive. My friends clamored for outings; I preferred to live in.

Even now I have to prepare for gatherings well in advance, the way athletes gird themselves for marathons. Solicitude is subtler and more tenacious than the "Come on!" that used to carry across the blacktop at recess. Especially at the end of the year, there is an epidemic of hospitality to contend with. I suppose it's being at the mercy of the room. While they settle in, I hang back with the coats, noting the way they've learned to breathe under water, naturally asserting their natural selves. A halo of dope does not discount this trick. A bottle of wine does not deny it. An uncompromising familiarity builds among them, incrementally, like a coral reef. I observe their movements, their prefab interactions—a bit scripted and artificial at this depth, perhaps, but consensual nonetheless, and adequate in a way mine are not, not to me.

There is an elsewhereness about me, an otherwise. It is a mystery to me the way they have managed to get so . . . located. While all about me loosen up, relaxing their collars, their behaviors, and their grammar, I remain firm. Entering into conversation is like trying to make a left turn into traffic, what with the sensation that my movements are at best allusions to established movements and my words are hedged by quotation marks.

That is not what I meant at all. That is not it, at all. I cannot interpret gestures from this distance, whether I am being beckoned or dismissed.

But you needn't stop on my account. Go ahead. Please, have another. And should the spirit move you, you might lift a glass on my behalf to salute the string of a thousand toasts I've lifted no glass to. You'll understand if I don't join you. For I am the sober one, the one who stands by the door, looking in, holding on.

19 Clique Song

There are days when you feel waylaid into your life, as if you'd been ambushed by conscription officers. You know the feeling, and you know it better as you age. Days when it seems as though you'd been dunted from behind on an eighteenth-century dock only to awaken on a whaler well out to sea. Yeah, *those* days. Days when routine settles into you rather than the other way around, the way nine degrees in December goes deep into your bones, shutting down the joints the way cops do when the health code's been violated. The polar opposite of salad days, when it's nothing but greasy bowls in the sink. Days you'd use the word "ennui" if you knew it, that is, if you were able to muster the energy or elegance it takes for even one word of French. Thursdays, usually, although they can be Tuesdays, too. Days when they've wiped the letters from the keys and silence seems to be the only sense you can make and the only eloquence left to you. Mondays, certainly. When you feel like checking your receipt because there must have been some existential bait and switch at your expense. Weekdays. Days ending in "y."

Fate must have mislaid your papers, you figure. There must have been a mix-up in the mailroom, for you undoubtedly deserve more and belong with wittier company, richer partners, loftier friends. You witness this man's art and that man's scope, and you tell yourself that someone hired his delinquent nephew, who mistakenly shredded your file or nodded off at the controls. So you never get to the soothing part of the sonnet.

On those indomitable days, you turn to tiny revenges. Although you can't match Fate in degree, you want to pay it back for its unwarranted ambush in kind. Then the paltriest plots absorb you. You imagine putting salt in the gas tank of the last salesman who made you stand at the counter like a criminal awaiting arraignment. When it comes to the secretary who met your innocent question with ice, you consider whether mustard or ketchup would prove most unsettling when she sat in it and leave the most indelible stain. Humiliated in public, you muse about glue on doorknobs and tacks under tires with the sort of pathetic relish conventional perversity would have you expend on the Playmate of the Month.

Or perhaps, acknowledging the consequences that even petty revenge might lead to, you simply settle for goosing the world when it goes against you. In the grocery store, you pretend to go woozy from the Muzak and urge a woman in the produce aisle to dance, confessing that the song they're playing makes your heart go softer than the mango she's squeezing. In the elevator, you pull a Salinger and like his Seymour Glass accuse your fellow passenger of looking at your shoes, then scorn her for not having the integrity to own up to her fetish. In the Dollar Store, you bring one item at a time to the cashier and ask how much it is, then act incredulous because of the coincidence. ·

When it comes to finding justice, the opportunities are sparse and the venues few; but if you are willing to take out your consternation in silliness or spitballs, stay alert. You can always deliver the snowball between the shoulder blades, make the phony phone call, ring the doorbell and run.

In short, on those days you've been denied significance, you can play a game of goose and duck. With checkmate impending, you can still topple the board. Feeling foreclosed, you can still take advantage of the opening, however small, when it comes.

On the day Deanne Solomon crossed her legs and set off puberty like a land mine below my belt, I began to realize what all that iambic caterwauling we had to bear in English had been caused by. I got my first glimmer of the urgencies poetry—in particular, poetry as practiced during the adamantine reign of Mrs. Devorah in seventh grade—was trying to disguise with simile and deaden with sentiment. Neither the dire revelations of Health class, replete with gruesome diagrams and wicked statistics, nor Biology's Delphic knowledge, imparted in difficult syllables and gnomic glyphs, caused anything near the turbulence and delicious distress Deanne did with her simplest repositioning in the desk next to me. Because of that single shift, all previous notions of extremity were invalidated. Here was a brand new intensity to be dealt with, which immediately became the measure of all future intensities.

"Down, wanton, down!" demanded Robert Graves, assailing with figures that fine and private place. Me, too, Bob. Mine, too.

Befuddled by my fervors, so exceptional that even the memory of
them doesn't stay put, I cannot help but embroider the moment that
lust first sank its fangs in. Post hoc fantasy supplies the hiss of silk I
never heard along her fish-netted thighs—a spectacular catch, unprecedented in any outfield and, for sheer value, outstripping any fisherman's haul.

Dismiss my suffering if you will. Accuse me of navel-gazing, or
more accurately, of casing the questionable vicinity somewhat further
south. But look to your own pubescent obsessions before you mock
mine. (You'll see: scratch the scabs on a cynic and his blood will run
red as any rose that ever set a poet moaning.) Had I been more sophisticated, I'd have realized that I was not the only seventh-grader hor-
monally stricken and straining to hold it together beneath his student
desk. And perhaps I'd have understood the paradox that only by virtue
of that sudden sense of deprivation did I finally, in terms of physical
maturity, become complete. Or as Yeats put it, in a poem that Mrs.
Devorah did not deem suitable to our curriculum, "Nothing can be
sole or whole / That has not been rent."

Unfortunately, although her desk was so close to mine that my appetite might have leapt the synapse between us, the disparate crowds
we kept to guaranteed our separation. In those unforgiving days, social groups were shops closed tighter against one another than Capu-
lets and Montagues. What had started in Middleton Elementary as
playground apartheid had spread throughout the school by junior
high and would soon infiltrate the entire neighborhood. Our different
cliques were so distant that classroom rows could just as well have been
a continent apart. Not only would my love go unrequited, news of it
would never get past the battlements. Deanne was one of the Popular Girls; I was an ordinary school citizen at best. Whereas I might
aspire to hitting a winning jumper at recess or celebrating an A on
my report card, Deanne was endowed with divine right, beside which
even my dreams were meager. Accordingly, as I joked and jostled in
the hallways, bumping and bruising with the regular guys, Deanne
Solomon, surrounded by sleek, unblemished Deborahs, Ericas, and
Cindys, moved insouciantly through school.

So we took our respective and ordained paths through junior high
and high school, and during the entire time I never once alluded to

my lust. I never searched out a knowing smile from her after class or offered one, never tried to brush up against her in line for the bus, never had a pal call me by a snazzy nickname as I arranged to pass her in the hall, never phoned her for the exhilaration of hearing her unmistakable "Hello?" before hanging up in a panic. I never stalked her—no, never even trespassed on her station. And she never knew that the reason she was getting on so smoothly with her life was that I was letting her.

I had the chance to tell her so at the one high school reunion I ever attended. Long past sharing grades with me, she was still unmistakably Deanne, and still a vision: all black tube beads and polished temperament. Only now she was Deanne Solomon Stern, her legendary legs holstered in nylon this time and, along with the rest of her, already spoken for. But of course, she had always been that.

As I say, life all too soon assails us with the knowledge of diminished possibilities and missed trains. However, what we lose in possibility we can occasionally compensate for in presumption. A combination of nostalgia, curiosity, brass, and an appetite for narrative resolution encouraged me to find an opportunity to catch Deanne momentarily alone and let her in on the alchemy she'd unwittingly performed in my lap all those years ago.

At this point, it might seem incumbent upon me to offer a transcript of the conversation that followed, the routine reunion talk: the how-long-it's-beens and how-well-you-looks and what-are-you-up-to-nows, all that conventional intercourse, sweet, predictable and unsuspicious as the red wine and sponge cake for six hundred that had been just as innocuously laid out for us. But I believe that the expression "if memory serves" refers to its willingness to extend hospitality beyond the regular menu, to provide amenities the actual event did not. Some days—Fridays, for instance, or Saturday nights when one has been thrust among long-deserted acquaintances—you've got to goose the truth a little. Writers call it "punching up the dialogue," and the most effective at it are handsomely rewarded. What looks like retrospect is always a result of many drafts. In the following scene, I perform the functions of actor, producer, director, editor, and usher all at once. So be advised.

"Anyway," I concluded, "that was thanks to you. I thought you might like to know. Well, I thought I might like you to know. So."

"Should I be flattered?"

"That's up to you. It's not as though I could have helped myself back then. Or helped telling you tonight, it seems. My suggestion is, enjoy it. I am."

A pause to gather herself, which was, as it always had been in Deanne's case, a treasure hunt. Then: "So tell me, why didn't you ever ask me out?"

Wait for it.

"You would've said no."

"Oh, yeah."

What I helped her recall was that by high school she had vanished into a caste system as intricate and absolute as any you'd have found in India. Even if she never gave it a thought, I intensely remembered that intersections between the Brahmins—boys who earned varsity letters and were spared the mundane requirements of ordinary gym class, as well as the inherently fetching girls with whom Deanne herself was numbered—and the Untouchables—introverted kids who clustered anonymously at lunch to play cards, conveyed and operated the audio-visual equipment, or vetted chess games in the auditorium before class—were rare and accidental. A Deanne Solomon might briefly consult with an emissary from below her station in order to pick up a missed homework assignment or to bum a quarter for a candy bar, but dating one would have been like letting her kitten escort her to Senior Prom.

Deanne's husband returned, drinks for the two of them in tow.

"Well," I began, which seemed both reasonable and strategic at the time.

"Mark, meet someone I used to know."

"Mark," he clarified. "Mark Stern." He put down a glass to free up a hand for me.

"Good to meet you, Mark Mark Stern." A man whose love did not alter her monogram a jot. "Let me congratulate you two," I continued. "Solomon and Stern. Solomon Stern. Think of the savings in towels alone."

"He was always clever," Deanne explained. "By the way, how has that worked out for you, Art?"

Thus it was I was once again deflated, for there was no denying that it was indeed one of those days. This day's undoing came courtesy of Deanne Solomon Stern, who implied that cleverness only became me so far, and did it in a manner that struck me nonetheless as both clever and becoming.

But beware my cunning, so subtle that no day of the week could have seen it coming.

"Fine and often dandy, Deanne. I work and wish for the weekend like everyone else. I buy groceries that cover all the major food groups, and even though I wince in line when the lasers seek out the product codes and skewer my meat like a magician's assistant in a coffin, I laugh over it with the next guy, and there's no harm done. I have a sensible sense of proportion. I don't complain when the woman in front of me has more than nine items in the Nine Items or Less line; nor do I mention to the manager that it should read 'Fewer.' I'm no fanatic, you see. I don't rush home to gobble the last Oreo even when I can make the argument that by all rights it's mine. I follow my teams on television, but I don't confuse their fates with my own, and I don't believe they can hear me when I plead with the screen. In no way nuts, not me. I use a handkerchief when necessary and hold open doors for the burdened and infirm. My hair and my teeth are original issue, and my car is mine outright. So are my biases, which are well within the realm of the acceptable, meaning that there are no flyers indicting my behaviors in store windows and on telephone poles. I have hands, organs, dimensions, senses, affections, passions, same as you. Not a single pathology to report, thank you very much. There aren't thousands of clippings about the same underage actress insidiously rippling against my bedroom wall. Nothing tabloid or trailer park operatic about me. No secret drawer with obscene trophies from women I've mugged to punish my mother. Oh, I'm the first to confess a tendency toward dreaminess, or among the first, surely—when it comes to recognizing my faults, I usually finish in the money—but I do my dreaming on empty stretches of highway, never when the traffic is tight. People trust me with good reason, you see. I might miss the odd odd-year election, but I weigh in religiously on presidents and school referendums. I pay taxes grudgingly but on time. I read the papers regularly, chuckling and grumbling at the appropriate parts. I show up when expected and keep apprised of the latest cultural breakthroughs without being indiscriminate about embracing them. I cheerfully endure the Girl Scouts that come to my door. I don't blow my salary on poker or drugs, but I am known to show up at restaurants with cloth napkins, real silver, and trendy gloom and ask, How's the swordfish today? I manage to keep up the three requisite dimensions, often all at the same time, though you wouldn't have recognized it when we were in school together. I don't keep my pee in labeled jars. You?"

"No. I mean, yes, I'm fine, too. No to the pee in jars part." Thus I'd completed a full reversal: in a matter of minutes, she had gone from issuing an affront to being taken aback. And even Deanne could not find anything to say that wouldn't sound effete or just plain foolish.

Give us this damaged-in-transit day our daily coup.

"Fascinating stuff, you two," inserted ever-helpful Mark Stern. It's a quality—his ever-helpfulness—that I extrapolated entirely from the fact that he brought glasses for the both of them, but I'd stand by it as firmly as he did by Deanne.

"Well," I said again, for it was still apt. "And what about you, Mark Mark? Do you but fumble in a greasy till?"

"Till what?"

"No, that's Yeats. I'm asking about the living you make and how you make it. 'But fumble in a greasy till / And add the halfpence to the pence.' Yeats, the poet, that is, as opposed to the butt fumbler."

"Listen . . . Art, is it? We'd love to stay and talk . . ."

"But that would prevent you from going somewhere else, wouldn't it?"

The beauty of the elevator goose is that after the goosing the goosed must ride all the way down with her gooser, trying to look steadfastly at the numbers above her while, giddy with insolence, he gloats and ganders. But because our reunion was as wide as it was long, the Solomon Sterns were able to withdraw at once to an unseen end of the room. Deanne, her legs, and her ride headed off for like-minded, like-careered, comparably bred companions, leaving me to craft the encounter I'd ultimately console myself with.

As for the status of the latest draft: I don't owe her an apology, but I do owe her a debt of thanks. I don't mean for detonating my sex life decades ago, but for finally releasing me from speculation about her, a release that she occasioned as unsuspectingly as she'd made me succumb to that sensual music back in seventh grade. No, that is no country for old men, as Yeats and anyone who's ever been young enough to have shuddered at the sight of newly bloomed bodies at recess could tell you. But I'm the sort who might light up an old longing he knows is no good for him, much like the habitual smoker who fumbles for a butt from the ashtray after he's promised himself to quit.

"What class are you in?" The question has another meaning now than it once did. Yet though as adults we may be divided by differ-ent criteria—the color of our collars, the make and model of the cars we drive, the vacations we can afford to drive them to—they can-not match for agony the initial cliques we kept to throughout that Deanne-torn, that bell-tormented season.

Yeah, it's Yeats again I fumble for, who indulges the old corruption. You can't retract the idiosyncratic course of your own education, you know. There's a protocol for reminiscence, too. Reunions can only bring us so close together, and for only so long. And there's only so much sponge cake to go around.

20 It Is to Weep

You weren't mistaken. That guy you may have seen trolling the hobby shop off Seventh Street a few weeks ago, looking puzzled and out of place among the master model-makers and mistresses of crochet? That was me.

When I get too splenetic or too grim about the mouth to win compassion or company, when I get too morbid for anyone's forbearance or my own good, my substitute for the pistol and ball, whether I am the one taking aim or being targeted, is to accept direction from someone with a talent for equanimity, or who can at least lift her sights higher than the tops of her shoes. I do not fool myself into believing that I can adopt a cheerful expression, let alone summon the authentic cheer that could sustain it, or that I can apprentice myself to that serenity that seems to me to lie just this side of a coma. I'm not looking for an overhaul of my leaden tendencies, only enough of a tune-up to get me through the next three months or three thousand miles intact. Leave it to Buddhists to envision reality as a perfect ball of light. Grown intolerably polar, I just want a few moments of sun every once in a while. More precisely, others want it for me.

Now, I have neither the patience nor the faith for a full-fledged evolution. But an occasional golfer might take a lesson or two from the club pro to correct his bad habits, not because he plans to chuck his teaching career for Q-school but because he wants to improve from awkwardness to legitimate amateur status. With similar logic, I stay on the lookout for pointers.

My girlfriend is just the sort of person to provide them. Without going so far as to pass out pamphlets, Joy is about as centered and sane a person as I know, so I'd be foolish to dismiss out of hand any advice from her that might make it out to the fringe where I usually camp. To my credit and good fortune, she never questions whether or not I possess a soul in the first place—she is convinced it's in there somewhere, banging blindly about like a bat in a cavern. The problem, or rather my problem, or rather hers with me, is that I cannot access it reliably and do not nourish it enough when I manage to do so. Joy insists that I need more spirituality in my life the way a doctor might recommend more fiber in my diet. Darkling, I listen, though your prescriptions are not always legible to my layman's imagination.

Fortunately, I could wish for no better guide than the woman who's volunteered for the job. Joy's own genius for maximizing her potential is at least as familiar among our friends as my relative contraction. Her natural propensity for occupying herself with self-actualizing activities—African dance, marimba music, and bird watching chief among them—makes her eminently qualified to lead me in the ways of healthy occupation. Just as important is the fact that she knows my grubby essence well enough to realize that I am not yet ready for serious supernatural shopping. I have observed squads assemble for Tai Chi, and the longer I watched them practice, the more it struck me as an elaborate, mysterious pantomime about requesting, offering, and denying one another invisible beach balls. I've tried meditation once or twice, but clearing my mind is about as successful an effort as spooning sand from a dune without spilling grains back down the bank, while my mantra devolves into an inventory of utterly worldly errands. ("Remember milk, remember milk, remember milk . . .") As for joining a drum circle, bathing in salts blessed by shamans, or imbibing my own urine—I have acquaintances who tout these and many other remedies for spiritual constipation—let's just say that I haven't the temperament for them. Unless my transports embark from a bit nearer my own idiom, I don't see myself buying a ticket.

In short, unable to stretch very far the tether that holds me back from higher consciousness, I have never been able to accumulate sufficient nimbus to satisfy my soul, or at any rate, a certain blessed person's estimation of its legitimate dimensions. Some people unselfconsciously accommodate themselves to the ethereal, as though they keep a ready reserve of ecstasy like an extra generator in the cellar for when the power goes out. Others like me can't automatically breathe the thin air up there.

Hence, the hobby shop.

According to Joy's diagnosis, a hobby might catalyze my elevation. Rather than task me with intangibles right off the metaphysical bat, she means to mesmerize me with macrame, seduce me with dowel rods, ply me with bicycle repair, or otherwise inspire me with the shelves of unassembled sundries assembled there, all in an altruistic effort to teach me wholesome time consumption. According to Joy, the specific hobby I opt for is less critical than the quality of concentration it would encourage and, by extension, the escape it might offer from the undeniable muck I've made of my psyche. Therefore, with the sole proviso that the activity I opt for be one I can play out alone—naturally shy about such things, I can't see myself om-ing except on my own, and like Glenn Gould, I believe that the ideal artist-to-audience ratio is one to zero—I agreed to christen my fiftieth birthday by beginning a new hobby.

I figure that Joy may be right: a continuum quite possibly connects *Popular Mechanics* and conventional prayer. Then might my soul fluoresce in stages comparable to and reliable as the step-by-step process by which a brick patio or a balsa wood biplane is put together. (The analogies are not arbitrary: both patios and model biplanes are among the contenders for my ultimate diversion of choice.) In other words, the weekend's satori is prelude to the transcendent journey, which begins with the first smudge on the canvas, the first coin in the collection, the first thumb plunged into clay.

From this perspective, a hobby diligently engaged in is so profoundly substantiated by philosophy that the ordinary connotations of "hobby" underestimate its value. Most of the time, our attentions and our resources are scattered, leaving us open to anxiety. But a focused force cannot so easily be deflected. In place of planting a shallow field of rice, you might say, the trick is to try to plant one redwood. The idea is to get absorbed. Desiring this man's art, and that man's scope, I might learn to delve so deeply into some new discipline that, at least for the hour or two I'm devoting to it, no disquiet could find me. Let it be something eccentric, whose sole justification is in the doing itself. Look at Sarah, who fashions dream catchers out of feathers and bones though there is nothing Native American in her background. Look at Carl, who makes barb wire in his spare time, which he hangs out near the garage like strings of ampersands in the sun though he lives nowhere near a ranch. It is the diligence that does them good. Thus might I whittle my way heavenward or seek out salvation in a handful of beads. Who'd have thought that epoxy and epiphany had more than proximity in the dictionary in common, or that through a tube of glue I might be so imbued?

But after a few days' surveillance in the local hobby shop, I came up empty. The avocations on display all struck me as artificial; the gadgets, handicrafts, and prospective fetishes, stubbornly unfascinating. The relevant section of the bookstore didn't help much, either. I noted that I might take up photography, refinish furniture, learn a foreign language, become an aficionado of almost anything French (including cooking, cinema, and wine), handicap horses, ingest nitrous oxide, or develop a mild case of alcoholism. But the conditional tense kept nagging at me: that I *might* consider all of these interests emphasized that I *needn't* undertake any of them.

I concluded that one does not adopt an obsession deliberately; rather, one is ambushed by desire. Just as you cannot script the course of romantic passions, you cannot predetermine a consuming interest in NASCAR replicas, metal gas station signs, or UFOs. The appeal of presidential signatures, circus posters, or horror film stills is born, not made. I'm afraid that no matter how many neighbors labor in their yards to produce a half dozen edible tomatoes this year, my own garden will remain untilled until my sense of its mandate sprouts of its own accord.

I confessed as much to Joy, adding that I felt that the connection between something like building a birdhouse and believing in God was at best obscure, but to her way of thinking, that shortsightedness is a symptom of my spiritual predicament. And based on where our respective ways of thinking have led us, she tells me, it would make sense for me to err in her direction.

Reasoning that my reluctance was in part due to a residual sexist concern that real men abjure watercolors and yarn, she has recently settled on woodworking for me. To demonstrate the seriousness of her campaign, she bestowed upon me an early birthday gift of tools. Having conspired with a friend who makes his living with his hands, she descended upon Home Depot, Visa card at the ready, with the apparent purpose of outfitting me to survive for years on nothing but lumber. She spread the Hephaestean plunder out on the floor before me just the other night. The booty included a chalk line, a retractable measuring tape, an assortment of nails and screws, a carpenter's square, and a professional level whose size and heft I equated with a girder from the Chrysler Building. Then, in a separate box, she presented the alpha male of the litter: a circular saw, heavy and malevolent-looking as a pit bull, complete with a carrying case comparable to what its owner would transport that animal in through an airport, along with an instruction manual as packed with precautions as a Puritan's bible. I'm still a little afraid just knowing that the menacing thing is in the house with me.

With no clear aspiration beyond the desire to be safe, I scour the manuals like an exegete.

Meanwhile, and at the risk of suspicion from my heightened reality instructor, I have come up with a recreation that is more in my line. It is unconstrained by the need for costly equipment or favorable weather conditions. It can be practiced at home or on the road, in a hotel room, a subway train, an office, or a toilet stall.

I've taken up weeping.

Immediately I need to respond to those who'll object that weeping is only a natural manifestation of my assiduous sadness anyway and therefore an intensification of my typical condition, not a liberation from it. There's a gaping hole where your agape should be, they say. Your heart's already a hamper full of sour towels—no one's mood improves when you air that sullen laundry, least of all yours. Buck up and unbuckle for once, boy! Or rebuttals to that effect. My answer is that a concerted lamentation exercised without instigation or aim is really an aesthetic gesture. Call it emotional yoga. With apologies to Sylvia Plath, who by way of contrast never blinked at all over her own poetry's funereal procession, crying is an art, like everything else. I do it exceptionally well.

In the movie *Broadcast News,* Holly Hunter plays a Type-A network producer. The hub of the behind-the-scenes wheel, she is the quintessential stress junkie. In order to ease the pressure on the dam, she schedules regular intervals during which she locks her door, unplugs the phone, and waits for the inevitable run-off. She cries loudly, chokingly, and most impressively for about sixty seconds, then she abruptly gathers herself for the next set of travails. At first glance, my own crying may appear to derive from that kind of "power weeping," except that Hunter's jags are an aspect of her careerism, not a departure from it. She wails the way that, during board meetings, executive officers might engage in butt-tightening exercises beneath the table. In other words, her tears are as goal-oriented and efficient as everything else in her life and, if you'll pardon the pun, a far cry from spirituality.

I might note that literature has offered fewer models than you might have anticipated for my aesthetic venture. You might have assumed that the nineteenth-century novel in particular offers a wellspring of exemplary criers, what with all of those scandalized, discarded, disappointed, and wronged-to-death women strewn throughout the canon. Someone like Thomas Hardy's ultra-humidified Tess might appear to be an ideal mentor for a would-be weeper like me. By my rough count, she cries a full forty-six times during the unabridged edition of *Tess of the D'Urbervilles,* thereby demonstrating a dedication to the drill that is nothing short of heroic. Unfortunately for my purposes, what she displays in abundance she lacks in discipline. Tess is continually on the verge of breaking into tears, and her artless dreads and unbidden desperation give little in the way of useful instruction. Although she could very well have inspired protégés in the truancies of the flesh as to how, when under duress, to properly quake the shoulders or quiver the lips, I decided against employing her services. Tess's waters are something of a natural resource. I am as likely to benefit from her example as to learn how to emulate a river.

This has ever been the case with fiction from that period, whose heroines evidently cultivated their orchid delicacy from birth. What modern reader can help but be overwhelmed by how regularly they are overwhelmed? Who can help but be distracted from the plot by their wild, wracking lamentations, or by sulks as luxurious as the silks they sound like, with tears so plentiful that, upon cracking the cover of the book, the reader would think he'd accidentally broken into the county aquifer. Indeed, the typical Victorian heroine is described like a weather system sweeping in from the gulf. One bosom straining after another, each a factory of agitation. All those resolute tears, sufficient to soak whole paragraphs at a time. Secret tears and scalding tears, tears that alternately burst, trickle, and blind. Devoted tears, intently shed. Tears violently triggered and liberally expended. Sobbing so dependable the rest of the community could time harvests and holidays by them. Really Olympic suffering. A pioneering mournfulness, I mean, ranging from secret secretions behind the bedroom door to clamorous, triumphal cries for attention, as if the blighted heroine were a barker before a booth at a trade show. Or sometimes, for effect, instead of a flood, just one stately, sculpted, totemic teardrop, the lone indulgence the stricken woman allows herself like one luscious chocolate before resealing the box.

This is no mere prejudice on my part. My colleague is a specialist in the British novel, and she herself admits that for weeks at a time her syllabus seems almost wholly comprised of crying. Each sodden plot is a primer of human frailty and melodramatic grief; each abused heroine inhabits her own private little circle of havoc, where the forecast is always "chance of showers." Maybe it was because the corsets of their protagonists were too tight or because they unwisely eschewed red meat, but these novels are rife with sighs and sumptuous swoons. Evidently all over Europe during the 1800s women were dropping to scrubbed oak floors, collapsing picturesquely onto divans, losing consciousness in the midst of italicized chatter between Lady Higginbotham and Lord Sinclair, and flinging themselves onto one or another patch of the local variety of receptive heather. You can't pass more than two chapters without the thud of someone succumbing to a spell, vapor, or faint.

And of course, the chief appurtenance of these plunges is a seemingly inexhaustible supply of salt water. What with so many heroines so quick to liquefy, what with the incessant sluices incessantly described, it is a wonder that every reader doesn't emerge from a session on Victorian fiction absolutely drenched. You don't have to enter Melville to be washed overboard. From elegant country estates to dank city streets, the whole syllabus is leaking.

But if Holly Hunter's punctual evacuations are too contrived— releases that do not ruin her makeup or disturb her pleats—this sort of despair is altogether too unrefined to be of any use to me. Not only are these bouts of tears initiated by romantic or financial devastation, they are messy, earthbound affairs, about as transcendent as tuberculosis (another probable cause, by the way). Again, there must be a method to my sadness if it is to lead me above as well as inside myself. Without strategy, without style, there is no mourning glory.

Hence my somber hobby's increments, the stations of regulated distress. As a novice, I needed an artificial stimulus to begin the flow. I would listen to Samuel Barber's *Adagio for Strings* or focus on the concluding scene of *To Kill a Mockingbird;* I might picture my little girl's expression as she colored a birthday card for her mother, or arrange my own funeral in my mind. Stanislavski would forgive my ploys, I suppose; so, I believe, would a guru or the grad student who teaches pottery classes at the Y on Tuesday nights. Sometimes I would just place my hand on my heart, which I found out as a child saying the Pledge

of Allegiance never failed to elicit my tears. (I am convinced that physiology, not patriotism, accounted for it.) But now that I am a seasoned
weeper, I have dispensed with those devices. I need only breathe slowly, deliberately. I relax my features. I relax my grip. In a minute or so,
the ducts open, and a modest yet steady seepage starts like drops eventually grown too heavy to keep their hold on the window after a rain.
Ideally, it's a quiet, measured event—to borrow the airline euphemism,
a controlled flight into terrain rather than a crash.

Let me note that there is no need to take a physical exam before
beginning a program of weeping. There is no preliminary stretching
to do. Arguably, there is the possibility of its becoming habit-forming,
but in the sense that distance running sometimes does, except that
here it isn't endorphins that provide the rush. As a practitioner myself,
I may not be objective, but I would suggest that chemicals alone can't
account for the soothing, stabilizing, clarifying effects of twice-weekly
weeping. While I hasten to add that the activity does not solve your
troubles, free you, or permanently deflect the quotidian, it does ease
(using the most optimistic definition of that word here) the contours
of your captivity (using the direst definition of *that* one). All I can do
is report my own experience: I haven't found a better decongestant
(using the broadest definition, as spiritual growth warrants). This is
not evangelism, only testimony.

While I've been honing my crafts, both the one peculiar to my disposition and the one bestowed upon me by Joy, science has weighed
in on the immaterial. Interest in the nature of human spirituality has
reached a kind of critical mass in the scientific community, leading to
a new coinage, "neurotheology," and a recent cover story in *Newsweek*.
Are our brains hard-wired for mystical experience, or do heavenly
manifestations result from shorts in the circuitry? Is God the electri-
cian or the glitch in the system?

Some brain specialists are satisfied to equate religious or quasi-reli-
gious sensations with neurological (and explicable) occurrences. They
analyze the amygdala, parse the temporal and parietal lobes, keep a
vigil on their monitors so relentless one might call it religious if he
didn't know better, and, briefly put, are at peace with a faith that
comes down to brain functions. They have audited the human mind
and declared that the true artist-to-ideal ratio is one to zero. They de-

liver this news matter-of-factly and with dry eyes, seeing no need to cry over spilled divinity.

Some of their colleagues in the field, however, are not convinced that God's center and circumference do not exceed our skulls. Dr. Andrew Newberg, of the University of Pennsylvania, speaks on behalf of those who hesitate to join with the abolitionists. He explains, "It's no safer to say that spiritual urges and sensations are caused by brain activity than it is to say that the neurological changes through which we experience the pleasure of eating an apple cause the apple to exist." As to whether or not we will have to find an alternative to church—making quilts or tying flies, starting a drug habit or a collection of Hummel figurines—the jury is still out.

Perhaps it does not matter whether the apple is imaginary or real, created or perceived. What matters is whether or not we feel full.

So far, there is no definitive answer as to whether the brain is transmitting or receiving when it tingles, much less whether it can be conscious of the difference in consciousness or wants to be. We can't necessarily distinguish whether we are witnessing the visionary gleam or whether it's just our own eyes shining. But there is consensus that whatever its origin or ultimate significance, spiritual experience can be courted, and we can intensify our orientation toward it. We might begin to content ourselves with the available intimations.

What are the chances that nirvana is not amorphous at all but the zenith of geometry? Admittedly, I find church architecture forbidding, and the Tower of Babel was notorious for being too ambitious. But I think I could handle the sublimity of a good bookcase. Once this week's paperwork is out of the way, and assuming my eyes are dry, I'll get to work on building one. After all—I'm using the most forgiving definition here—what have I got to lose?

21 On Reading with a Pen

I used to teach an introductory course in film, which proved more popular among freshmen than alternative introductions to fiction, poetry, and drama because it promised to circumvent the principal drawback of more traditional literary studies—namely, an emphasis on print. Even as far back as the 1970s, students often viewed encounters with the printed word the way they did get-togethers with their grandparents: respectable by reputation, but tedious company, and smelling of neglect and decay. When the week's feature was a silent classic or a foreign film, more than one student was heard to moan in the darkness about having to contend with subtitles: "Hey, if I'd wanted to take a course where I had to *read* . . ." But the most frequent complaint I received after the course was over was that those students upon whom I'd for sixteen weeks inflicted awareness of montage, lighting, camera angles, *mise en scene,* and so on could no longer just watch a movie anymore. They couldn't help *seeing* what they were seeing and seeing why they saw what they saw the way they saw it. It sullied their enjoyment, they said, to be infected with terminology, the movie-viewing equivalent of crab grass or mange. It forced them to re-evaluate the movies they once enjoyed, not to mention the uninitiated dating partners they once enjoyed movies with. Because of me, movies were ruined for them, and they, too, were ruined. "Like you!" they accused, the fresh undead indicting the vampire who'd done them in for eternity.

In other words (though other words did not soften the suffering they'd been sentenced to), they had become readers.

Now rumor has it that even conscious, critically endowed readers are occasionally able to shut the valves of their attention and surrender to the massage. I am sure that that is what my students are getting at when they ask me what I read for pleasure. It is too strenuous or just plain ridiculous to imagine an English professor in the midst of a disco, an orgy, or a hardware store, but the idea of Doctor X in his recliner enraptured by Raymond Chandler, lathering to a romance novel, or slumming with science fiction occasionally sparks some curiosity. But for me, it has never been a question of what I read for pleasure but how. This is not to say that I take no pleasure in reading or no longer do. Not being able to read for pleasure is not the same thing as not taking pleasure in reading. Quite the contrary: although as an English professor I am by career and craving as reliant on reading as a medical doctor on drugs, I still relish the prospect of settling down with a new novel, an event I prepare for the way one does for a first date. I select the setting, lighting, posture, and even the bookmark with care; I deploy pillows and snacks with deliberation; depending on how imperative the worldly affairs I'm absconding from, I set the cordless phone at arm's length or ensure that it's sufficiently distant so as not to disturb me. Despite their close correlation to the occupations I'm paid for, I mind mindful pleasures with the scrupulousness of the committed golfer who during a Sunday thunderstorm consoles himself by lovingly debriding his irons as he prays for the return of clement weather.

So do not confuse me with students saddled with core requirements who complain that literature is a chore on the order of weeding the yard. The truth is that I cannot, or at least can no longer, read simply for pleasure, not if by that one means a reading free of interpretive agenda or unaffected by ulterior motives. It isn't guilt over the guilty pleasure of reading for pleasure that prevents me. Instead, it is that my love of reading is a love fraught with purpose and profession. Reading for me is invariably reading *for*. I am always asking myself what I can *do* with the book I'm indulging in—no surveyor digs solely for the visceral satisfaction of how the dirt gives beneath his spade—and so my delving is never entirely outside the perimeter of career. Accordingly, I treat every book I buy as a future tax write-off, and my conscience remains clear. No manuscript is an island, entire of itself. At least for me, every text implies its commentaries. Thus I am something like the gynecologist who eagerly beds down with his beloved yet cannot rid his mind of expertise when he does so.

And what does the retired *professional* golfer retire to *do*, anyway? Does he live out his golden years practicing cost accounting?

No matter how comfortably I'm burrowed into blankets or enfolded in the wings of the armchair, I always have a pen at the ready.

Indeed, I feel uncomfortable—incomplete—if I settle down without one. I keep it clipped to my collar, teetering on my lap, stuck like a dagger in my pant cuff, or trapped by the elastic band of my watch until it's required, which, depending on the incitements of the book before me, may be anywhere from a few times per chapter to several times per page. (I sometimes think I should have one depending from a chain like a sommelier's cup.) I retrofit and recondition, fiddle and tune. I turn over curious paragraphs like stones for the rally of insects and grubs I might uncover. I "Hmm," "Huh?" and "Aha!" in the margins, fidgety as any kid forced to wait in a hallway. With an auditor's crotchety resolve I worry the text with checks and asterisks, insistently twitchy before the text and tilling it obsessively. I pen in lively insights like prize colts. I escort model sentences, proud just to be in their company, my underlining serving the way the red carpet at the Oscars does to consecrate their progress. I lasso, underline, and arrow, marking my trail, keeping tabs on provocative cases like ex-cons so I might find them again if I need to after returning to the world. Mothers fussing with their sons' cowlicks and collars before church have nothing on me. I spruce, groom, primp, parent, and implore with the most obsessive of them. After all, I may take the book out in public one day.

Even the king who has every dish at the feast tasted for possible toxins does not outdo me for scrupulousness. The customs officer who feels for hidden compartments in your luggage is cousin to me; the master chef on the sniff is kin.

This in part explains my prejudice against audio books. While tapes and compact disks are arguably just as permanent as paper, the impact books produce upon me through those media are not. That is to say, my interactions with audio books are not preserved, which strikes me as too dear a sacrifice to make to the opportunity to drive while I catch up on my reading or read while I catch up on my driving. One cannot annotate the air. Enough said.

Authors, be warned: I meddle in the proceedings like a jealous member of the wedding. Do not leave your precious books in my charge if you value them unblemished, lest I pull back the covers and molest them.

Was I ever abducted by a book I didn't feel compelled to embellish? There must have been a time when I swam contentedly at the surface of the sublime oblivious to depth charges. There must have been a time when I was so blown away by a book that I didn't return to the epicenter of the blast to take its measure. (Emily Dickinson spoke of knowing she'd experienced poetry because she'd lost the top of her head to it and left it at that; I, on the other hand, recover my scalp and jot down a reminder to "cf. Dickinson.") But while I might hypothesize, say, a volume of unvetted verse, while I might once have been capable of an unwrought, unrecorded reaction, I cannot recall when it could have been or when that capacity deserted me. Likely I'd have made a note of it, which would have defeated the effect. At some point I must have broken off the key in the cognition switch. As a result, I would no more let a telling metaphor go unattended than abandon a baby in her stroller outside while I went into a bar. No, if a book has served as my cloister for very long, you'll find my graffiti on its walls.

If you stripped me of sharp implements like a suicidal patient, if you divested me of my pencils and pens, I would scar the margins with my teeth or engrave the pages with my nails, registering where I've been impressed with my impressions. Sever my tendons and I'd still smudge the page with unopposable thumbs.

My particular police work may be identified by a variety of signature incisions, as unique to me as a surgeon's stitches. For example, when a given image asserts its power or a passage proves so inviting that I suspect I might plan a return trip through it, I may stamp it with one of three fundamental commemoratives. These are the dash, the bracket, and the star. Three categories of reciprocity, if you will, between the engaging reading and the engaged reader. The dash, slipped like a shim into the justified margin, is designed to be a practical reminder that there's work still to be done here—I'll want to refer to this in class, effect some connection to a previous point, develop an essential echo elsewhere in the book. Driven in like pitons, dashes help guarantee me purchase as I make my way over the sheer face of narration. A dash functions as a simple machine as well, in that here I mean to lever open room for my own relevant observations, or possibly, by inserting it at a slant, to intrude according to my own inclinations. Here is a cryptic instance I need to jimmy open: Pynchon has holed up, his meaning taken hostage, or Joyce has barricaded himself behind a pile of allusions and puns. I'll be back with the proper tools.

If dashes stake out territory for utilitarian purposes, brackets make more aesthetic claims. When a bracket bites down on a savory phrase, it represents my desire to make the meal last and, if fate is kind, dine at that choice spot again one day. I'm reading along, then: a sudden blow.

A shudder in the lines engenders there, and I cage the insight like an endangered species before it can escape. (An obstreperous text will try to throw off the handler who is trying to help it. Be patient but firm.) "Vela was especially beautiful when she was silent. Silent, she seemed to be praying to her beauty." Bellow's chiasmus not only complicates the nature of the woman's silence and beauty both but also confirms the self-interment those qualities establish. In that same novel: "My belief is that on the side he grew a little herb garden of good, generous feelings." The twin victories of metaphor and alliteration earn the author another bracket, another stripe for valor. On occasion, even a word or two—Bellow refers to the "threshing and bickering" of certain birds—are so winning as to compel me to clamp them off. When an author continually requires bracketing, the pages look as if I've proofed a blueprint for a building by showing where the windows are located. Whereas in murky or pedestrian prose the paragraphs are bricked in like interior offices or prison cells, ingenious writing opens out onto a hospitable climate, so the light is let in everywhere.

There's a moment in Salinger when Seymour Glass says something about carrying the evidence on him of all he's ever touched or been touched by. I remember loving that line, and I remember cordoning it off somewhere in that novella—a lower right-hand page, I believe. It is not enough that I once loved; the true proof of fidelity is that I can recover the trappings—that amethyst pendant, that perfect aphorism—of intimacy.

You could say that the star is an exceptional bracket, a bracket with additional charisma. If the bracketed aspect is deft, the starred is dazzling—writing that preens for me, expensive and unexpendable. Flipping through an otherwise unexceptional novel I've read, I might come upon a single star—a Polaris interrupting the dark, signaling hope and providing adequate rationale for restraining me from cashing the book in to fund lunch. Of course, the shapeliest sentence-makers I've enjoyed have spawned galaxies. John Updike, for example, who coincidentally can count among his literary prizes a small but enviable bracket for "stark, plummy stars" in *Rabbit at Rest,* is among the most star-crossed authors in my library. William Gass's *The Tunnel* shines with over one hundred and fifty stars; Don DeLillo's *Underworld* is studded with at least that many, rendering even the darkest musings delivered there luminous, too. At the risk of slighting the composite

brilliance of the full universe of books, I snatch a star at random from
the Paul West constellation:

> He longed with almost childish wistfulness for the
> life he used to have, when there was no need to talk
> to anyone save the grocer and the milkman, when he
> could put the Ripper behind him and be the painter
> all in all, awaiting the tutelage of certain moments he
> did not mind calling vision, which was when he both
> saw things and saw beyond them: almost complete. In
> a way he envied Gull and Eddy and the women, with
> a final date appended to their strivings, even if stones
> filled Gull's coffin and Eddy was bellowing like an in-
> fected heifer on the Isle of Wight, and the women were
> peaceful as carbon during the first unalloyed privacy
> in their lives.

Prose that soars and stuns, arriving with wings and a hammer. We find
ourselves just a shade this side of purple, where the art's emboldened,
not bruised. To anatomize the grandeur, the *rightness,* of this passage
any further would be, in Emily Dickinson's own stellar words, to split
the lark in order to discover the source of song. Some passions are too
pure to gloss. What couple would corrupt their honeymoon night by
letting a French theorist through the bedroom door? Take him and cut
him out. In little stars I map but do not conjugate my joy.

And should I one day get to edit heaven, I would not have it be the
consummate library where Wim Wenders' angels preside over infinite,
untouched texts. I'd tweak the miracle a bit to let my special penchants
in. The afterlife may find me in the ultimate used bookstore, all of
whose volumes show human use. They display the unique cuneiform
of those readers who owned and exchanged them; not just each authorized writing but the added material as well represents a conversation
in search of an understudy. Here a reader once landed with an elegant
hand, his perfect cursive incursions aimed at posterity. Here a reader
with a tremor took hold, controlling as best he could his response to
the illness or the argument, depending on the cause. Here a reader
took offense, and a wrathful stabbing took place. Here *A Farewell to
Arms* bleeds red ink between the lines and into the gutters of several
pages as though the novel had passed through triage instead of English
282. Here in a copy of Conrad a reader all in green went writing, and

the green ink grows so profuse that by the end it seemed as though *Heart of Darkness* were yielding to jungle. Here a reader spilled his idiosyncrasies into a subscript running from pages 112 to 126; another set of tidy revelations on 134 and 135 betray the book's consultation with a second analyst. Here a reader composed her wedding vows.

Doodles and due dates, personal connections and question marks, verdicts and ventured guesses, cautions and caricatures, imprecations and praise—the collusion continues, the insider scribbling persists. There is an eternity worth the lingering, a Book of Life to be inscribed in. No matter if no one returns to the pages I've collaborated on, only let me be bracketed in that holy context and among such holy company saved. The pious carver understands that the stones he sets unseen to make the roof of the cathedral are no further from worship than those apparent to the congregation. So let my destiny be to eavesdrop among the erudite immortals, who from behind faultless ears or the folds of glorious robes produce the pens they need to do their adoring properly.

22 Time Out

Sophistication is relative. Cable television and the Internet notwith-standing, your kids do not know about record players or the LPs played on them. They do not ask how cell phones invisibly thatch the empty air, and the sight of a rotary dial would utterly flummox them. Weaned on Velcro, they do not master the technique of tying their shoes, much less appreciate the longstanding debate between advocates of the One-Loop Method and the Two, until they are much older than you were when you mastered and appreciated. Surrounded by unprecedented sexual reference, the whole spectrum of seduction from explicitness to innuendo, they remain mistaken in their assumptions about sex (although it must be admitted that they make more inge-nious mistakes than we did). And they cannot tell time.

Well, they can, but the time they tell is different than the time we told and have continued to tell ever since. In fact, the time that presides over their lives is more specific than what gets us up for work and occupies the actuaries. Thanks to their having been principally exposed to digital clocks, time points at them more sharply than our own appointments do. While adults typically divide their days into segments no smaller than ten minutes or so, kids can tell you down to the very moment when they drifted off last night. "I fell asleep at 9:53," my daughter once told me, and I imagined her keeping a diary like the docket book of an IRS agent. Indeed, there are digital clocks that report second-by-second read-outs as well, so that the obsolete ticking I remember as a child punctuating my fading concentration in the dark has been replaced by a device that pinches off and disposes of the tiniest increments of time like so many embedded ticks.

But even though today's kids may know their component moments more precisely than we did or do, it is a different kind of time they abide by. Because of the clocks and watches I grew up with and still en-vision when I encounter "clocks" in conversation or witness "watches" on the page, I think of time as progressing and departing in a circular fashion. For me, time moves like a hoop rolling toward a vague horizon. Digitally defined children, on the other hand, must perceive of time as numberless instants milling at the edge of a cliff and dropping off, like regimented lemmings, one by one. Or as meat sliced to transparent thinness by the butcher, who is the closest counterpart to Atropos they understand. Or as passengers abandoning the sinking ship of their lives yet keeping the line straight, maintaining decorum, as they meet the sea. So it goes for them, snip, snip, snip, while our hours more or less ooze away. The point is that when we refer to time before them, how it passes and passes us by, so that we feel the way we feel when a stranger rubs across us on a subway, a stranger whose face we might have stopped to ponder, whom we might even have come to love, if only we had realized, if only we had had the time, they do not know what we are talking about.

According to the International Bottled Water Association, whose business it is to know, the average adult body is composed of between fifty and sixty-five percent water. As it happens, men are more watery than women, which is something of a surprise in view of the notorious tidal proclivity of female biology, but no matter. Babies, meanwhile, weigh in at an astounding seventy percent water, the better to cushion them during birth and other inevitable early-life buffeting. Our blood is eighty-three percent water, our muscles seventy-five percent. Even our bones, our supposed solid-state circuitry, are twenty-two percent water. It is amazing that we circulate intact; it is a wonder that whenever we step we do not slosh or pool where we sit. According to the International Bottled Water Association, we are pretty much bottled water, too. Eulogists may measure our progress "from dust to dust," but it is likelier to think we liquefy.

Given this affinity, I wonder why I found it so hard to snatch that rubber ring from the floor of the pool in summer camp. All of us had to pass the test before moving on to the landed activities I preferred and for which I felt I was better suited. But while the rest of the campers had managed to accomplish the task and were off hiking or playing ball, I was dunking myself all morning with no success, the only kid who foundered at the five-foot level—just me and the counselor who'd been exiled with me and likewise denied the day's pleasures.

It was apparent to both of us that persistence was futile. Although I could vaguely aim my way toward the target, I could not open my eyes under water, so my efforts were never better than hypothetical. And the water would not have me: I had barely begun to flail blindly about the bottom for the sunken lifesaver before I burst up gasping again. Going by the force of his encouragement and ridicule, I realized that the counselor's honor and mine were at stake; my own stubbornness, not any physical law, was preventing us from joining the others. He suffered my clumsy plunges over and over again. But the water kept refusing me, and each time, except for a throat full of it, I came up empty.

Years later, I would read about how Virginia Woolf, like a freshman hazed into daring, loaded her pockets with stones so the Thames would accept her into the sorority of the dead. The "down-soaring dead," James Dickey calls them, supreme in their sinking. I would read about the boy in Flannery O'Connor's story who kept being denied the Kingdom of Christ he believed lay beneath the river's surface; he, too, had to prove his worth before he could earn the afterlife. If you buy such examples, drowning can be a gathering into something greater and serene, an insertion as smooth as a letter sliding into its envelope, tucked away for eternity. Then every day from that death on will be lost on you, and innumerable nights. Such a soft and dreamy end must be nothing but parenthesis, a permanent state of afterthought. But the metaphor must take you in before the water will.

On that summer day, I failed to live up to my nature. "Such is the endlessness, yea, the intolerableness of all earthly effort," confessed Melville's Ishmael, who also ended his efforts dazed and waterlogged. After wasting over an hour trying, I was finally fished out for lunch.

In 1993, spring rains so inundated the Upper Midwest that the earth began giving up its coffins. Unleashed from the long bad dream of death, they rose through the water, tumbling upward and blind— organisms still and after all they'd succumbed to—noiseless and inexorable, obeying invisible laws, they climbed, until they broke the surface of a decade not one of them had ever expected to see. (Olly, olly oxen free, we would call, surrendering the game because the day had grown dark.) It was the way fish might die, ascending to drown against the atmosphere; think of hundreds at once swooning out of their element, dying toward the light. As though prematurely summoned to Judgment or rehearsing for Glory, the dead departed their sodden graves and, having to improvise in the absence of a Savior, made their aimless way over the flood plain. (Oly, oly ocean free, as a different dialect would have it.) A lavish, epic ascent, with each coffin a Cleopatra's barge laid against a vertical axis, indolent though on the move.

They took their cue from Ishmael aboard Queegqueg's coffin, riding their destinies, or like Viking warriors made their last voyage out. Seven hundred caskets deserted Hardin, Missouri, alone. A flotilla out of a horror film, a veritable exodus of the dead, their devoured bodies roused to unpredictable business in the world they'd presumably left forever. One newspaper recalled *Night of the Living Dead,* the cult film in which some radioactive glitch rouses a ravenous band of corpses to leave the ground and come after us. (All, all out are in free.) Religious leaders had to quell rumors among their congregations, assuring them that, in spite of the symptoms, it was not time for resurrection yet.

Prompted by local psychologists, parents promised their children that there was no need to fear either the undead or the eternal, depending on the particular nightmare they had to contend with. Depending on the particular nightmare, they promised that we won't stay buried or that we will.

The phenomenon is more common than you might think. Research reveals that in cemeteries everywhere the dead refute their tombs. In Pineville, North Carolina, for example, Hurricane Floyd sprung so many coffins that the Coast Guard had to be called out to corral them. Fortunately, the practice of stamping coffins with ID numbers helped facilitate the process of tracing them back to the funeral homes they had originated from and, ultimately, to the families who had purchased them. Andrew Ritter, executive director of the North Carolina Board of Mortuary Science, made a point of assuring the local community that the caskets posed no health risk.

"That corpse you planted last year in your garden, / Has it begun to sprout? Will it bloom this year?" England is a civilization so old and whose space for corpses is so compacted that it is said that undertakers would routinely dig up coffins to re-employ the graves. In doing so, they often discovered scratch marks on the undersides of the lids, meaning that those folks had been buried alive. To combat this problem, they would sometimes tie a string to the wrist of the seemingly deceased, which led up through the ground and was attached to a bell. That way, someone sitting the "graveyard shift" could be alerted by that "dead ringer," who would then have a chance to be "saved by the bell."

Thus we may be spared the hazard. Thus we are assured.

Some ran aground and burst, producing spawn too awful for the television news to show, lest the children ask questions, lest they have to bed down with that imagery and intimations of mortality, the sullen ultimacies, which are the things that go bump in the night. (Andrew Marvell contemplated "The mind, that ocean where each kind / Does straight its own resemblance find." Imagine that the earth itself were such a mind, with all of us afloat in that massive and restless limbic system.) When the waters receded, some of the cadavers had docked in people's yards or even shunted up against their front doors, like accusing ghosts who come knocking in a tale by Poe. (First, a preemptive thunk too heavy for a human hand to produce. Parents tell their children to pull up their covers—it's nothing, they say—then close the curtains and secure the locks.) Some settled against the bases of trees as if staking out shady picnic spots. Three came to rest in a grocery store parking lot. One, when the waters receded, was found stuck in the branches of a tree, further complicating the fate of Milton's Lycidas, who had also "sunk low, but mounted high."

They entered the rushing water like drugs dissolving in the bloodstream, time-released.

What haunted us most of all was that there were so many of them. So many still demanding, denying their final resting places, departing their plots. So many prodigal among the fatally impacted and prone to embark. Street gangs do not match them for delinquency, these emergent, unmurderable forms. "Unwept, and welter to the parching wind, / Without the meed of some melodious tear." The stealth and errancy of the dead. Their waywardness does not end with the end of them.

Some cemeteries in Mississippi that date back to the eighteenth century have been regularly gutted by catastrophic weather, revealing how many of the dead had turned over in their beds, slipped into adjoining graves—promiscuous even as they moldered—or broken out altogether. Because of the water table, the instability of the dead is so frequent a problem in Louisiana that people have their loved ones encrypted above ground, thereby shortening by a few feet, anyway, their leap into ether and the after all, out of consequence and out of time.

"Ask me what's the key to comedy?"

"What's the . . ."

"Timing."

Looking into her mirror, Sylvia Plath would have gotten that one. Seeing into her age that way, her amortization schedule laid out before her like that, she finds the layered skins of resident selves awaiting her and already dying. The mirror becomes a lake where a young girl has drowned, a grown woman treads water, and an old woman whom she recognizes and denies rises toward her daily from the depths of reflection "like a terrible fish." Plath would have appreciated the joke at her expense. As for the precise image she saw when she struck through the mask, we must depend on conjecture, for she was barely thirty when she ended it, and all the pictures we have of her show her still brimming with possibility, and so young. Plath, who wrote as though she were being pursued, whose poems were at best a rickety bridge over oblivion. Lazing about, people talk about killing time, but the truth is that it's always the other way around, and Plath would undoubtedly have gotten that one as well.

Ishmael reminded us that every man is a Narcissus fixed by his own features: "We ourselves see in rivers and oceans." The watch we keep is relentless.

What arrested Plath was nothing she could see for sure. Put it this way: she could not discover a philosophy to save her in time.

Physics would have us believe that what looks like a solid form is not solid at all. This goes beyond erosion and entropy, whose thieving we've long been familiar with. It goes beyond the steady, radiant decay of subatomic structures, as everything leaks out of a hole in Creation's pocket. I mean that what seems solid ground is really as restless in its packing as a subway platform at rush hour. And every object's rush hour is ongoing. Atoms are always on the move, reconnoitering and wedging against each other like the crowd at the World Cup, so that, in theory, one might pass his hand through the molecular bustle of a brick if he timed it right. With luck he could draw it back out again intact, or as intact as things ever pretend to be.

My grade school marked an anniversary of its founding with the burial of a time capsule. We composed the past, as it were, a la carte: the capsule contained a conventional set of readily obtained mementos, which I will not bother to list. Suffice to say, they were not missed by those chosen to inter them, nor could I envision any future generation designated to unearth them anticipating the date with any eagerness. To impress upon us the profundity of the occasion, our class was assigned the task of devising and burying time capsules of our own. In this business I sided with the coffee can contingent, disdaining those who opted for cigar boxes as shortsighted. Troweling in the empty lot behind our condominium for the better part of an hour, I managed to core out a hole sizeable and deep enough to contain it, and I stuffed it in and covered it up without ceremony. But I never had the chance to determine how effectively my booty would brook time because I kept digging it up. It must have been because I hoped to catch posterity in the act. Lying in bed at night, I would imagine some secret subterranean turbulence assaulting my stuff, and a shiver would go through me. I'd let only a few days go by before I was back at the site, poking my nose in, fuddling the experiment. (It doesn't take a physicist to tell you that observation tickles the event, and the hand of the scientist soils whatever it sets in place and is tainted in turn.) Unearthing the can and peeling off the plastic lid, I was satisfied and disappointed at the same time to find my key chain, class picture, plastic decoder ring, dollar bill, and baseball cards unchanged, while the apple I'd deposited with them had altered no more exotically than it would have on the kitchen counter.

Over time I've lost touch—I no longer have the can or its contents, and I cannot recall exactly where I'd planted and replanted them in that vacant lot behind our building, which may not be vacant anymore anyway. (I haven't lived there in thirty years and haven't been back to see.) One way or another, I can't disturb the experiment again. It has all been consigned to time. Which is to say that the experiment in the end has been useless or successful, depending on your point of view.

What I have located, however, is a passage I'd been looking for in Marilynne Robinson's novel, *Housekeeping,* in which heaven is highlighted by the prospect of recovering all that's ever been stolen, misplaced, or squandered. All that's drowned or fallen away, all the perishables in our experiences and on our shelves, all the orphaned universe salvaged from the catastrophe of time. At least, that's the question the author begs: "What are all these fragments for, if not to be knit up finally?"

Discovering the line you're looking for when you're groping about in your books—confirming that it hasn't been distorted over the years or dissolved altogether—is heartening. It tempts me to speculate about the rest of what's lost to that conjectural heaven, warehoused there among the missing rings and revenants, the artifacts, attachments, and angels. I suspect that I might eventually lay my hands on them or, barring that, remember. I'd like to think it is only a matter of time.

23 Falling with Style

Of all the perennials at the Illinois State Fair, Sam the Chocolate Man stands out most prominently in my mind. It isn't his girth, which even in the midst of scores of penned-up pigs and cattle competing for prizes on the basis of sheer poundage, is impressive. It isn't his paddling through his copper vat of inchoate fudge, over which he warbles like one of *Macbeth*'s witches grown bloated over her own magical brew. It isn't even the fudge itself—"The Finest Fudge Anywhere: That's Sam's Guarantee"—a dollar clot of which goes down about as fast as a rat passed through a python, ruining dinners all over the Midwest no matter how many hours away those meals might be. No, it is the way Sam ladles and spreads the chocolate over the slab that, according to the banner above him, will one day serve as his tombstone.

We know that ancient civilizations sought chocolate as an aphrodisiac, but for Sam it serves as a memento mori, acknowledging a darker fate for the body, answering another appetite altogether. "The last dessert you'll ever want! The best you'll ever eat!" he cries. If we cannot make our sun stand still, yet we will make its run scrumptious. So for his profit and our delectation every summer, Sam the Chocolate Man demonstrates that death is always with us and, despite our bias to the contrary, sweet.

It is a lot of consequence to lay upon a confection, I know: to face up to Henry James's "distinguished thing" and, through arrogance and flair, to face it down. Now arrogance and flair do not make a *saving* combination, mind you, but there is satisfaction to be had in bucking against proper conduct when propriety conducts us to the grave anyway. Watching a moth expend its tiny ration of being, Virginia Woolf mused how "one is apt to forget all about life, seeing it humped and bossed and garnished and cumbered so that it has to move with the greatest circumspection and dignity." We are not exempt: our verve failing, we might first take refuge in good behavior, but we feel beggared by the consolation. Better counsel might be provided by Sula Peace, who in Toni Morrison's novel delivered several lectures on the subject of the fortunate fall. Not just a "fortunate fall," in fact—a passionate one. Her stubborn thesis: since mortality is the wicked given, from which neither virtue nor valor grants reprieve, the question is not if you will die but whether you will die like a star blazing its way out or die like a stump slowly cringing into itself. Why die down to our deaths when we can live up to them?

In the end, there is still glamour to be had. This may be the attitude that distinguishes us from the distinguished thing, after all, or right up to it, as well as from those efforts and enterprises that are in their essence the furthest things from either distinction or dessert. I mean the way Sam's "I am" issues from the very same dais where his death will eventually have the floor, no matter how diligently the Chocolate Man filibusters for the time being. I am speaking of style, which does not guarantee the wave of the future so much as it does the surfer's antics upon that dissembling, disintegrating wave.

Keats eulogized himself by saying that all his efforts were writ on water, and so it is with every art, and every artist, too: conceived in solvents, destined to succumb to shore. Flaubert presumptuously dreamed of a novel so pure that style alone might suspend it, but I refer here to even riskier novelties and last vanities, the sorts of flourish best reserved for our exits.

And many would choose to end the suspense anyway, elevation for them being but a point of departure. For example, the California Highway Patrol has recently reported a considerable increase in the incidence of corpses washing up near the Golden Gate Bridge. Their statistics do not differentiate between deliberate jumps and accidental tumbles, between suicide attempts, over-eager sightseeing turned tragic, or drunken revelry gone wrong. There is no telling daring from despondency at this range, no distinguishing those who'd had enough already from those who'd wanted it all at once: everyone obeys the same laws of descent, accelerating at the same legislated rate, reaching the same terminal velocity before impact. (Brinkmanship is both a science and an art.) Psychologists have tried to define or anticipate the onset of desperate weather in vain. What we do know, however, is that whether, inebriate of air, one rushes to greet it, or whether one draws anxiously back from the windswept barrier, gravity is the great equalizer.

The leading edge is the crumbling edge. It's a two hundred and twenty-foot drop to the water, further and as fatally mesmerizing as the view from the crow's nest of the Pequod. Under these conditions, a slip or a swoon is as good as a vault, and for lethal results will as well suffice. But whatever the explanation or incentive, we are definitely in the midst of an epidemic of southbounding into the Pacific, and it has been under way for generations already. Only a four-foot safety railing separates onlookers from the outermost reach of the bridge, a beam which is itself a mere thirty-two inches wide and which serves as a last platform for an average of about two dozen jumpers per year. The figures come from a recent article in the *New Yorker,* in which we learn of the Golden Gate Leapers Association, a rather ghoulish group that takes bets on what day of the week the next attempt will take place. Bay-area newspapers and radio stations initiate countdowns as milestone suicides—the five-hundredth jumper, the thousandth—grow near. So common has the phenomenon become that there is a special code—a 10–31—to alert police to a jumper.

And it isn't only an American phenomenon, as reports from Europe confirm. The Seine runs heavier than ever nowadays with anonymous dead, or so the current rumor goes. Trawl the Thames, and you'll come up with a catch so large that you'd think someone had shaken the cast of the collected Dickens overboard. Experts attest to a world-wide plague of jumpers, diverse and densely gathered, like lemmings enticed by altitude and the company of so many others opting out. We might imagine them leaning like dowsing sticks toward the water, answering some shared seduction, taking the measure of the impending descent.

Bluntly put, falls are definitely on the rise.

Even so, "fall" may underestimate the strange nature of the season, which often features stylish demises and extravagant declines. In one of her poems, with typically mordant whimsy, Stevie Smith referred to "waving while drowning," which will do to describe the sprung rhythm of lovers who not only plight their troth but plunge it. Last year, the national news ran a wholesome counterpart to just such a story, in which two committed skydivers decided to have their wedding mid-air. The entire wedding party conspired with them, and so one night the ten o'clock news ended with footage of a ceremony conducted entirely in the upper atmosphere. Those in attendance made a kind of human constellation around the fluttering bride and gravity-defying groom. The splayed father passed his daughter, her veil snapping like a flag, through a gauntlet of tightly clasped well-wishers into the hands of his plummeting son-in-law. The minister, one hand clutching the Bible, the other firmly affixed to his ripcord, appeared to be screaming what TV viewers could only surmise was scripture. No doubt he ran a reform ceremony, combining predictable devotions and acrobatics. Possibly the newlyweds shouted their vows, with "till death do us part" taking on special resonance as they returned to earth.

If we cannot fly, in other words, we can fall with style, facing down gravity with elegance. Dylan Thomas said that words "make our ephemeral lives dangerous, great, and bearable," but for those who cannot marshal sufficient lyricism to lift them up, there are literal sorts of soaring that at least temporarily will do the trick. Sticklers would not include in this definition the inadvertent splendor of people who leap from burning buildings, sporting a pyrotechnic aura as they drop, or the ruined investors who choose to bottom out artlessly with their stocks. They wouldn't accept descendants of the descents of the women forced to step out the windows of the Triangle Factory, their bodies flaring, their petticoats opening into parachutes too flimsy and too late. But they would admit people who obviously prepare their dives like Olympians, on the order of those "lords a-leaping" we celebrate in the holiday song, intending to represent in death the comeliness they could not manage in life. And mightn't they honor Hamlet, whose play became an anthology of prologues to fatality? He grew more and more obsessed with the trajectory of the dead king, the Hamlet who went before him, and soon saw in every sheer drop or unsheathed sword a seduction. Poetry, not policy, decided his rise and memorialized his fall. Praise him, on his way down.

There are many ways to compose oneself for the inevitable, and they range from slapstick to sublime. Once their exits have been ordained by the physician or the judge, a few choose to go out on a witticism as they go out on a limb. Remember Gary Gilmore's "Let's do it," which he declared at his execution with the aplomb of a sovereign decreeing from his throne? Dashiell Hammett never boiled a detective hero so hard as that. In fact, all manner of gallows humor fits the category I'm describing. Such as the last words of the man going to the gas chamber: he poked his head out just as he was being escorted into the door and said, "This is definitely going to teach me a lesson!" What film star ever issued so quotable a quote over the shoulders of her handlers as she entered her limousine? And what about the man who as he was being strapped down was asked, "Do you have anything you wish to say?" "Not at this time," he replied. With the scene so perfectly sealed, any director would call out "Cut." Sylvia Plath, who in these matters had more relevant experience on her resume than most, wrote that "Dying / Is an art, like everything else." Well, with sufficient preparation and an audience alert to irony, perhaps it can be.

Yet this isn't the message the authorities would hope to send to citizens straddling the railing, who could go either way. School boards fund assemblies so students can hear would-have-been suicides discuss their good luck in having survived their own attempts. "I instantly realized that everything in my life that I'd thought was unfixable was totally fixable—except for having jumped," explained Ken Baldwin. He is one of several who, having jumped, had mid-air collisions with regret and lived to be fished out and to testify to anyone who might be considering just such a decision. It is sensible strategy and common practice to refer to people like Baldwin as "survivors," not "failed suicides." For whether one's desire is to make a political statement, to escape an unwanted pregnancy, or to avoid the collection agency, "successful suicide" is a contradiction in terms. At least that's the lesson the school boards that underwrite their visits would have the kids take away from them.

Besides, the blissful image of free-fall to the contrary, there is nothing clean or crafted about the landing. In the few seconds it takes from the height of the Golden Gate to hit the water, leapers reach expressway speeds, and the result is gruesome: their flesh rips, organs rupture, bones obliterate. Also, there are sharks and other marine opportunists eager to dine on the stew the impact makes of them. The logic of "so far, so good" lasts only about as long as the gasps from onlookers do. Forensic photos always refute the sentiment.

Nevertheless, voters consistently reject proposals to build viable barriers around their bridges. Most people don't want to insult city icons by girdling them with cyclone fences or barbed wire. As far as less obtrusive or more architecturally ingenious alternatives go, they either would fail to deter would-be jumpers or would prove too expensive for those already overtaxed citizens who actually do want to keep on living.

I suspect that there is another reason as well, one that doesn't make the editorial page. It has something to do with our fascination with elevation, however artificially achieved and all too briefly maintained. It has something to do with the way faith aims upwards always, physics and the disasters of the flesh notwithstanding. And it has something to do with a hope that Toni Morrison—evidently a frequent flyer among contemporary authors—offers in *Song of Solomon* as the book's first principle and closing line: "If you surrendered to the air, you could *ride* it."

Toward that lofty end, and at the same time that the lines are getting longer at the world's largest bridges, an increasing number of people are arranging to have their remains launched into space. The cost is high, but when you take into account the fact that it is the last expense they will ever have to shoulder, coupled with the fact that they can amortize over eternity, it does not seem unreasonable. In effect, those who opt out in this fashion are performing a public service, what with the steady decrease in the number of available earthbound vacancies. More and more cemeteries are overbooked, with even the most luxurious family crypts packed tight as fish with bones. (And as I've noted, although census-takers neglect San Francisco Bay, it, too, hosts a growing population.) The groundwater grows dense with ancestors. Cremations choke the incinerators, as though human corpses were so much Halloween candy gone down the wrong pipe.

Yet it isn't altruism that accounts for this kind of rising to the posthumous occasion. It isn't civic duty that sets them off. Call it an aesthetic of uplift, which deems "down-to-earth" derogatory—the resigned state of beasts forced to walk on all fours. Their ashes are loaded into labeled cylinders that look as if they held expensive cigars. Thousands at a time are torpedoed toward whatever heaven they might have aspired to as they passed away, their final prayers detailing ideal flight paths. Some may have sought to speed the transmigration of their souls; others just to broadcast their obituaries beyond what their local papers could accomplish.

Meanwhile, those who'd been interred before this option became available, buried by convention face up, wear their last expressions of longing as they gaze blankly afterward.

How serene the telemetry of deaths expelled like that seem from this distance, unagitated in spite of space's hollow spaces, transfigured among the transfiguring stars. We cannot know all of the motives implied in that cargo, the expensive jetsam of the dying animals all of us are fastened to but for which only a few can afford such a send-off; we are puzzled apart from the urge to ascend that survives them now. Maybe they have taken their cue from Elijah, who was likewise lifted into the afterlife and thereby spared the indecencies of decay. Once they've taken the leap, of course, they are beyond the reach of interview. Like E. E. Cummings's sweet spontaneous planet, these especially intrepid dead answer us only with spring.

Meanwhile, back at ground level, Sam the Chocolate Man makes a scumble of fudge upon the tombstone he treats like a palette, loading his every indulgent rift with an oar. His hearty come-hither song and heavenly coating divert us from the somber marble he makes his art upon. Kids who'd been pinballing all about the midway slow down for Sam. The aroma of fresh fudge redirects teens originally headed toward Happy Hollow or the live bands, unravels families who'd had the horse show in mind. (Sam's recipe is secret, which tantalizes, too.) Old folks arrive in their dazed way. Even lovers find themselves looking away. "The last fudge you'll ever want!" he sings. It is much too early to think about it. We should know better. Nevertheless, the lines grow longer every day. And maybe just to see what's so marvelous—oh, maybe just this once—we come closer.

24 What All the Fuss Is For

I remember Clarence and John, who once occupied an office adja-
cent to mine, with a fondness that they'd hardly suspect and never
welcome. Cynical as only instructors with temporary contracts can
be, they were notorious for treating sentimentality—toward their colleagues, toward their students, toward baby pictures and pets—as an
irritation on the order of a Gummy Bear stuck in the teeth. Both wore
expressions permanently set on "sour." John, a transplanted Georgian,
knew that the one true barbecue featured a pig seared in a pit and
saturated in vinegar, and so could not stomach the culinary crimes of
Missouri, where a dastardly fate had landed him among barbarians
who worshipped beef steeped in red sauce. Clarence, an enormous,
bilious Oklahoman with the mass and implacability of an idol presid-
ing over an Asian temple, thought all administrators unfit to address
him, much less offer advice, and told the student reporter who came
to profile him for the campus paper, "I eat freshmen for breakfast" (a
diet that might have accounted for the regular seismic activity that
sounded from his welling belly). John and Clarence. Clarence and
John. They shunned department functions and personal hygiene; they
disdained bureaucratic procedures and the subtleties of other people's
feelings. Individually severe, truculent together, they were the Scylla
and Charybdis of the English Department, and wise students sailed
wide of their door, lest they run afoul of their dependably foul mood.

Seldom would anyone earn any more empathy from either of them
than they would from the basement vending machines that gobbled
their dollars. Nevertheless, from time to time I trespassed on their
premises to watch them smoke. This was back in the pre-Enlight-
enment era when smoking was not generally prohibited on campus.
(Subsequent policy changes might well have chased Clarence and John
from employment there even if contract realities hadn't destined them
for departure.) Both men were pipe smokers of supreme dedication

and long standing. Having discovered this second reason for solidarity—their transitory status at Missouri Southern being the first—they came in early one morning and, in a joint demonstration of exertion that was unprecedented and never to be repeated, slid their metal desks together so that they faced one another, swept away any and all ungraded papers, memoranda, and other evidence of our profession, and transformed the space into a two-man smokers' lounge. Like twin pashas, they draped themselves on opposite ends of their hastily constructed oligarchy, a miniature dominion where overcast was the only weather and which no undergraduate dared cross or dean felt obliged to invade. There, in actions at once lavish and specific, they pooled their pipes and related paraphernalia—the tamps and picks, the shellacs and chamoises, the walnut racks like dugouts along both baselines, in which as many as a dozen pipes apiece awaited their turn—and began what was to become a daily ritual.

Their procedures did not soften the countenance or the character of either man—John was just as gelid as ever when he indulged, shaping and sucking at his tobacco with lizard diligence, while lighting his pipe kept Clarence's scorn perpetually warm instead of relieving it—but I was so taken by the pains they took that I willingly suffered the grumbling and the smog of Room 309 just for the pleasures of sedulousness on display. They concentrated on their materials like Japanese performing a tea ceremony or Jesuits bent over exegesis, and one had to respect the intensity of the devotion even if he did not join in the particular faith. Repellent in many ways as the witches in *Macbeth*, they were no less dependent than those scabrous creatures on method, and for that reason, they were just as fascinating to me.

As does any uncompromising behavior, this one had its drawbacks and its detractors. There were the inevitable sediments and drools associated with smoking, which typically manifested on John's sleeves and in Clarence's moustache, distracting students from their lessons and generally testing their digestion. Many in Hearnes Hall found the sounds emanating from 309 just as unnerving: on many mornings we could hear the matins of their hacks from well down the hall. However, if the smoking habit itself made me gag, their careful protraction of it kept me going back. I doted on the drawing out of effort like a steady inhalation of a premium blend, luxuriating in the half-hour's focus upon preparing, packing, and scrupulously appreciating each pipe even before it passed each man's lips. I admired the delectation of

Clarence and the fondling of John—qualities they exhibited nowhere else. That is to say, I loved the fuss.

"Don't make a fuss," we say by reflex when someone surprised by our visit rushes off to better their dress or offers to cook. We assume that fusses are undesirable by definition. Too much fuss makes us feel uncomfortable, forced to wait on the sofa while the host hurriedly works up dessert. For doesn't "fussy" hiss with "prissy," as if alliteration made the precision seem too effeminate and mincing for men to defend? By that reasoning, any fuss at all presumably puts us over budget; certainly, Clarence and John, whose respective salaries barely broached five figures, would have found almost any purchase other than what subsistence required extravagant; yet when it came to smoking accoutrements, they spent unashamedly. Experts on leaf grade and provenance, grand masters of the craftsmanship of stem and bowl, they were as obsessively drawn to the local tobacconist's as motorheads to the Harley-Davidson showroom or perverts to the adult video stores barnacling Highway 44. There they lingered like addicts to something more sublime than mere nicotine; like acolytes they dedicated hours to debating relative pipe properties and pipe imperatives. There they compared seasoned cedars richly finished and lovingly sculpted, whose tapers runway models might envy. They pined for the dearer Meerschaum-lined pipes, the Mediterranean briars, and the Tiger Eyes, praised upgrades in design and mourned the country's refusal to revise the trade policy with Cuba. They deplored among like-minded deplorers the philistinism of mass production and of tobaccos available at any convenience store and, for the sake of keeping their elitism aloft, spent time and money beyond their means but which they would never think of spending any other way. Let their cars rust out and their children put up with hand-me-down clothing and public school if it meant sustaining this single form of election, this one tiny protectorate where quality control reigned without concession. (And were the university to burn, which was a fate neither John nor Clarence would have regretted and, truth be told, might both have been questioned about by the authorities, I have no doubt what equipment they'd have rushed to save and what they'd have blithely consigned to the fire.) When they brought the bounty of those visits back to Hearnes Hall, they spread their wares like winnings to divvy over their connected desks. Then, treating each pipe as dearly as if it were a piece of Etruscan pottery newly redeemed from the earth, they scoured, cored, filled, packed, and arranged, ever vigilant to prevent the least particle of those estimable leaves from being lost. They lit and coaxed and quaffed their expensive smoke from tobacco unaffordable even for safely tenured professors and that came from pouches made of leather finer than anything either of them ever wore.

Don't make a fuss? No, not if you can *engineer* one. Not if you can establish an Eiffel Tower's worth of fuss, a fuss a Louis Sullivan would envy or that would make a Frank Lloyd Wright go weak at the knees.

And that incremental effort is what enchanted me enough to brave the second-hand smoke and arrogance of their office. I would ignore the mephitic mess for the sake of the industry that caused it. I would give in to the abyssal drift like a contact high. Tender in no respect— the same smoke that clouded their air and yellowed their teeth must have toughened their skins over time—Clarence and John allowed me to sit in on their proceedings because they recognized that in me they had found, if not someone ready to light up at their level, a legitimate witness to their wholly rococo art. Truly I had a privileged view of the only intimacies they engaged in and, as I believed, the only love they ever expressed. (I don't imagine that they ever mooned over their wives the way they did over catalogues featuring bowls of rarest bone, stems fluted by Renaissance artisans, gorgeous humidors reminiscent of crypts fit for pharaohs, orgies of insider accessories and plushest stuff—the pipe aficionado's porn.) By ten o'clock, their browned, besotted desks were a darkling plain of pipe appurtenances; by noon the whole office was dark with it, a veritable Morlochs' lair; however, by virtue of the epicurean attentions that established it, it seemed strangely, seductively graced. No lotos-eaters' island or opium den could have been more intoxicating or inertia-producing than Room 309, where hour after hour John and Clarence bothered about their pipes. The opposite of delicate in every other way—bulbous Clarence had hands like hams, whereas John, missing three fingers since birth, had to make do with a sort of articulate flipper—they husbanded and colluded over their pipes, making each mandatory office hour pass not only palatably but in a manner that was aesthetically pleasing as well. (One man's reek is another man's rectitude.) And the bothering raised the habit to eccentricity, then, no matter the studied grubbiness of the two of them, to something I chose to call elegance, though never in front of them. For as a guest in their domain, I had only to sit quietly amid the meticulousness and dream.

On their behalf, let me pre-empt anyone who might find prolongation of this sort exasperatingly pointless. "Spare me the details," he might say, and thereby reveal himself to be someone who thought a box score equivalent to the entire ball game. In fact, Clarence and John obeyed quite the opposite priority: they would sooner sacrifice some of the gist than risk the loss of a single detail. That commitment places them squarely in the camp of those sentinels of minutiae whom Nicholson Baker deems "busy, cheerful angels." Note that Baker believes such compulsions, whether inspired by bird calls or by home brewing, by the evolution of the cricket bat or by preferred techniques of embalming, to be heaven sent. He makes the crucial distinction between being small-minded—a hellish situation, surely—and being mindful of small proprieties. Admittedly, neither denizen of 309, however assiduous he might have seemed on a given day, could ever have been characterized as cheerful or angelic, but I could discern through their mutual fog a clear kinship with Baker's exemplary creature of detail: "that excellent low-key sort of man who achieves little by external standards but who sustains civilization for us by knowing, in a perfectly balanced, accessible, and considered way, all that can be known about several brief periods of Dutch history, or about the flowering of some especially rich tradition of terra-cotta pipes."

Clarence, John, and Baker's Dutch and plumbing specialists share a temperament for pickiness about what's important to them—an importance conferred, commemorated, and consecrated by their pickiness—with ritualists ranging from racehorse handicappers to grammarians, from gourmets to rabbis. They would prefer the anonymous sailor who didn't come ashore until all of the knots securing his ship met the standard in the manual to the celebrity who left his Ferrari's rear wheel lipping the curb when he disembarked; they would have presidents and kings hang fire while they honored a lowly stonecutter for having incised faultless glyphs into granite facades. I bet that membership in their exclusive mix must have been tendered to Anne Fadiman, who explains in *Ex Libris* how for years she reserved the same fountain pen, which she plied in the same fashion, for every first draft of a poem: "Like a dog that needs to circle three times before settling down to sleep, I could not write an opening sentence until I had uncapped the bottle of India ink, inhaled the narcotic fragrance of carbon soot and resin, dipped the nib, and pumped the plunger—one, two, three, four, five." Too autistic for your taste? Too insular to survive the open air? What about Hemingway's Robert Wilson, the very model of machismo in "The Short Happy Life of Francis Macomber," who can barely go on with the safari he's been paid to conduct because Macomber is so obtuse about the way of things. The hunter manages to rein in his outrage when, for instance, Macomber wonders why they don't just shoot their prey from the safety of the jeep or when he suggests that they set fire to the grass to bring a wounded lion into the clearing rather than go in after it. "It isn't *done*," is all he says to his employer, but he knows that only a fellow club member, someone who *already understands* that, would appreciate (and never need) the reproach. Let him content himself with the commiseration of Baker, Fadiman, and the other exacting company at their next meeting.

I wonder if fussiness creeps through the genes. Did John father a child who lined up his rattles in his crib according to color, size, or decibel potential? Did Clarence help to conceive a budding curmudgeon who would not sit down to breakfast unless his eggs and hash browns didn't touch one another and who demanded that the milk be poured clockwise around the perimeter of his Cheerios, not smack-dab down the middle of the bowl, so as to even out the sogginess as the meal progressed? Did each fetus fetishize in its respective womb?

And if these routines are inheritable, perhaps the capacity to be enthralled by them is inheritable as well. Watching a barber observe the protocols of shaving with a straight razor, of a pharmacist parceling out pills on a plastic trivet, of a gunsmith dismantling and reassembling his weapon would make me glaze over with contemplation. At parties in graduate school I'd get high watching the host cut, cull, and fabricate his stash into reefer form—high enough that, so far as I was concerned, doing the actual drug was superfluous. There's not much that's incendiary about me, but I'd half-consider sitting in on a terrorist organization just to study someone wiring a bomb. Maybe this characteristic harks back to a time when ancestral Saltzmans counted it a good day if they got to spend it meditating the operations of tinkers, coopers, cobblers, or other masters of intricacies now obsolete. Who knows but that a Saltzman a couple of hundred years removed from me was hypnotized by the sight of a writer whittling new nibs for his favorite quills? Who knows whether he conjectured whether another twenty generations further back some Medieval Saltzman sat rapt before an armorer whose job it was to forge corselets and breastplates and the daily mail?

What I do know is that Clarence and John, my private icons of discernment and systematic exercise, who plied their pipe cleaners like regimental caterpillars and their corers and tamps like jewelers tools, represented a small but dependable contingent of this country's fussers. Secreted inside a contemporary society that is commonly maligned for its sloppiness, diminishing standards, and a widening gyre that threatens to render all standards obsolete is another society whose initiates are more tightly wound about their activities. In extolling the finicky interest enjoyed by Clarence and John, I would by no means slight other "just so" stories that come from other disciplines. They include the one about the fly fisherman who devises his lures and practices his casts until both ends of the enterprise are surgically exact; the one about the chef who is as choosy about the plating of his food as he is about the preparation that preceded it; and the one about the grandmother who is never judgmental about the grandchildren, whom she praises indiscriminately to all and sundry and who win gifts and kisses at each of her visits despite their domestic transgressions or their grades, but who, when it comes to knitting is more fastidious than technician about computer circuits as she ignores the effects of arthritis to observe the stations of the cross stitch. Praise those who manage to trump the random with the overwrought! "Oh maculate, cracked, askew, // Gay-pocked and potsherd world," sighs Richard Wilbur, seemingly resigned to there being no alternative. But here and there, on chessboards and watchmakers' tables, in English gardens and, occasionally, the groves of academe, a John will try to edit or a Clarence counteract Wilbur's jerry-rigged, ramshackle reality, positing against the ramshackle rest of life a decorous little acre of his own. That a couple of short-timers, their careers and contributions to the university slighted as a matter of course, made a haven of coherence for themselves deserves commendation however else one feels about John, Clarence, or the legalities of smoking in a public building. Cinder-blocked inside of one hundred square feet, pressed together John's hollowed cheek by Clarence's ample jowl, they found refinement nevertheless. Yet today the institution neglects them as relentlessly as it did during their abbreviated stay. Deprived in most things as every state school is, we are unaccountably blessed with custodians who keep the place cleaner than a surgical field. As a result, within a week of their leaving us, not a name plate, not a scorch mark on a desk edge, not a brown dot on the linoleum remained to mark John and Clarence's passing there.

Although it's been more than twenty years since their involuntary departure from the English Department, more than twenty years since I battened onto Clarence and John's expertise, I still think of 309 Hearnes as the ultima Thule of by-the-bookishness. Writing this now, I trust that somewhere John is berating a tobacconist for his pedestrian holdings, stabbing indictments with his stained and scabby claw. I trust that somewhere Clarence, like stout Cortez, is contemplating an exotic brand with a satisfaction that, naturally, he doesn't share with or show to the dullards who otherwise populate the shop. Better yet, I imagine that they have found employment together again, so that in some unknown office their sooty plumes continue to silently collide, braid, and lift for, perhaps, one or two attuned and lucky others to wonder at.

Meanwhile, although I have never been tempted to take up smoking myself, I have more than once at an antique shop run a thumb down the length and about the bowl of an especially fetching specimen. While visiting larger cities, I have credibly nodded and frowned over the provisions at a tobacconist's stall, stopping to pass judgment rather than just passing by. I have equated the legitimacy of certain heroes of films that predated the surgeon general's warnings with how elegantly they managed their pipes (Walter Pidgeon and Gregory Peck, those stalwart smokers whose blazes audiences trailed out of World War II, rank among the most impressive) and supported or dismissed their chances with women or in war accordingly. And when, say in a faculty lounge or upscale bar, a venerable blend ascended—beckoning, so it sometimes seemed to me—I have surrendered my attentions to it. On behalf of absent colleagues, I have let myself imagine a higher plane of ideal forms, to which the smoke aspires, rising in a measureless, perfect curl, elaborate and essential, that, magically, does not buckle or fade, but keeps climbing to define and appraise the upper air. It persists, a nimbus that nothing disperses, ever, toward a regimental heaven, where it reaches a connoisseur God Who, like His fussiest subjects, gets it, too.

25 Much Obliged

Opportunities for dedication arise everywhere. Books, obviously, as well as individual stories, songs, or poems composed by artists who fear that the full-length enterprise is too fond or far away. Some will choose to craft the dedication first, in fact, by way of igniting the incentive required to complete a text to append to it. However, it must be noted that for some this strategy proves paralyzing, landing them in the predicament of the consumer who maxes out a credit card and only then worries about finding the funds to handle his debt. These premature dedicators could be kin to the boy who commits his savings from working after school at Hardee's to a leather jacket and motorcycle helmet months before he's old enough to obtain a driver's license. They might mimic the girl who practices her married name on paper napkins before her dream mate has even asked her out. The point is that dedications page us when and where they will. Like the birthdays of relatives, they often approach inconveniently, often regardless of our having sufficient gifts to give.

One author's stimulus is another author's trauma. I've heard of would-be writers who spent weeks recasting their dedications well in advance of having authored any draft to attach it to. They hone the consonants and trim the vowels, guard against crumple and smudge, only to discover that they've exhausted their inspiration, and their craft ends up becalmed while still in port. When the dedication becomes the whole of the duty to be discharged, it makes the same claim to permanence as a stack of unpaid bills. Surely there are less implicating shows of love.

For example, for next Valentine's Day, the entrepreneurial romantic who hasn't the talent or the time to apply to creative endeavors anyway might decide to give something celestial and comparatively lasting. Eras ago, mythic proportions had to be met for one to earn the status an entire constellation confers, but there remain smaller plots of

firmament just waiting to be mortgaged out. Those attuned to sublimity might consider naming a star for a loved one.

Adam entitled all over the earth, but he left the heavens relatively
unreserved. As a result, and for a mere $54 paid to the International
Star Registry (a pittance, when seen from the broader perspective) we
can scissor, cultivate, underscore, and apportion there with impunity.
We can stipple and stipulate the sky, contracting for personal excep-
tions against the obliterating rule. Talk about the gift that keeps on
giving! Truly, any other gift pales against the light of a star placed in
one's beloved's keeping, without which one and beloved alike are destined to become nondescript drops in the consummate black bucket.

The International Star Registry invites the buyer to invest in the
galaxy: for $54, he can select an astral body to place into nomination
and thereby lay claim to permanence, or as much imperishability as
the universe might provide for $54, at any rate. (Another disclaimer:
the term "international" may sound deficient, in view of the scope of
the registration the buyer has in mind. But passion transcends legal
and lexical issues alike.) Shipping and handling are covered in the cost,
and while a moment's caprice may mislead one to wish the designated
star delivered to that fragment of sky visible to his or her own neighborhood, the location charts and certified documents that "shipping
and handling" actually refer to do add substance to the sentiment.
Flowers fade—though lest we forget, hundreds of hybrid roses have
been named to remember everyone from recently graduated daughters to English queens—and chocolates last less than a week once the
calorie-conscious lover retrieves them from the freezer. But the stars
won't wink out for epochs yet, and as the International Star Registry
reminds us, the vast majority of vastness is still unspoken for. So why
not pit the personality of your choosing against the indifference of
immensity? Why not contest the annihilation to come with the self's
most fundamental anthem and ode?

What's in a name? For $54, the corroboration of the cosmos.

At the other, humbler end of the infinite, the last twenty or so
entries at least in the Periodic Table bear the surnames of scientists.
Although many of these elements cannot be sustained for more than
a few seconds in the lab, they will sustain their namesakes forever,
or at least for so long as the planet's components endure to warrant
them. And not to exclude folks from the artsy edge of the Quad from
eligibility, the name of poet Diane Ackerman officially designates a

molecule—definitely a boon to any resume regardless of whether it's an art or a science one chooses to pursue.

Set a precedent in nearly any discipline and yours is the coinage, yours the noun to come. Add a special twist to a figure skating routine or an innovative flair to your minute's maneuvers on the pommel horse, and imitators ever after will contort in your name. Recognize a chemical process, invent a chess defense, refine a wrench, recast a confection, or alter a sauce, and chemists, chess masters, carpenters, chocolatiers, and chefs will not long endeavor without echoing you. Sponsor an expedition and your reward will include autographing any territory you find. (Just think how many hills, craters, and culverts the cartographers have missed and await someone's signature.) Scale a mountain and monogram the peak. Penetrate a molecule, a mathematical puzzle, or an enemy army's flank and copyright the move. The cliché speaks of how the bullet with your name on it marks you for extinction, but logic argues the opposite: with such an engraving, so far as mortality allows, one trumps the grave.

Any surface is susceptible to inscription if the desire behind it sufficiently burns. How else explain how someone was able to emblazon a highway overpass over night or to steal his way into your screened-in porch to initial the wet cement? How else explain how graffiti was found on the side of a skyscraper sixty stories up or how the subway train was tagged by gang members under the very noses of the cops stationed beneath Fifty-Ninth Street? Poet C. K. Williams marvels at the way children will invade a work site immediately after the roofers have left for the day to mark "the leftover carats of tar in the gutter, so black they seemed to suck the light out of the air." The kids resist that malignancy with their own mischief, ensuring that "every sidewalk on the block was scribbled with obscenities and stars," which for them may be two sides of the same signature.

Some say that the most honorable form of charity is anonymous, but how honor the donor who endows undesignated? While it goes without saying that committing to a box of Thin Mints from the Girl Scout at the door should go without saying, even a modest contributor rightly gets his name on a patio brick in front of the new hospital wing. Arguably, part of the good the donor lavishes is the opportunity he provides the rest of us to bask publicly in his favor. Largesse should be writ large. If we would force the benefactor to endure a ceremony honoring him with his name above a reconstructed viaduct or a refurbished stretch of expressway, accepting the dedication is the least he can do after the most he has done.

Reluctance to do so is certainly the exception. Given half a chance, most of us would incise any tree, tenement building, or curb with our Kilroy, would hammer, paint, print, or otherwise impose ourselves on posterity. Unique to writers, perhaps, is the dream of rising up adjectival some day. To so thoroughly influence the field that a fresh modifier becomes as necessary to literary discourse as new sewer lines to a growing metropolis! Had Faulkner known that "Faulknerean" would follow his involuted fictions into the academy, he'd have undoubtedly found succor where his catastrophe-haunted protagonists never could. Had Hemingway known that "Hemingwayesque" would derive from his notoriously terse line segments, it might have steadied his hand on the trigger, if not stayed it. My one-time colleagues, Professors Bright, Stern, and Harder, affixed with ready-made modification like characters out of Restoration comedy, for all the predictable punning their names required them to put up with, had respective legs up when it came to ensuring that their prose would resonate long after their retirements. In my own case, I suspect that campaigning for "Saltzmaniacal" would be in vain. It is hard to imagine anyone aspiring to that description, much less that adjective motivating a writer so described to persist at his desk.

As for what motivated basketball phenom Kobe Bryant to excel at his profession, he says it was the dream of eventually having a shoe named after him. The designers at Nike came up with a miracle of slipstream iridescence: a silver, zippered basketball shoe that resembles the protective garb a worker in a nuclear facility might wear. If you buy Bryant's testimony on his commercial for "the Kobe," along with the $110 pair of shoes themselves, the idea that kids all over the world now chase across the court with his name on their heels satisfies him as thoroughly as any of the championships he has won with the Lakers.

Then there is the issue of deciding what to name the baby—at once the most common and the most profound of dedication ceremonies. One can always whitewash a boat if the woman he christens it for betrays him for someone whose craft proves more impressive. He can similarly remove a tattoo pledging his commitment if he decides that the acids required will prove less painful than having to see "Darlene," who'd deserted him for another man's arm, still attached to his own or peering over his shoulder for the rest of his life. But we sense that when we confer a name on a child we confer an inflexible destiny along with it. That is probably the reason so many of us cringe when we see the Boggle combinations some parents come up with for their kids or the inventive spellings that do not strike us as clever but as dyslexic. It is as though Mom and Dad forgot that their wriggling little Ridgemount or bundle of Bathsheba would in a few years have to survive grade-school recess, where onomastics can be a terrorist activity. (Both Ridgemount and Bathsheba managed to do so, I'm relieved to report, both of them having later appeared on one of my own college rosters.) Some parents overcompensate, of course, dubbing their young with honors they haven't yet earned. I've had a "Sir," a "General," and a "Doctor" in class, all of whom persevered, it is true, but none of whom prospered so automatically as his name promised.

Nor are girls exempt from their parents' urge to guarantee them distinction at the start. Comb out the tangled halls of a typical grade school and I'm willing to bet that you'll come up with a pig-tailed Lucretia, Phyllida, or Clytemnestra, her post-elementary class asserted and consequence ratified as if every constituent letter were an emerald entrusted to her keeping. What were her parents thinking? you wonder. Perhaps that thanks to their foresight a child born to a schoolteacher and a secretary just outside of Portland, Oregon, will alchemize into a woman of pedigree notwithstanding their middle-class standing. Perhaps that she'll preside over a society set high above the concussions of the daily news, her longevity adorned by symphonies and consistently quotable conversation. She will never exit a room without announcing "I must fly!" and leaving in her wake the unmistakable aroma of station. She will ladle her urbane observations out, will our Thalia, among steadfast companions who'll appreciate her essential worth and her allusions. Our Clarissa will inhabit a climate-controlled future, enjoy privileged attachments and detachments. She will live, in a word, an assured life—a life assured in a word. Or perhaps they just liked the look of "Clarissa" on the birth certificate or the way "Thalia" and "Torkelson" blended in the ear. In either case, they needed to intuit that their daughter's name would know her as surely as she would know her name.

This is to say nothing of the ignominies and gaffes that constitute folklore in neonatal wards. One wonders what ever happened to baby Female (rhyming with "Emily"), so named because her semi-literate parents liked the way it looked on the hospital chart; or to One-Eighth

Brown, whose mother had meant to honor her husband with the hope
that her son would match even that fraction of his father's virtue; or
to offspring named not only after consumer goods ("Can Pepsi come
out to play?") but also after pharmaceuticals ("And here are the twins,
Vioxx and Viagra. Aren't they adorable?") and even the diseases drugs
are designed to combat ("Angina! Chlamydia! Hurry up! You'll be late
for school!"). God help them all. Whereas we are dumbfounded when
a Jennifer takes an overdose of sleeping pills or a Jason takes aim from
atop his dormitory, we might be distressed to learn that those oddly
denoted kids came to such ends, but hardly astonished.

Jews customarily reduce the innumerable options for naming the
impending baby to the commemoration of dead relatives. In this way,
in addition to the savings bonds and money market accounts they
keep on behalf of the impending generation, each Jewish family has
a private repository of names awaiting embodiment, on the order of
a stockpile of Mordecais, Aarons, Elis, et al, anticipating conscription into the Israeli army. Some parents confine themselves to using
just the initial letter of a relinquished name to cue the coming son or
daughter, which gives them some room to maneuver. Some choose to
duplicate the Hebrew name of the deceased for later use in synagogue
and for the odd *aliyah* while granting themselves greater versatility
and the chance to participate in seasonal trends when they confer the
English name the child will be known by in homeroom. (This compromise accounts for any Amber Leavitt or Travis Kornblum you may
happen to encounter.) The practice of naming for the deceased merges
inheritance and offering. If it does not go so far as actual reincarna-
tion proposes, it does let the dead rest in their descendants, not just in
the dirt.

Not that the living are any less demanding about being identified
by those devoted to them. Assure your beloved all you like about how
she starts your heart each morning and lifts it like a chalice through
your waking hours, but unless you document the debt by name, your
poetry won't hold up in the court of her affections. Splendor seen must
also be cited. "You know who you are" is a transparent, useless finesse
on the order of failing to sign the check you promise the collection
company is already in the mail. When Elton John sings, "And you can
tell everybody this is your song," the unspecified subject would not be
blamed for preferring that the singer would do the telling himself on
the record. In fact, after the umpteenth consecutive concert in which

he's sung "Your Song" to mass after mass of unsung fans, one begins to wonder just whom it is Elton John has been honoring all this time. If the poet John Ciardi is correct when he writes, "The camera always photographs the cameraman," it may follow that the love song actually consecrates the singer.

For the model of bait-and-switch dedications, let us consult the Bard. Critics have struggled with Shakespeare's sonnets for generations, debating their origin, their order, and the true target or targets of their ardor. But for our purposes, we might focus on Sonnet 55 for the cagey way in which Shakespeare bends his dedication back toward his own talent. Ostensibly, he is going about the predictable Petrarchan business of certifying and preserving the person who has inspired his love. On closer inspection, though, it is the poem, not its prompter, which wins the greater honor. What neither "marble, nor the gilded monuments / Of princes shall outlive" is "this powerful rhyme." It is not the enchanting qualities of the person being enclosed in the poem but the sublimely shaped confinement that person is lucky enough to live in that the laurels are really reserved for. It is Shakespeare's praise that makes someone praiseworthy, not to mention guarantees that someone matchless, immortal eloquence. Love may have begun with the beloved's virtues, but it endures as art through the author's cadences and vocabulary. It is the master poet's polished "contents," his "living record," that confers the qualities he celebrates, against which fire, enmity, oblivion, and "sluttish time" shall fail though they succeed in overcoming every stone idol. Shakespeare sets the pace, provides the stage, compels critics and classrooms, and tutors lovers to come. "So, till the judgement that yourself arise, / You live in this, and dwell in lovers' eyes," he concludes, the couplet cinching the case for his own genius, while the suppositious muse enclosed there remains unidentified and (the final "judgement" not having arrived so far) unavailable to testify.

As for going beyond the initial nod to "the onlie begetter of these insuing sonnets, Mr. W. H.," or shedding explicit light on the Dark Lady the last couple of dozen sonnets are apparently addressed to, Shakespeare kept his own private counsel. If memory serves, based on how that lady's "worser spirit" is characterized, it's probably just as well that he gives her a low profile.

For a dedication can be an indictment, too. The weatherman who started the practice of naming hurricanes did so to scandalize politicians who'd inflicted their own brand of damage on the community. A bus explodes on the West Bank, and we wait for the perpetrators to phone in on behalf of their faction, which report comes as dependably as a DJ's lead-in to the next ballad he'll play: "This long-distance dedication goes out to Sherry in Tucson, from Jimmy." Indeed, if the evening news is a reliable indication, for every congregation that builds a temple in the name of one god, there is another group ready to bomb it in the name of another. Part of piety is the eagerness to ascribe it. But while no mother ever complained because her son said he owed his college diploma or game-winning basket to her benign effects on him, the mention of John Hinckley's name must still, even decades later, send a shudder through Jodie Foster, to whom he dedicated his attempt to rid the world of President Reagan.

And what about Odysseus, who while he escaped him couldn't resist goading the gouged Cyclops by crediting the wound he inflicted? As his remaining men frantically rowed, he stood up and cried, "Cyclops, if anyone ever asks you how you came by your blindness, tell him your eye was put out by Odysseus, sacker of cities, the son of Laertes, who lives in Ithaca." It was not enough for Nobody to provoke the monster; Odysseus had to affix his true name and address to the deed. Thus he ensured that Polyphemus would be able to better direct his curses and more accurately hurl his stones. Homer doesn't mention his crew shouting out, "Sit down, Odysseus, you're rocking the boat!" but all of them must have thought it.

As the balked and blinded Polyphemus cast about wildly for ammunition, each sailor pulled at his oar for all he was worth, praying that the next thrown boulder didn't have his name on it. (The epic makes no specific mention of this in any translation, but there can be no question of the strength and nature of each man's dedication under duress.) But the very ocean was the monster's father, in whose name the Cyclops rampaged and promised revenge. Behind each heave was the thought, This one's for you, or something to that effect—the epic is mute on that account, too. Nor is there any reference made to the hero's men taking consolation from their share of glory, going under into unlabeled graves. All we'll ever know of the lost ends with Book IX. Odysseus himself hesitates for only a moment over their memory. The poet's implication is clear: if it is the hero's responsibility to acknowledge whoever brought him to this pass, it is also his prerogative to press on with the story that will bear his name.

About the Author

In addition to *The Obligations of the Harp,* Arthur Saltzman's previous books include the collections of essays *Solve for X* (2007, University of South Carolina Press), *Nearer* (2006, Parlor Press) and *Objects and Empathy* (2001, winner of the First Series Creative Nonfiction Award), and six critical studies of literature and writers. Recognitions for his writing include the 2005 Columbia Nonfiction Award, the 2003 Victor J. Emmett Memorial Essay Award (from *Midwest Quarterly*), the 2002 Nebraska Review Creative Nonfiction Award, and the inaugural Ames Memorial Essay Award (from *Literal Latte*). He was a Professor of English at Missouri Southern State University at the time of his death in 2008.